Swing Along

Swing Along

The Musical Life of Will Marion Cook

Marva Griffin Carter

OXFORD
UNIVERSITY PRESS

2008

OXFORD
UNIVERSITY PRESS

Oxford University Press, Inc., publishes works that further
Oxford University's objective of excellence
in research, scholarship, and education.

Oxford   New York
Auckland   Cape Town   Dar es Salaam   Hong Kong   Karachi
Kuala Lumpur   Madrid   Melbourne   Mexico City   Nairobi
New Delhi   Shanghai   Taipei   Toronto

With offices in
Argentina   Austria   Brazil   Chile   Czech Republic   France   Greece
Guatemala   Hungary   Italy   Japan   Poland   Portugal   Singapore
South Korea   Switzerland   Thailand   Turkey   Ukraine   Vietnam

Copyright © 2008 by Oxford University Press

Published by Oxford University Press, Inc.
198 Madison Avenue, New York, New York 10016

www.oup.com

Oxford is a registered trademark of Oxford University Press

Library of Congress Cataloging-in-Publication Data
Carter, Marva Griffin.
Swing along : the musical life of Will Marion Cook / Marva Griffin Carter.
p.   cm.
Includes bibliographical references.
ISBN 978-0-19-510891-0
1. Cook, Will Marion.   2. Composers—United States—Biography.
3. African American composers—Biography.   I. Title
ML410.C7545C37 2007
780.92—dc22   2007020402

1   3   5   7   9   8   6   4   2

Printed in the United States of America
on acid-free paper

To my father and mother, Marvin and Lois Griffin,
who have given me life and love

To my husband and son, Lawrence Carter, Sr. and Jr.,
who have supported me tenaciously, and—

To musicologists Eileen Southern and Samuel Floyd, Jr.,
who have inspired me to tell the untold stories
of African-American musicians

ACKNOWLEDGMENTS

This study represents the culmination of conversations with informants, including scholars, and discoveries in newspaper accounts, letters, and other primary sources. The work began as a musicological dissertation and has undergone radical surgery before recovering in its present form. I am indebted to Lawrence Gushee for originally shepherding this project and to committee members Bruno Nettl, Charles Capwell, and David Stigberg for their amendments. Samuel A. Floyd, Jr., and Sheldon Meyer deserve special thanks for acknowledging its publication value.

Cook's biography would not have been possible without the able assistance of many librarians. Most instrumental in this regard were Wayne Shirley at the Library of Congress; Joellen Elbashir, Donna M. Wells, Ida E. Jones, Deborra Richardson, Denise D. Harbin, and Esme Bhan at the Moorland-Spingarn Research Center of Howard University; Archie Motley at the Chicago Historical Society; W. E. Bigglestone and Roland Baumann at Oberlin College; Wendy Warnken and Marty Jacobs at the Theatre Collection of the Museum of the City of New York; Richard Jackson at the Lincoln Center Branch of the New York Public Library; and Vera Mitchell, Rosemary Stevenson, Jean Geil, and William McClellan of the University of Illinois at Urbana. Other archives used include the Driscoll Collection at the Newberry Library; the James Weldon Johnson Memorial Collection of American Literature at the Beinecke Rare Book and Manuscript Library of Yale University; the Music Library and Theatre Collection of Harvard University; the Institute of Jazz Studies at Rutgers University; the Schomburg Center for Research in Black Culture of the New York Public Library; and the Vivian G. Harsh Collection, Carter G. Woodson Branch of the Chicago Public Library. European archives include the British Library of London and the Hochschule für Musik of Berlin.

Other persons who shared valuable knowledge and resources were Dwight Andrews, Valerie Bada, Richard Barksdale, Adrienne Fried Block, Rae Linda Brown, Sterling Brown, Mellonee Burnim, Richard Crawford, Dominique DeLerma, John Graziano, Thornton Hagert, Eva Jessye, Richard Long, Josephine Harreld Love, Doris McGinty, Carol Oja, Lee Orr, Thomas Riis, Lawrence Schenbeck, Ann Sears, Eileen Southern, Jean Snyder, Judith Tick, and Mark Tucker. European sources were contributed by Jeffrey Green, Howard Rye, and Karl Gert zur Heide. Penelope Williams and April Grier served as research assistants and gathered data on Cook family history and legal records. Clinton M. Schaum and Paul DeAngelis provided editorial critiques, Irmgard Immel submitted German translations, and Stuart Feder offered medical interpretations.

Funding for this project was obtained from Georgia State University, Morris Brown College, Oxford University Press, the Smithsonian Institution, and the University of Illinois. I am particularly grateful to Maureen Buja, Sheldon Meyer, Maribeth Payne, Kimberly Robinson, Norman Hirschy, Suzanne Ryan, Robert Milks, and other Oxford University Press staff for their competence and patience in this endeavor.

Special thanks to Michael and Rickie Byars Beckwith, Alice Holliday, Clarence and Pearl Hollis, Vivian Taylor, Veola Tinsley, Pat Williams, and Robert O. Young for helping me to maintain body and soul.

CONTENTS

Photo gallery follows page 90

Swing Along

Prelude

EXHORTATION

My love affair with the musical life of Will Marion Cook began when I was a doctoral student in a history of jazz class at the University of Illinois in Urbana. I became intrigued with the unique career and personality of this artistic trailblazer through the lectures of Lawrence Gushee. Moreover, in most jazz histories there were brief references to Cook's contributions to early syncopated orchestral music and to his role as mentor to Duke Ellington. Theatrical sources pointed to his pioneering 1898 Broadway musical-sketch *Clorindy—The Origin of the Cakewalk*, and to his substantial influence on the golden age of black musicals in the early 1900s.

Fascination with Cook's life led me on an exploratory trip to Washington, D.C., where I met his son and pursued the feasibility of writing Cook's biography. Dr. Mercer Cook, a distinguished retired Howard University professor of Romance Languages and former ambassador to Niger, Senegal, and Gambia, was charming, engaging, and encouraging. We spent hours discussing Will Marion Cook's unfinished autobiography, family papers, and musical legacy. Six months later I returned to the District of Columbia as a Smithsonian Institution Fellow to spend the summer interviewing Mercer Cook and delving into his father's life and works. This experience was ideal—conferring almost daily with my subject's next of kin. Mercer Cook and I also played and sang his dad's music between trips to the archives of the Library of Congress and of Howard University. Our collaboration continued over the next several years through telephone calls and a myriad of correspondence now housed with the Mercer Cook Papers in the Manuscript Division, Moorland-Spingarn Research Center at Howard University.

The publication of this biography fulfills several dreams that have been long deferred. More than sixty years ago Will Marion Cook began writing his autobiography on scraps of paper, envelopes, musical scores, and the like. Ill health, fatigue, and a largely transient lifestyle contributed to its unfinished status. Even though he did not maintain many primary sources, through the urging of his son, certain aspects of his life were preserved from interviews and woven into a story line by Mercer Cook. Further gaps were filled in by the unpublished memoir of his wife and lifelong companion, Abbie Mitchell. In 1944 his son assumed the charge to complete the manuscript, in addition to his university and governmental responsibilities. When pneumonia snuffed out Mercer Cook's life after a fall in 1987, his father's memoir was still incomplete. I then assumed the challenge of bringing Will Marion Cook's biography into realization.

There has been a resurgence of recordings, publications, and live performances of Cook's works. Tenor William Brown and pianist Ann Sears have recorded a two-set CD "'Swing Along'—The Songs of Will Marion Cook" (Albany Records, 2006). Tim Brooks has published *Lost Sounds— Blacks and the Birth of the Recording Industry 1890–1919* with companion CD reissues of Cook recordings (University of Illinois Press and Archeophone Records, respectively, 2005). Terry Gross produced a "Fresh Air" National Public Radio program devoted to Cook's life and music (May 18, 2000). Thomas L. Riis published the *Music and Scripts of In Dahomey* (A-R Editions, 1996), Cook's most outstanding musical, as well as additional song facsimiles in *Just Before Jazz: Black Musical Theater in New York 1890–1915* (Smithsonian Institution Press, 1989). The Black Music Repertory Ensemble of the Center for Black Music Research performed and recorded Cook songs on *Black Music: The Written Tradition* (Chicago: Columbia College, 1990). Moreover, the historic Clef Club Concert of 1912 was recreated at Carnegie Hall in 1989 with Maurice Peress, Jester Hairston, Wynton Marsalis, and the Morgan State University Choir performing Cook's works. Even a historical and biographical novel, *Dvořák in Love*, written by Josef Skvorecky, imagines that Cook first met Dvořák while studying in Berlin (Toronto: Lester & Orpen Dennys Limited, 1983).

Beth L. Savages's *African American Historic Places* (Washington, D.C.: The Preservation Press, 1994) indicates that on December 8, 1976, the house at 221 West 138th Street in New York, where Will Marion Cook lived from 1918 until his death in 1944, was designated a National Historic Landmark (B5/11/76 NHL, 76001238).

The colorful subject of this biography represents the first generation of well-educated post-Civil War blacks who were born free. With this newfound liberty, Will Marion Cook became an advocate for racial uplift in the entertainment transition from the minstrel show to the black musical. His syncopated orchestral achievements paved the path to the Big Band phenomenon. Furthermore, as the surrogate son of the outspoken abolitionist Frederick Douglass, Will Marion Cook sought to secure racial equality for his people through music, in the wake of Reconstruction, so they could "swing along" the road to freedom!

Chapter I

BOYHOOD

Howard University is a special place. It nurtures and respects those who
pass through its gates. It is free of oppression. . . .

                                                            H. Patrick Swygert

Four million African Americans were free by the late 1860s, and
their cumulative wealth was not insignificant. Those who lived
in the District of Columbia owned property worth more than a million dollars. They supported twenty-one churches and twenty Sabbath schools and
belonged to thirty benevolent and civic organizations. The eagerness of
blacks to secure an education that promised "freedom from the bondage
of ignorance"[1] led to the establishment of Howard University in 1867.
William Mercer Cook, who was to become Will Marion Cook, was born two
years later on the stormy 27th day of January in 1869.[2] Because of the District's war-torn, overcrowded conditions, William's birth took place in a sol-
dier's barracks, behind the university's campus. This academic backdrop
presaged the prominent place that education and the Howard University
environment would play in the lives of the Cook family.

Civil War General Oliver Howard, the school's heroic namesake, served
as the commissioner of the Freedmen's Bureau, which was established to
improve, protect, and employ the newly freed men and women. Among his
early recruits was William's father, John Hartwell Cook, the able 1864 graduate of Oberlin College, who had been teaching in Louisville, Kentucky,
from September 1864 to July 1866. He and his wife, Isabel, were summoned
to Washington, D.C., where he began a five-year term in 1867 as chief clerk
of the Freedmen's Bureau by day and was a law student at Howard University by night. At the age of 32, John Cook was one of ten students to obtain
a law degree in the first graduating class of 1871.[3] (At that time, the degree

could be obtained in two years.) He and eight fellow graduates immediately began to practice law in the District of Columbia. Cook was elected to Howard University's Board of Trustees two years later and was professor and dean of the Law School from 1876 to 1878.[4] He also maintained a distinguished law practice at 1511 Pennsylvania Avenue, opposite the Treasury Building.

When William turned five, his father sent him, along with his brother John, to a small school that he helped to organize on an interracial model. The brothers were consistently sent home from school early for a week, because the whites believed that the time wasn't ripe for an experimental interracial academic environment. Records do not indicate what alternative school the boys attended. Be that as it may, John and Marion Cook's future never looked brighter. Soon they outgrew their home in the barracks, following the birth of three sons—John Hartwell, Jr., in 1868, William Mercer in 1869, and Hugh Oliver in 1873. (A fourth infant did not survive.) This bulging family moved to a dwelling overlooking the reservoir near Howard University, and they later purchased a home at Sixteenth and M Streets in northwest Washington. Just as their lives appeared secure, John Cook's health began to wane. Overwork had weakened his resistance to tuberculosis, causing his untimely death on March 9, 1879, at the age of forty. By then he had earned a "reputation as an honest lawyer, a conscientious teacher, and a gentle father who never whipped his sons with anything heavier than a lead pencil!"

John Hartwell Cook "won the respect and confidence both of bench and bar" through his devotion to the profession of law, his honesty and purpose, and his acknowledged ability.[5] Upon his death, Chief Justice Carter adjourned the Circuit Court with a testimony of the esteem with which Mr. Cook was held. In the Criminal Court, Thomas Miller announced his death by revealing that Cook "was prompt to do justice to the deserving. He paid a glowing tribute to his ability, energy, high moral character, and general popularity."[6]

The final rites for John Cook were held at the First Congregational Church, officiated by Pastor Andrew Rankin, assisted by the Reverend F. J. Grimke of 15th Street Presbyterian Church and President William Weston Patton of Howard University. At the ceremony's conclusion, the slim, diseased body of John Cook was interred at Graceland Cemetery in Washington, D.C.

The family was devastated by the loss of their husband, father, and primary breadwinner. Now widowed in her mid-thirties, Isabel Marion Cook suffered from a touch of lung fever from having nursed her husband. She was not strong enough economically, physically, or psychologically to assume the mother-father role of rearing three sons alone. Mrs. Cook, therefore, decided to rear ten-year-old Willie herself and to send eleven-year-old John, Jr., and six-year-old Hugh Oliver to live with other relatives.

We do not know what persuaded this mother of three to care personally for young Willie over her other two sons. Perhaps she sensed that he would have the greatest adjustment to make in losing his father. Perhaps she empathized with his precarious birth position as the middle child, fighting for and needing more attention. Or perhaps she simply favored this fair, handsome, wide-eyed lad over the other two sons.

Regardless of her motive, mother and son traveled first to Denver and then to Kansas City, where she became an educator and he became a student.[7] Willie advanced normally in his class until one fateful day when his teacher tried to discipline him with a strap; he retaliated by attacking the instructor's head with a wooden plank. Still grieving the loss of his father, who never adhered to corporal punishment, Willie was determined not to succumb to his teacher's lashing. Thus began a series of school expulsions.

Out of desperation, Isabel Marion Cook sent her son to Chattanooga, Tennessee, to be reared by her parents, William and Jane Lewis, in the hope that their two-parent home would provide more discipline and stability for the young boy. This proud black Northerner was sent, at great risk, to the South on a Jim Crow train in the early 1880s. His journey began in first class, but as he descended into the *real* South, he was ordered to ride in the "smoker" coach ahead. Willie refused to move to cheaper seating, since a more costly train ticket had been purchased for him. As the train descended toward Chattanooga, the conductor pleaded, cajoled, and finally threatened to throw him off. Traveling fifty miles per hour, in a heated exchange peppered with profanity, Willie held his ground. Biting his lips until blood trickled onto his woolen shirt, hands clenched until they ached, too frightened to sleep for fear of the KKK, Willie was not ready to die, but less ready to live in a society of racial injustice. He finally arrived in Chattanooga, in a first-class coach, unharmed, but shaking in his shoes.

Grandfather Bill had been born in 1809 as a slave to Colonel Lewis of Winchester, Tennessee. He had learned the blacksmith trade during his youth, working extra odd jobs to save enough money to purchase his freedom and that of his wife, mother, brother, and sister. Such acts of courage caused his offspring to be born free. William Lewis established himself in 1837 as one of the founding black fathers of Ross's Landing. He purportedly created the bell that rang to call the town meeting when the official name was changed to Chattanooga. Lewis's entrepreneurial vision led to the purchase of land from William Crutchfield for $2,000 and to the building of a blacksmith shop at Seventh and Market Streets. Here he monopolized the horseshoe trade during and after the Civil War. His blacksmith business prospered, enabling him to send three of his nine children to be educated in the North. One of his offspring was Isabel Marion, the mother of Willie Cook.[8]

By all accounts, Bill Lewis was an unusually bold and accomplished man. His character was as strong as the horseshoes he made. This strength was about to be tested, as his defiant, undisciplined namesake came to live with him.

Initially Chattanooga provided the optimum setting for Will's adolescent maturation, particularly with regard to his precocious erotic adventures.

He began to delight in the company of the opposite sex. Beautiful, blue-blooded Hattie "instructed" him in his first sexual encounter:

> a woman of the world, aged thirteen, a Cleopatra in all but age and throne, an octoroon with the best and worst of the Creole and African rising to the quintessence of passion. . . . This thirteen-year-old, raven-haired, red-lipped Cleo was the tops. She was a volcano, and her eruptions brought to a head the Battle of the Chattanooga Marne.

Willie's second cousins by marriage, Renee and Kate, were also among his companions. Renee was only fourteen, but her full breasts, big legs, and shapely hips caught Will's roaming eyes. "She was beautiful and she was good, but it was mating time for animals, and she was a healthy animal, a luscious Georgia peach, fully ripened, and waiting to be squeezed, bit, and torn apart."

Willie slept in a room apart from the rest. One evening as he prepared for bed, a large black snake darted from his covers. Terrified, he ran into the kitchen, interrupting his cousin's tub bath.

> I was so frightened that Renee, alarmed, forgot her nakedness. Like a little mother, she sat down on the floor, drew my head gently to her gorgeous breast, and crooned to me as you would to a baby. My fear quickly left, for there, against my lips, was a firm, warm, throbbing breast. Beneath the body of a Madonna, with all the best maternal instincts of the healthy and virtuous: love, mating, babies, and plenty of them. I kissed her breast with hard spasmodic sighs that made her grip me with muscles of iron. I forced my lips deep into that cream-colored nipple. It must have hurt like exquisite pain. Quickly stifling a scream, "Go back," she whispered, "I'll come right away." Gone was my fear of snakes: big snakes, little snakes, any old snakes. Renee was coming and I was ready. She came in her flimsy cotton nightgown, oh so clean, so wholesome, so deliriously happy, yet so humbly submissive. Was I not to be her man, married or not, was I not to be hers, to give her beautiful babies?
>
> Remember, dear reader, and be lenient: this was but a few years after slavery, where a woman and man, or boy and girl had but to say, "That's my man," or "That's my woman," and thus they mated. . . .
>
> So Renee got into my shake-down, her eyes swimming, her arms reaching out to embrace me and hurry to the final consummation of human bliss. If our bodies had joined, if we had spent the night in a truly youthful fervor of love, maybe many of the heartbreaks, the bitter disappointments, the disillusions, and illnesses that have been my fate might never have materialized. Instead, I remembered a warning my mother had given me. "People closely related should never marry." Just how close was a second cousin by marriage? Neither Renee nor I knew, but we both agreed it would be awfully bad to defy mother's warning and get any closer.

This short-lived romance ended when Will moved away and Renee subsequently was the victim of an incestuous relationship with her half-witted uncle, resulting in a severely retarded baby and Renee's premature death.

After nearly a year in Chattanooga, Grandpa Lewis, who in his life had outwitted the Confederates, overcame a myriad of drawbacks, and reared many children, decided he had met his match with Willie. His usual disciplinary tactics—depriving Willie of pocket money, dessert, or special privileges, locking him in his room, lashing him, or knocking him down with his fist—all proved futile. During his last whipping, Willie was stripped of his clothing and thrashed with two dozen switches from the pear tree, pared with their prongs protruding, all to no avail.

> The first blow he struck, the prongs cut into my body like a knife, but I felt no pain, only rage. I had never been struck like that. Slavery was over, abolished. Again the swish, the cut . . . this time I felt it good, but only hissed with set teeth to keep from sobbing. "You gray-haired son of a bitch!" And I kept saying it more and more weakly until I fainted. Yes, I shall always remember that beating, though for the life of me I don't recall why I got it.

Grandpa Lewis truly loved his grandson and probably admired his courage and stubbornness. If the truth be told, they were two of a kind—like grandfather, like grandson.

Will learned to shoe horses, chop wood, and repair wagons but still failed to learn discipline. He was punished frequently, with no effective result. Grandpa Lewis soon realized that the South was no place for Will's kind of Negro. He had already been in half a dozen fights with white boys who insisted upon calling him a "nigger." Bill Lewis knew that sooner or later Will would get into serious trouble. So he wrote his daughter Belle this missive:

> I am sending Willie back to you. I think he needs his mother. Today he sassed me and I whipped him. Then he sassed me again and I whipped him again. Then he cussed me and I knocked him down. He got up, looked me in the eye and said when I grow up I'm coming back and kill you. And he meant it.
>
> He's the damnedest child I ever saw, but I'm glad you named him after me. And I'm sending him back before one of us kills the other.
> Your Father

Two days later Willie was returned to his mother. As he awaited his train's departure:

> "Goodbye boy," Grandpa Lewis said, holding out his rough hand.
> "Goodbye, Grandpa," the lad replied. Now there was no holding back those damned tears. As the old man turned to leave, Willie sobbed, "Grandpa, we'll just call it a draw, huh?"

For a second Grandfather Lewis didn't understand what the lad meant, then suddenly comprehending, he smiled. "Yeah, call it a draw, son, call it a draw."

The youth began this journey in the smoking car of the Washington express train. To justify his presence, he furiously puffed on a three-cent black cigar.

Willie Cook had many experiences in his new home in the South. He "heard real Negro melodies for the first time," which caused him to characterize this interlude as his "soul period."[9] He not only had been infatuated with the charm of the Tennessee girls, he had been impressed by the natural splendor of the vast terrain. He would run off and gaze at the apex of Lookout Mountain and envision himself becoming a prominent musician, eradicating racial unjustness. Somehow he believed that Negro melodies "might be the lever by which my people could raise their status."

After a brief reunion with his mother in Washington, Willie decided to pursue his latent desire to study music. Since both his parents had been educated at Oberlin, it would become the natural setting for his musical education. If he had inherited any artistic ability, it no doubt had come from his paternal grandfather, who once organized an orchestra in Detroit composed entirely of Germans (except himself), wherein he played the violin and clarinet. Similarly, the violin was to become the instrument upon which the young Will would choose to express his musicality.

Chapter 2

FROM OBERLIN TO BERLIN

Plato and Socrates knew that the study of music is one of the finest disciplines for the adolescent mind.

Leonard Bernstein

In the early nineteenth century Willie Cook's paternal family was among the free African Americans of Fredericksburg, Virginia, who were fairly prosperous contractors. As a result, they were able to provide private education for their children. Many free as well as enslaved black families employed private teachers to instruct their young until Virginia's General Assembly passed a law in 1819 prohibiting this practice. When learning became increasingly more dangerous and difficult, free families such as the Cooks migrated to Detroit. There Willie's father was educated in private schools before entering Oberlin College.[1]

Located in Ohio's Western Reserve, the secluded town of Oberlin was merely 35 miles southwest of Cleveland and shared its name with the college. Both were founded in 1833 by the missionaries John J. Shipherd and Philo Stewart, who were inspired by the Alsatian pastor John Frederic Oberlin to cherish and institutionalize a strong religious belief in God and a deep sympathy for others.[2]

In the two decades preceding the Civil War, Oberlin township became a temporary haven for as many as 3,000 escaped slaves who were seeking freedom in the North. Six routes of the Underground Railroad ran through Oberlin—three from communities to the south, one from Norwalk to the west, and two running north to nearby ports on Lake Erie. The Oberlin community was "second only to Canada as an asylum for the hunted fugitive."[3]

The integration of its African-American residents was remarkable:

You could not only see black men and women in the classrooms of the college, sitting next to white students, but you could see black youngsters in the public school as well—a marked contrast to public schools elsewhere in Ohio, which were separate but hardly equal. . . .You could find black families in First Church, praying next to white parishioners. You could shop in one of their stores on South Main.You could hire a black man as a lawyer. You could find their names on voter registration lists at a time when black men did not enjoy the franchise in Ohio. And you could stroll through Westwood Cemetery and see the gravestones of both black men and women beside those of whites. At a time when blacks were not welcome or encouraged or respected virtually anywhere else in the United States, Oberlin was—in spite of some shortcomings of its own—an integrated community.[4]

Beginning in 1835, Oberlin College took a firm stand for abolition and was among the first to enroll students regardless of race or color.[5] It even elected John Cook's friend John Mercer Langston to its first Board of Education and made him its secretary. Consequently, hundreds of blacks made their way to the Oberlin College campus to study. The school also pioneered in the education of women, becoming the first coeducational college in the country to award bachelor's degrees to them in 1841. Few Oberlinians could boast of the number of ties to the college as could the Cook family. Both of Willie's parents took advantage of Oberlin's open door policies toward blacks and women, and they both matriculated there. His father received an A.B. degree in 1864 with highest honors, and his mother graduated from the "Literary Course" in 1865.[6] His uncle, George Frederic Thompson Cook, attended the college in the late 1850s and received an A.M. (honorary) degree in 1877, and Will's older brother, John, also graduated from the college.[7] When Willie arrived in Oberlin in 1883, he lived on North Main Street with his paternal Aunt Jennie Jackson and initially enrolled in the public school system. On one occasion, however, he swore at his Latin teacher for refusing to acknowledge Hannibal as a member of the darker race. He was immediately expelled. Soon, however, he was permitted to matriculate at the conservatory. Here he satisfied his musical interest by seriously studying the violin from 1883 to 1887.

When he entered Oberlin as a full-time student, Willie was fourteen. No doubt he studied harmony and counterpoint, pianoforte, and violin during the next four years; unfortunately, no transcript is extant. The 1880s were an optimum time in the conservatory's history for him to be studying there. Frederick G. Doolittle had arrived just the previous year and was given the task of developing the violin department. Heretofore harmony classes (including counterpoint) had consisted of ten students, who met for two one-hour sessions and were taught by the conservatory's director, Fenelon Rice, along with piano teachers L. Celestia Wattles and Calvin B. Cady. All three had been students at the Leipzig Conservatory, which became the standard of comparison for Oberlin's music faculty. The harmony text, *Lehrbuch der harmonie*, by former Leipzig professor Ernest Richter, was an English translation of the most popular manual of the period.[8]

Prior to Willie's arrival, Calvin Cady (who taught between 1874 and 1879) voiced his dissatisfaction with the pedagogical approach to theory at Oberlin.

> In the first place there is not enough practice in connection with it; too little is done to call out the inventive faculty of pupils. Then there is too much study of the representation of music and too little of the essence of it. The course progresses too rapidly and does not give opportunity for cultivation of the ear and the ability to *think* music.[9]

By the time Willie entered Oberlin, the conservatory had adopted a new syllabus for music theory, extending the course over nine terms or three years, and including ear training.

Willie may have taken his first piano lessons at Oberlin, where he would have played scales and exercises by Koehler and Spindler with rounded fingers and hands able to level a coin on their backs. He would have played Bach, Mozart, and Beethoven sonatas, as well as salon pieces by Mendelssohn and other early Romantics.

Applied music instruction was based on the European design, whereby two students were assigned the same hour with a given teacher. While one performed, another listened, watched, and hopefully benefited from the other's performance. Frederick G. Doolittle, Willie's violin instructor, taught for thirty years at the conservatory, chairing the violin department for the last half of his tenure.[10]

The 1880s were a time of transition for the college as it reexamined its conviction that education should be founded upon faith and introduced: better methods of teaching, stricter academic requirements, and a more enthusiastic spirit of scholarship. The advent of Darwinism at the college contributed to a rebirth of science instruction and a theological transformation from evangelicalism to the liberalism of Henry Churchill King, the mathematics and philosophy professor who would later become the college's president. New professors and equipment made scientific instruction competitive with that at colleges everywhere. Ohio Congressional Representative James Monroe, an endowed professor of political science and modern history, became the first teacher to lecture at the college on the contemporary times (including John Brown's raid at Harper's Ferry and the Abolitionist movement). Students began to grope for answers to questions as their social conscience found expression in community service and a kind of systematic study of society that would ultimately become the social science curriculum. Furthermore, with the construction of the Spear Library and the 1887 appointment of its administrator, Azariah Root, the college began to build a first-rate library.[11]

Willie Cook's education at Oberlin coincided with the end of James Harris Fairchild's tenure as Oberlin's president from 1866 to 1889. This was the post-Emancipation era, before Jim Crow began fully to spread his wings. Black students were given the same privileges as others, and whites determined for themselves how they would interact with blacks. No white was obliged to sit next to a black, since students were not assigned seats alphabetically. Apparently, "an unwritten rule" specified that blacks and whites should not room together in the dormitories, but they customarily ate side by side.[12]

President Fairchild believed that Oberlin students should be involved with the great moral issues of the day. The ideal student was to be both activist and judge, forcefully applying Christian ethical principles to all institutions and circumstances. Fairchild was convinced that a moral commitment brought vigor to the acquisition of knowledge and the disciplining of the mind.[13] The Oberlin milieu during Fairchild's presidency helped to solidify Willie's moral commitment to fight against racial inequality wherever he encountered it.

Despite the shifts in definition of what constituted a true Christian faith, the college maintained its mission of cultivating Christian character. Prayer or hymn singing opened each class. Revivals and prayer meetings, as well as mandatory chapel services, were frequent occurrences. The Congregationalism of the college's founders enhanced the student body's participation in their local churches.[14]

Willie Cook was afforded various opportunities to play at Oberlin's First Congregational Church, pastored by the renowned evangelist Reverend Charles G. Finney. The orange-brick edifice was the oldest and grandest west of the Allegheny Mountains. Willie would often arrive so late for his violin postlude that on several occasions the already dismissed had started to scatter in the churchyard; when he began playing Schumann's *Träumerei* or other similar work, however, many returned to the sanctuary to hear his soulful rendition.

In early 1884 Willie was also cited in the *Oberlin Review* as a member of the Double Quartette, which included Messrs. Koons, Buckley, Loomis, Hamilton, Kimball, Bunker, and Swift, a group that gave six concerts during their vacation in Eastern Ohio and Pennsylvania. Inclement weather affected the turnout in two cities, but the other four had large and appreciative audiences. There were numerous encores and many expressed a desire to hear the ensemble again. In rendering the selections, "they proved themselves to be thoroughly prepared and well qualified to perform their part."[15]

The conservatory students were required to attend Wednesday evening "rehearsals," opportunities for them to hear their fellow students perform, sometimes assisted by faculty. One such public "rehearsal" that Willie Cook may have heard attracted a respectable audience in the chapel in May 1884:

Polonaise in D Minor (Chopin) played by Miss Regal; Miss Boise rendered the very difficult "Sonata Pathetique," first two movements by Beethoven;

Miss Hottenstein gave the favorite "Spinning Song" from *The Flying Dutchman* in her usual charming manner. Miss Dennie sang an aria, "Mia Piccerella" by Gomez. Messrs. Andrews, Doolittle, and Cheeseman rendered Bach's "Sonata in G Major." Miss Nettleton sang Elsie's "Prayer" from *The Golden Legend*. Prof. Kimball rendered two songs, "The Dew Is Sparkling," by Rubinstein, and Siegmund's "Love Song," by Wagner. Miss Hamilton, with violin obbligato by Prof. Doolittle, rendered in her rich tones two songs by Weil, "In Autumn" and "Spring Song." Miss Taylor and Prof. Blakeslee played the duet "Repitio Me," and lastly came Mozart's "Symphony in G Minor" by the Conservatory Orchestra.[16]

Such performances as these were coupled with a series of Artist Recitals which had begun in 1878. Students heard such performers as Clarence Eddy, organist; Gertrude Stein, Ffangcon Davis, and Mr. and Mrs. George Henschel, vocalists; Leopold Godowsky, Teresa Carreno, and Mrs. Edgar Sweet, pianists; Carl Halir and Charles Gregorowitsch, violinists; the Kneisel (string) Quartet Club; and New York's Metropolitan Orchestra with Anton Seidl conducting. The Fisk Jubilee Singers also attracted a large audience in 1884, a performance Willie no doubt attended.[17]

Oberlin's most popular organization was the Musical Union, whose membership numbered up to 200. They performed four concerts a year and secured the best soloists available. Handel's *Messiah* was presented during the holidays, and another large choral piece was performed at the commencement. Their concerts included such works as Verdi's *Manzoni Requiem*, Brahms's *Ein deutsches Requiem*, Mendelssohn's *Elijah*, and Saint-Saens's *Samson and Delilah*.

The Cleveland Vocal Society held its May Festival at Oberlin in 1884, during William's first year. There were five grand performances, with three evening concerts and two matinees featuring some of the most eminent artists of the day, including Henrietta Beebe, Agnes Huntington, R. W. Britton, Albert L. King, and S. E. Jacobsohn. The chorus of 300 voices rehearsed for more than a year in preparation for the festival. They performed such works as Mendelssohn's *Hymn of Praise*, Macfarren's *Cantata*, and Rubinstein's *Tower of Babel*. This festival exceeded "all previous ones in the character of its singers and general musical magnificence."[18] Additionally, there were lectures on acoustics, aesthetics, and music history.

Willie was an active performer throughout his years at Oberlin. According to one reviewer, "Willie Cook, who is creating quite a sensation as a violinist," performed Deberist's "Sixth Variation" and Wieniawski's "Legende" at Weisgerber's Hall on October 12, 1886. His numbers "were among the best of the evening and were encored."[19] Two months later, on December 14, he appeared in concert at the same hall with African-American soprano Maudie Adair. His renditions of Vieuxtemp's "Romance" and Raff's "Tarantella" were described as good, given his limited performing experience. One critic observed: "The young man has natural ability, which is being developed by good tutoring. He plays with expression, excelling in legato passages. His age [nearly 18] and short time at his chosen instrument should be taken into consideration. . . . He will undoubtedly one day rank among our first violinists. The concert was a financial, artistic and social success, and can be numbered among the best given here."[20]

The outcome of this performance was soon marred by a controversy portrayed in *The Cleveland Gazette* under the title "The Cook-Adair Squabble." The performers disagreed about who was to collect the income from the concert and how it was to be distributed. Willie reported that he made "no promises in regard to dividing the proceeds" and that he expected to use them toward his studies.[21] The Adair perspective was that both parties "willingly agreed to divide the proceeds equally."[22] In the end, Adair was allowed to keep the funds she had acquired from her individual ticket sales, while Master Willie Cook felt deceived: "She had spread the rumor in order to stigmatize and place me in the wrong," he argued.[23] This dissension was symptomatic of episodes throughout Cook's life during which he usually considered himself the victim.

Willie's student days at Oberlin enabled him to foster a relationship with the editor of the African-American *Cleveland Gazette*, whom he visited on several occasions.[24] This was the beginning of a lifelong practice of using journalistic opportunities and promotional advertisements to keep his name in public view. Willie Cook also performed at a Christmas church benefit, during which "the charming violinist gave a fine rendition of the 'Mazurka;' and at the Excelsior Reed Band's Grand Concert and Ball at Haltnorth's Hall on March 23, 1887. The following month he appeared in concerts at Doan's Armory in conjunction with other performers.[25] He also played with Wendell P. Dabney, the uncle of the dance-band leader Ford Dabney. Cook created the ensemble, featuring himself on the violin and Dabney on the guitar, while his brother John played the piano.[26]

It is not fully known to what extent Willie participated in extracurricular activities. No evidence exists that shows him active in social clubs or the student newspaper. The literary societies introduced some of the best orators, the most famous singers, and the finest orchestras to Oberlin; Oberlin's fraternities, on the other hand, were often censured for their gluttony and drunkenness.[27] Willie seems not to have been attracted to either kind of group; he was throughout his life never a "joiner" of social clubs or organizations.

According to Cook's memoir, he eventually outgrew Professor Doolittle's violin instruction. The suggestion was made that he matriculate at the conservatory in Cincinnati, but race relations in Ohio's southern city were as prejudicial as in Chattanooga. Doolittle then advised Will to study at Berlin's Hochschule für Musik under the Austro-Hungarian violinist Joseph Joachim (1831–1907). In 1887 he was sent home to Washington with fifteen dollars borrowed from Professor Doolittle and a note explaining that, in light of his unusual talent, he should study abroad.

By now Cook's mother had remarried and was the wife of Dr. James H. Howard, a physician alumnus of Howard University.[28] Despite her husband's income and even though she taught sewing many years in Howard's Industrial Department, the couple did not have sufficient funds to send Willie abroad. Therefore, Mrs. Howard approached Frederick Douglass. For many decades the First Congregational Church of Washington had been a dynamic artistic center featuring frequent concerts of well-known musical artists. Frederick Douglass was instrumental in arranging a recital there for Willie. The performance netted almost $2,000.[29] It also exposed his uneven violin technique, which was somewhat camouflaged by broad, soulful tones that dazzled most of his listeners. One exceptional critic[30] noted that the boy "has great talent, but must study, study, study. He has many faults: bowing, interpretation, stance, everything except tone and time."

Upon Will Cook's arrival in Berlin, Professor Doolittle's introductory letter was given to an Oberlin native, Mrs. John Morgan, who had relocated there. She recommended that he study with a certain Herr Moser before auditioning, advice that Willie took.

William found a Berlin culture that had been saturated with the legacy of the French Revolution's calls for liberty, equality, and fraternity. Although these ideals were more concerned with class than with race, they fostered a more liberating climate for the African-American William Cook, who interpreted the rallying cry of liberty as giving each artist the right to develop his unique artistic expression. The experiences of the heart took precedence over those of the head, and the flame of romanticism was kindled.[31]

Berlin offered many outward signs of progress in the late 1880s. Its economic prosperity made it an attractive site for actors, singers, musicians, and performers. New museums and galleries, cafés, beer halls, and concert halls enriched and entertained its diverse population of one million. Many artists had contributed to its cultural landscape. Mozart had performed there before the court of Friedrich Wilhelm II in 1789, as had Beethoven in 1796. The flamboyant violinist Paginini had given eleven public recitals before the Prussian royal family in 1829. During the following year a procession of dazzling pianists, including Clara Schumann, Sigismund Thalberg, Ignaz Moscheles, and Friedrich Kalkbrenner, graced Berlin's concert stages. These recitals culminated in the brilliant virtuoso performance of the pianist Franz Liszt in 1841. French composer Hector Berlioz also visited Berlin in the same year and wrote in his memoirs:

Music is in the very air. One breathes it in theatres, in churches, in the street, in public parks—everywhere. For everyone respects music in Berlin, rich and poor alike, clerics and soldiers, the common people and the King. The monarch above all brings to the cultivation of music the same passion as he devotes to science and the other arts, which is saying a great deal. Hence the attraction that Berlin holds for great artists, and the remarkable popularity of music in Prussia.[32]

The Berlin of William's sojourn offered well over a hundred musical performances a year. Impressive concert halls were built to dazzle audiences, including the Mozartsaal, the Beethovensaal, and the Bechsteinsaal, along with two dozen theaters. William witnessed the charisma of Hans von Bülow, who conducted the Philharmonic Orchestra to packed houses in Philharmonie Hall. Von Bülow's orchestral concerts ran the gamut from classical to modern repertoire conducted with intensity and without scores. When asked once about the challenge of performing from memory, he replied, "One must have the score in one's head, not one's head in the score."[33] Hans von Bülow further transformed the Philharmonic's orchestral concerts by shortening them and providing a musical centerpiece, usually a symphony. His concerts typically began with an operatic overture by Mozart, Verdi, or Meyerbeer, followed by marches and polkas, and ending with battle music in the tradition of Beethoven's "Wellington's Victory." Von Bülow also promoted the New Music cause of Liszt, Berlioz, and Wagner. William also saw performances by conductors Arthur Nikisch, Emil Paur, and Anton Seidl and heard such artists as Amalie Joachim and Lillian Nordica sing Italian opera at Kroll's Summer Garten. By the late nineteenth century, Berlin had at least two opera houses—the Royal Opera House on Unter den Linden, where Italian, German, and later French works were performed, and the Schauspielhaus on the Gendarmenmarkt, a venue primarily for spoken drama and the home of Singspiel.

Berlin had also nurtured the arts through the founding of a leading school of instrumental music in 1869,[34] coincidentally the year of William's birth. This Hochschule für Musik was led by Joseph Joachim, friend of Johannes Brahms. As one of the greatest solo violinists of his day, Joachim had previously worked under Liszt in Weimar and at the court of King George V of Hanover. He remained director of the Hochschule until his death in 1907, while concertizing internationally both as a soloist and with his quartet.

By the time of Cook's arrival, the Hochschule's enrollment had gradually risen to about 250 students, with four separate departments in composition, voice, orchestral instruments, and piano and organ.[35] The school had become known for its pedagogical effectiveness and had enjoyed international renown for decades. Eventually, William mustered enough courage to take the entrance audition for the Hochschule. He chose a very technical composition, resulting in extreme stage fright after hearing younger competitors render Fiorillo and Paginini exercises with superb technique. When William's moment arrived, he could hardly hold the violin in place, appearing to have lost awareness of where he was and what he was doing. Crying and cursing beneath his breath, he tucked the violin under his arm and started to leave the podium. A deep voice asked him if he could play anything else. It was the master teacher and founder of the Hochschule, Joseph Joachim himself! William's confidence, soul, tone, and talent returned as he began to play Beethoven's "Melody in F." The judges no doubt sympathized with this nearly twenty-year-old African-American youth, who was in a foreign city, a foreign culture, and a foreign conservatory. Cook reports that the following morning his name was at the top of the acceptance list (incidentally, it's also near the beginning of the alphabet). This may have been a sympathy vote for William, since there were many who surpassed him in everything but soul and tone.

William Cook from Washington, USA, appears among the pupils in the *Jahresberichte* of the Hochschule für Musik. He is reported to have studied with Heinrich Jacobsen, who from 1887 to 1889 had been a pupil of Joachim. Jacobsen was head of the "Direktorium" and Departmental Chairman of Orchestral Instruments.[36] In *The Cleveland Gazette* of March 30, 1889, Cook was described as "making rapid and exceptional progress with his studies with the master and virtuoso Joachim, in Berlin, Germany. His teacher takes a personal interest in him and compliments him highly, which is much when it is known that the great master never flatters." No doubt this item was submitted by Cook himself. There is no documentation that he was taught by Joachim at the Berlin Hochschule, nor that he was among the published prizewinners (an assertion made in his memoir). Perhaps he took private lessons with Joachim, in which case his name would not appear. This seems plausible, since another pupil asserted that because of Joachim's overactive lifestyle, "students never had fixed lessons but were summoned by a servant at short notice."[37] Besides,

> Joachim was not a pedagogue who gave graded lessons from the foundation onwards till mastery was achieved, but restricted himself to giving advice and guidance to specially talented and advanced pupils. . . . Some of them used his name for publicity purposes.[38]

Of course Cook's association with Joachim immensely enhanced his marketability and reputation.

Mary Church (Terrell), who was to become a well-known civil rights activist, was a senior at Oberlin when William was a freshman. Writing in her autobiography of a surprise encounter with him on the streets of Berlin, she noted that he was studying violin at the Hochschule für Musik with Joachim when many others with more impressive credentials were denied that opportunity.[39] *Time* Magazine, in its obituary of the composer, made the unsubstantiated claim that Cook played in the Berlin Symphony.[40]

While in Germany, William did become fluent in the language, learned the social graces, and fraternized with both men and women. One such friend he met on a park bench was Max Adler, a real estate agent from Chicago, who was also Sears Roebuck chairman Julius Rosenwald's brother-in-law. He advised William to wear high-collared white shirts instead of flannel ones if he wished to be treated more seriously by the public.

Cook confesses:

I had plenty of money and when that was gone, presto! More would somehow come in overnight. Thanks to Max Adler, I knew how to dress. My
brown complexion and bushy hair made me something of a novelty with
the frauleins. By this time my German had become fluent: I could make
love in two languages. What more did a young man about town need?
Since the early experience with Hattie, I had played around with other
girls in Washington and Oberlin, but never had the pickings been so plen-
tiful. It wasn't that I preferred white girls, as the Negro stereotype is sup-
posed to; there simply weren't any brownskins around. Totally unpreju-
diced in the matter, I just liked girls, period! A good dancer, I met most of
my conquests at balls, public or private.[41]

On November 30, 1889, *The New York Age* disclosed that William had just
returned to Washington after a year's study in Germany[42] and was "A musical phenomenon performing some of the masterpieces upon his violin
with one hand." Presumably his departure from Europe occurred because
he had depleted his funds, become ill, or both.[43]

Soon after Cook's homecoming, he began to conduct. The following September *The Freeman* announced the formation of a new Washington, D.C.
orchestra with Frederick Douglass as president and Willie Cook as director.[44] Their first concert was on September 26, 1890, at the Grand Army Hall,
with E. Hoffman as the soloist; the concert marked the saxophone's debut in
an African-American Washington orchestra.[45] The Cook ensemble was
credited with having "an excellent reputation for its ability to interpret and
render well the better class of music. . . . Mr. Cook plays so well and throws
so much spirit in his work that the rest of the orchestra cannot but partake
largely of his enthusiasm and strive to do good work."[46]

As William Mercer Cook acclimated himself to being back in America, he
made a dramatic name change. He had been named by his parents for his
maternal grandfather, Bill Lewis, and the Dean of Howard Law School, John
Mercer Langston, who was elected briefly in the late 1880s as a black con-
gressman from Virginia. He now abandoned the middle name, Mercer, in
favor of Marion, in honor of his mother:

The change came one day after I had heard Langston deliver an address.
I wanted to vomit! There he was, my father's friend, the great race leader,
my namesake, publicly boasting that he got his lovely hair, his tiny feet
and hands from his white ancestors! I rushed home, told Ma about it, and
concluded: "My bushy, wiry hair certainly didn't come from any white
ancestor; my hands are small enough, but look at my feet (my feet were
then as large as they are today, and I wear a man-sized eleven shoe). You
named me after the wrong man, Ma. From now on I'm Will Marion. If
Marion's good enough to be your middle name, it suits me to a 'T.'[47]

Whether or not Cook misinterpreted Langston's remarks, it is clear that his racial consciousness and pride were dramatically sensitive aspects of his personality. His assuming of his mother's name took courage, pride, and love of the highest order. Ironically, Cook's features were not stereotypically Negroid. His passionate rhetoric may have been means of overcompensation. By now he strutted along with a curled-at-the-end moustache, symbolic of his manhood and distinguished good looks.

By the time William Mercer Cook reached his twenties, he had chosen a new name and a new career as conductor/composer. His maturation progressed from Master Willie at Oberlin to William in Berlin, and ultimately to Will Marion on Broadway and beyond. The discipline of music had become the stabilizing force in his ever-changing status, a means to overcome the loss of his father and family and the unstable environment of his youth. As Cook traveled from Oberlin to Berlin, music and music making remained the common denominator in his life.

Chapter 3

THE CHICAGO WORLD'S
FAIR OF 1893

Nationalism provided purpose for progressive change.

Reid Badger

Will Marion Cook's whereabouts during 1891 and 1892 are a mystery. *The St. Paul Appeal* of January 31, 1891, indicated that he was considering a proposition from Orpheus McAdoo to sign a two-year Australian-tour contract with his Virginia Jubilee Singers. He was not in the traveling ensemble. His name appeared prominently, however, with those providing entertainment at the greatest international fair of its time—The World's Columbian Exposition, which took place in Chicago in 1893. The spacious lakefront city of Chicago was chosen over Washington, St. Louis, and New York as the best urban center for mounting the stucco exhibition temples and showcasing the most impressive artistic and scientific global accomplishments of America's four centuries of progress. Chicago became, literally and figuratively, a "white city," with its white architectural structures and the exclusion of almost all black Americans in the planning and execution of the fair's exhibitions.[1] Race leader Frederick Douglass and anti-lynching crusader Ida B. Wells orchestrated the publication of a pamphlet *The Reasons Why the Colored American Is Not in the World's Columbian Exposition.* In it they argued:

> The exhibit of the progress made by a race in 25 years of freedom as against 250 years of slavery would have been the greatest tribute to the greatness and progressiveness of American institutions which could have been shown the world. The colored people of this great Republic number eight million—more than one-tenth the whole population of the United States. They were among the earliest settlers of this continent, landing at

Jamestown, Virginia in 1619 in a slave ship before the Puritans, who landed at Plymouth in 1620.[2]

The pamphlet's introductory statement, written by Frederick Douglass, was peppered with eloquent sarcasm:

> We would like for instance to tell our visitors that . . . two hundred and sixty years of progress and enlightenment have banished barbarism and race hate from the United States; that the old things of slavery have entirely passed away, and that all things pertaining to the colored people have become new; . . . that here Negroes are not tortured, shot, hanged or burned to death, merely on suspicion of crime and without ever seeing a judge, a jury or advocate; that the American Government is in reality a Government of the people, by the people and for the people, and for all the people.

To combat this exclusionary climate, some black musicians, artists, and writers would have a special African-American day at the fair that would resemble those honoring the Swedish, German, Irish, and other nationalities. Among them were Will Marion Cook and Paul Laurence Dunbar, a young black poet. In fact, Cook was escorted to the White House by Frederick Douglass to meet with President Benjamin Harrison, with a view toward ensuring Cook's participation in the fair's events. Douglass had campaigned for Harrison, who in turn appointed him minister-resident and consul-general to the Republic of Haiti and chargé d'affaires for the Dominican Republic.[3] The president issued Cook a letter of permission enabling him to sponsor concerts within the fairgrounds.[4]

When all was said and done, August 25, 1893, was designated "Colored American Day" and Cook persuaded Frederick Douglass to be the keynote speaker. Douglass proclaimed that the day should be celebrated "in a way that would reflect the highest credit upon the Negro in the eyes of assembled nations."[5]

Not all African Americans were enthusiastic about this idea. Douglass's co-pamphleteer, Ida B. Wells, led those who opposed a "Colored American Day" and initially urged blacks to boycott the fair. Wells and her faction feared the event might provide whites with ammunition to mock the race. She believed that a segregated fair day was patronizing, and she particularly dreaded watermelons donated for the occasion; the prospect of blacks munching them was reason enough in her book to cause whites to continue withholding equality from African Americans.[6]

As it turned out, "Colored American Day" was observed in a dignified manner and the appearance and demeanor of the participants brought honor to the race. After a successful parade through the main streets of the city, several thousand colored people came to the fairground gates at Jackson Park. They were well dressed, prosperous looking, and courteous. Many were visitors from other parts of the country who were able to afford train fare to Chicago as well as the fair's fifty-cent admission fee.[7]

"As a concert of very high order," Colored American Day's presentation "was a glittering success." An audience of 2,500 (two-thirds of them black) assembled in Festival Hall to hear music and oratory. On stage were Fredrick Douglass, Isabella Beecher Hooker (sister of Harriet Beecher Stowe), and the daughters of Colonel James Beecher, the famous writer's brother, who had been commander of the first black North Carolina regiment. Listeners included such notables as Richard J. Rust, the first president of Wilberforce University, and Lieutenant J. H. Alexander, the first black graduate of West Point.[8]

> There was classical music rendered by black men in a way that would grace the grand opera stage, and there was an oration, which, with its fervid eloquence, burned itself into the memory of those who listened. . . . First on the program was a tenor solo by J. Arthur Freeman. He sang Buck's aria, "The Shadows Deepen," in good voice, Maurice Arnold Strothotte, Professor of Harmony in the National Conservatory of Music, accompanying on the piano. But the musical treat of the afternoon came later when Sidney Woodward of Boston, a tall and very black young Negro, was presented. He sang one of Verdi's arias in the tenor that for sweetness and purity of tone has rarely been equaled at the Exposition. Of course he was encored, and so insistent was the audience that they called him out five times to bow his appreciation. Paul Dunbar of Dayton, Ohio, another tall young colored man, the author of *Oak and Ivy*, was presented and read an original poem on "The Colored American."

Mme. Deseria Plate sang the aria "Lieti Signor" from the *Huguenots* in lieu of Sissieretta Jones and, as an encore, "Nearer, My God, to Thee," "with tender and touching effect."

"The succession of talented black artists who graced the stage that afternoon was unmatched," according to one reviewer.[9] Perhaps the most unusual and ambitious of the numbers on the program was the performance by Harry T. Burleigh of the National Conservatory of Music of America with selected songs from Will Marion Cook's opera *Uncle Tom's Cabin*. It appears that a performance of this entire work was once envisioned but had to be abandoned because of disputed payment (discussed later in this chapter). Dramatic selections were recited by Hattie Brown, and several classical violin numbers were performed by Joseph Douglass, Frederick's grandson.[10] (The Fisk Jubilee Singers were also scheduled to perform, but it appears that they did not.)[11]

Why was Cook drawn to *Uncle Tom?* He may have seen an earlier production of the play, based on Harriet Beecher Stowe's novel, during its many performances through the country. There were themes of family separation after slave auctioning; loyalty toward slave owners in spite of cruel treatment; and perilous journeys to freedom. Critic John William Ward characterized the novel's movement theme as people in constant motion "seeking a resting place, seeking no less than a home." He suggested that "The tragedy of the Negro is that he has, quite literally no home." Cook identified with this "longing-for-home" motif as manifested in his life since the loss of his father and the subsequent dispersion of his family.

The status of *Uncle Tom's Cabin* as a milestone in American literature also obviously appealed to Cook, who wanted to be taken seriously as a composer of serious opera. One even wonders to what extent he envisioned its staging. No extant score exists, nor evidence of an entire performance ever being presented; Still, it seems certain that Cook did indeed write an African-American opera as early as 1893—if nothing else a significant indication of his compositional aspirations.

After the concert, those present listened to Frederick Douglass, who took this opportunity to condemn white supremacy in his speech on "The Race Problem in America." The famed abolitionist orator passionately intoned:

> Men talk of the Negro problem. There is no Negro problem. The problem is whether the American people have loyalty enough, honor enough, [and] patriotism enough, to live up to their own constitution. We fought for your country, we ask that we be treated as well as those who fought against your country. We love your country. We ask that you treat us as well as you do those who only love a part of it.[12]

Paul Laurence Dunbar reinforced this patriotic theme in his reading of his "Ode to the Colored American:"

> And their deeds shall find a record
> In the registry of Fame.
> For their blood has cleansed completely
> Every blot of Slavery's shame.
> So all honor and all glory
> Tho those noble sons of Ham–
> The gallant colored soldiers
> Who fought for Uncle Sam![13]

Despite the noble words, the event remained clouded by controversy. Ironically, a day designated to showcase African-American cultural achievement in reality demonstrated how well blacks could perform European genres—Italian arias, Protestant hymns, and the like. Acculturation was the avenue to greater acceptance into the larger social order. Some black newspapers were openly critical. The following day *The Cleveland Gazette* (August 26, 1893) reported that ""Colored Folks' Day" at the world's fair was a farce. Hardly one of the prominent persons advertised to participate—to speak, sing and play—was present. Even the promised watermelons were conspicuously absent."

The most noted absentee celebrity was Sissieretta Jones, better known as "Black Patti" (after the Italian soprano Adelina Patti), who had been given a prominent role in *Uncle Tom's Cabin,* a work she declared "to be the most beautiful music she ever heard."[14] Manager Charles S. Morris apologized to the audience for her absence. According to at least one source, she had been influenced by the opponents of the occasion and had chosen not to perform, even though she had been advanced $300 on an $800 contract for three appearances.[15] But Black Patti had other reasons for not showing up as well. In an irate letter to the editor of the black newspaper *The Conservator,* the letter writer claimed that Cook and Morris, although they had prior knowledge that Sissieretta Jones would not appear as scheduled, prominently continued to advertise that she would be singing a leading role in *Uncle Tom's Cabin,* in order to increase ticket sales. Furthermore, the reason Mme. Jones did not appear was that her fee had not been sent in time. Morris and Cook had forwarded $100 with the promise of $200 more to come. The letter writer speculates that they intended to win the latter amount in a "craps" game; and when that sum did not materialize, the funds had to be hurriedly secured from Frederick Douglass. In the end, Black Patti kept the $300 for damages and divided it with her manager. Ultimately Morris and Cook drew down over $500 from their brilliant success. Their integrity was blemished, however, for the opera did not appear on the stage.

Nor was Will Marion Cook at the performance, according to the letter writer, "The folks wanted to hear his violin, but it or its master or both was 'on a tare' and not a single note did the opera get from manager Cook." The writer further acknowledged: "Cook is fairly well known in Chicago where he is considered a kind of good natured crank who can get more music out of a violin than any colored man that ever came here."[16]

Cook may have been too embarrassed to put in an appearance at the program, which failed to present more than a few songs from his advertised opera, but he and his contemporaries seized both the cultural and employment opportunities at the Columbian Exposition. James Weldon Johnson, then a student at Atlanta University, clinched the chance to earn money for the coming school year as a "chair boy," carrying fairgoers around the grounds in wheelchairs for seventy-five cents an hour.[17] Similarly, Paul Laurence Dunbar secured an assistantship with Frederick Douglass at the Haitian Pavilion; Dunbar hoped that fair patrons might want to purchase his recently published first book of poems.[18]

There were also those who were employed as Creole waitresses in checkered bandannas and starched white aprons, in the restaurant inside the Louisiana Building. They served gumbo, red beans and rice, and opossum stew under the watchful eye of their white bosses. Two black men dressed as slaves sold miniature souvenir cotton bales for the Brinker Company.[19]

Opportunities were also available away from the fairgrounds in the Tenderloin District, where itinerant musicians could be heard throughout the night as they eked out a living. Relatively obscure players such as Scott

Joplin (later dubbed the "King of Ragtime"), "Plunk" Henry (named for piano ragtime rhythms transformed from his banjo), and W. C. Handy (who was to become the "Father of the Blues") earned pocket money performing in gambling dens, saloons, and houses of prostitution.[20]

Maurice Peress's *Dvořák to Ellington* convincingly describes the emergence of ragtime as an important outcome of the Columbian Exposition. He includes two press interviews with Will Marion Cook in which Cook describes the significance of the fair for the emergence of ragtime. In the 1898 interview, Cook is quoted as follows:

> This kind of movement, which was unknown until about fifteen years ago, grew out of the visits of Negro sailors to Asiatic ports, and particularly those of Turkey, when the odd rhythms of the *danse du ventre* [belly dance] soon forced itself upon them; and trying to reproduce this they have worked out the "rag."
>
> During the World's Columbian Exposition at Chicago, the "Midway Plaisance" was well filled with places of amusement where the peculiar music of the "muscle dance" was continually heard, and it is worthy of note that after that time the popularity of the "rag" grew with astonishing rapidity and became general among Negro pianists. [The Midway included Cairo Street's "hootchy kootchies" and their *danse du ventre*.]

Similarly, in a 1915 *Chicago Defender* interview, Cook indicated that "at the World's Fair in Chicago, "ragtime" got a running start and swept the Americas, next Europe, and today the craze has not diminished."[21]

Ragtime was not the only cultural innovation in the air. *The Creole Show* also was playing at Sam Jack's Opera House during the Columbian Exposition. This historic production successfully departed from the traditional minstrel format in giving prominence to beautiful black women at center stage, with a female interlocutor and at either end. Bob Cole was one of several comedians in the production, which climaxed with a grand cakewalk finale in which a cake was the winning dancing couple. This show was an important first step toward the development of the black musical comedies of Will Marion Cook, Bob Cole and J. Rosamond Johnson, Bert Williams and George Walker, and Ernest Hogan.[22]

The Dahomey Village at the fair may have been the inspiration for Cook's most significant musical, *In Dahomey*, of 1902. This exhibition featured West Africans, who periodically broke into tribal songs and dances around their authentic-looking huts. Reactions to their display ranged from amusement to revulsion.[23] The distinguished music critic Henry E. Krehbiel recorded his observations of the West Africans over several days. He noted the singing and harp playing of one of the minstrels. Even more striking were the war dances, performed several times each day and accompanied by unison singing, drums, and bells. Krehbiel was most impressed with the polyrhythmic skills exhibited by the singers performing in duple meter and the drummers performing in triple meter. He and John C. Fillmore attempted to transcribe these musical events, but when their transcription books appeared, the natives immediately altered their style of playing.[24]

"The World's Columbian Exposition was not meant to be a stage for black Americans, but a stage it turned out to be. It was the greatest gathering of singers, musicians, composers, poets, suffragists, lawyers, journalists, educators and clergy of the nineteenth century."[25] The fair also proved significant for Will Marion Cook's compositional career. Besides the probable influences of *The Creole Show* and *In Dahomey*, he later collaborated with Paul Laurence Dunbar, Harry T. Burleigh, Bob Cole, and James Weldon Johnson in the writing and performing of black musical comedies and popular songs.

It is further possible that he caught sight of the composer Antonín Dvořák on "Czech Day" (August 12, 1893), while Dvořák was conducting the Festival Orchestra in his *Symphony in G Major, Op. 88, Slavonic Dances (6,2, and 3), Op. 72*, and his overture *My Country, Op. 62*. Burleigh addressed a letter to Dvořák the next day:

> Dear Doctor,
>
> I want to introduce to your consideration Mr. Will M. Cook, a former pupil of the great Joachim. Mr. Cook has marked ability in the line of composition and desires very greatly to meet you and speak with you about his work. He has composed an opera, the principal role of which I will sing. . . .
>
> I am going away from Chicago today but will leave this note for you and Mr. Cook will call and see you.
>
> I sincerely trust you will listen to his work and give him your opinion. . . .[26]

Apparently Cook impressed Dvořák, both personally and musically, for soon Cook journeyed to New York City to study composition with him and to play at least occasionally in his orchestra.

Chapter 4

THE NATIONAL CONSERVATORY AND
BEGINNING OF MUSICAL CAREER

To this day no institute of musical instruction can be said to have surpassed
The National Conservatory in potentialities.

Edward N. Waters

The visionary New York teenager Jeannette Meyer was pro-
foundly influenced by her experience as a music student at the
Paris Conservatory in the 1860s. Upon her return to the States, she married
the wealthy food merchant Francis Beattie Thurber, and in 1885 she founded
the National Conservatory of Music, located at East 17th Street and Irving
Place in Manhattan. It attracted a brilliant faculty, offered a comprehensive
curriculum, and was a vital force in the development of music in America.

A liberal admission policy was maintained in order to augment the conservatory's 600 white students with "as many Negroes of positive talent as
may apply." These pupils were recruited for the purpose of producing black
professors of merit.[1] Similarly, women and the physically challenged were
admitted in significant numbers. The general student tuition was $100 per
semester, with competitive scholarships available for the musically gifted.
Recipients were to perpetuate the scholarship fund by contributing a per-
centage of their income during their first five years of employment. Needless
to say, these return contributions did not always materialize.[2]

Mrs. Thurber knew that an outstanding faculty would be essential to the
success of the school. Toward that end, she explored abroad and was successful in attracting the Bohemian composer Antonín Dvořák as director
in 1891. His arrival was arranged to coincide with the celebrations com-
memorating the 400 years since the "discovery" of America by Columbus.
He was also expected to found a school of composition that was *truly* na-

tional in character. In a letter to *The New York Herald* (May 28, 1893), Dvořák acknowledged:

> It is my opinion that I find a sure foundation in the Negro melodies for a new national school of music, and my observations have already convinced me that the young musicians of this country need only intelligent direction, serious application and a reasonable amount of public support and applause to create a new musical school of America.[3]

Composition courses became the principal venue for developing this school. At the time of the Chicago World's Fair, Dvořák had seven pupils and expected to have more the following year. He once told a reporter, "I take only those far advanced in composition; that is, understanding thorough bass, form and instrumentation."[4] Only highly gifted students were privileged to study with him.

> [T]hey had to have an adequate mastery of counterpoint, the determination to work hard, and sufficient natural ability to give a reasonable guarantee that they would be likely to succeed in the musical profession. He made considerable demands on those he accepted, both as regards quantity and quality of work, and according to Harry Rowe Shelley, expected his American students to produce a piece of composition at each of their three weekly classes.[5]

Students were well aware that if they brought unsatisfactory work, they would be dismissed without hope of reprieve.

Dvořák taught an impressive array of American composers, including William Arms Fischer, Rubin Goldmark, Harvey Worthington Loomis, Harry Rowe Shelley, and Henry Waller. Goldmark's achievements were particularly noteworthy; he later became director of composition at Juilliard and exerted a major influence on many of the younger generation of American composers, including Aaron Copland, George Gershwin, and Frederick Jacobi (who also later taught composition at Juilliard). Dvořák himself identified the African-American Maurice Arnold (Strathotte) of St. Louis as "the most promising and gifted of his pupils."[6]

Composition students would have taken classes in sight-reading and ear training using solfeggio (do, re, me, etc.), history of music with Henry Finck, who was music editor of the New York *Evening Post,* elocution, and piano. The first two courses were mandatory. This curriculum, with its humanistic foundation, positioned The National Conservatory in the vanguard of theoretical pedagogy for musical studies.[7]

Unfortunately, little evidence survives that reveals much about Will Marion Cook's first-hand experience at the conservatory. On December 4, 1893, National Conservatory students performed a musical program under Antonín Dvořák's baton at the Scottish Rite Hall in Madison Square Garden. Among the black students performing were Will Marion Cook, Harry

T. Burleigh, and Maurice Arnold.[8] Soon thereafter, on January 23, 1894, Dvořák directed the National Conservatory Chorus and Orchestra in a benefit concert for the *New York Herald* 's Clothing Fund at Madison Square Garden in which Cook may have participated.[9] Cook apparently disagreed with Dvořák about his obligation to perform in concerts. In one published account, he described his conservatory experiences as "a bit of composition under Dvořák, harmony and mighty little counterpoint under John White."[10]

> I went on to New York to study at the National Conservatory of Music— endowed by Mrs. Jeannette M. Thurber. . . . She made no distinction of color, creed or state of good looks. She didn't even care much about the money. Jews, Negroes, real white people. Fact was a little bit of everything and everybody was in the musical melting pot. All she and Dr. Dvořák asked was talent—heaps of it—and the power of concentration on the subject at hand.
>
> Burleigh was the pet. I [was] the outcast of the whole school. Burleigh ran errands, played the tympani (extremely well) in the school orchestra, sang baritone and bass in [the] school Negro Chorus. And smiled his way into the hearts of all. . . . I had forgotten how to play my fiddle. Not have seen it in many years. Fact [is the] last good one was pawned and never redeemed. I couldn't starve, could I. 'Twas tough going those blessed years.

Cook continues with accolades to his friend Burleigh:

> I know of no Negro (not even Coleridge Taylor) during the last 50 years so respected so loved—and who has done so much to lift his and my God forsaken Race out of the mire as has this grand old man—Harry T. Burleigh. And in passing long the road he has helped to lift plenty white folks. How they love him.[11]

Dvořák no doubt grew particularly fond of Burleigh as he spent many hours listening to him sing the folk songs of his people. This repertoire apparently inspired the writing of Dvořák's celebrated symphony *From the New World (No. 5 in E Minor)*, which thematically embraced the spirit of African-American folk melodies. A generation later, Burleigh reflected on the genesis of this work:

> There is a tendency in these days to ignore the Negro elements in the "New World" symphony, shown by the fact that many of those who were able in 1893 to find traces of Negro musical color all through the symphony, though the workmanship and treatment of the themes was and is Bohemian, now cannot find anything in the whole four movements that suggests any local or Negro influence, though there is no doubt at all that Dvořák was deeply impressed by the old Negro "spirituals" and also by [Stephen] Foster's songs. It was my privilege to sing repeatedly some of

the old plantation songs for him at his house, and one in particular, "Swing Low, Sweet Chariot," greatly pleased him and part of this old "spiritual" will be found in the second theme of the first movement of the symphony, in G major, first given out by the flute. The similarity is so evident that it doesn't even need to be heard; the eye can see it. Dvořák saturated himself with the spirit of these old tunes and then invented his own themes. There is a subsidiary theme in G minor in the first movement with a flat seventh, and I feel sure the composer caught this peculiarity of most of the slave songs from some that I sang to him; for he used to stop me and ask if that was the way the slaves sang.[12]

From the New World not only embodied African-American characteristics but similarly contained tone poems based on "The Song of Hiawatha" by Henry Wadsworth Longfellow. In an interview in the *New York Herald* at its premiere December 15, 1893, Dvořák described a quasi-programmatic intent in the second and third movements:

> It is in reality a study or a sketch for a longer work, either a cantata or an opera which I propose writing and which will be based upon Longfellow's Hiawatha."
>
> The *scherzo* of the symphony was suggested by the scene at the feast in Hiawatha where the Indians dance, and is also an essay I made in the direction of imparting the local color of Indian character to music.[13]

The exposure to Dvořák's philosophy of using the indigenous folk music of America undoubtedly gave Cook license to creatively exploit his cultural heritage in his own compositions that were published after his experiences at the conservatory in New York. "We're Marching On," published by George W. Broome, was designated as "A Colored American Hymn" and dedicated to Frederick Douglass. Although not published until 1896, this work may have been created originally for "Colored American Day" at the World's Fair in Chicago. His text sets forth a grand march to racial victory and liberty, recapturing the nostalgia for Africa, the pain of slavery, and the hope for interracial unity.

> When sorrow's deepest pangs do move,
> Until the heart doth swell.
> If visions of a distant home
> Should'st cause the tears to well,
> Mourn not for 'tis the work of God
> Who doeth all things well.
>
> *Refrain:* And we're marching on to victory,
> Ring out the joyful sound,
> Ask God for might,
> Then fight for right
> Till Liberty be found.

Those dreadful days of slavery,
When we apart were torn,
Were hated dreams of awful night
And centuries were borne,
But with the gleaming of the light,
There came a wondrous dawn.

I see a day, 'tis near at hand,
When all throughout this land,
Shall man to man as brothers be
In one united band.

Imagery similar to that in the refrain, "And we're marching on to victory," may be found in other song texts: for example, "Let us march on/Till victory is won" from James Weldon and J. Rosamond Johnson's Negro National Anthem "Lift Every Voice" (1900); and Scott Joplin's signature song and dance "Marching Onward" from the opera *Treemonisha* (1905). Cook's final stanza's theme of brotherhood is reminiscent of his hero Beethoven's "Ode to Joy" from the *Ninth Symphony,* which uses Schiller's translated text: "All mankind are brothers plighted. . . ."[14]

The introduction to Cook's "We're Marching On" appears to paraphrase Antonín Dvořák's *Largo* ("Goin' Home") from *The New World Symphony* (ex. 4.1); this introduction dovetails into "visions of a distant home" (Africa) in the first verse. A melodic quotation from the penultimate phrase "We Shall Overcome" is also apparent (ex. 4.2). Already in this early hymn, Cook demonstrates his penchant for nationalism and chromaticism. His decisive refrain embodies an essential *raison d'être* for both Douglass and Cook: "Ask God for might, / Then fight for right/ Till Liberty be found." This final phrase becomes even more poignant by its dramatization of "liberty" with an octave soprano leap and a cadential Picardy third (ex. 4.3). "We're Marching On" represents a pride-filled forerunner of "Swing Along," which Cook composed some seven years later.

An opposite racial polarity is expressed in "That'll Be All Right, Baby!" (1896), a song in a coon-style vernacular by Cook that depicts an unfaithful

Example 4.1 "We're Marching On," mm. 1–4 (Will Marion Cook [West Medford, Mass.: George W. Broome, 1896]).

Example 4.2 "We're Marching On," mm. 20–24.

courtship turned violent. This genre of comic songs was a prevalent late nineteenth- and early twentieth-century phenomenon that portrayed exaggerated negative images of blacks as violent and sexual as well as drunkards and thieves. The coon term was derived from raccoon, a meat apparently enjoyed by the slaves. The story unfolds:

> Late last night about eleven o-clock,
> Went to see my Lula gal, the door was locked,
> I peeped in the window a-meaning no harm,
> And yonder sat my Lula in another nigger's arm,
> My mind was agitated and my heart was sore,
> Got myself together and I busted in the door,
> My Lula gal's a black gal, but I gave her such a fright,
> I hope I'll never leave here if she didn't turn white.
> Such queer foolin' now I never could stand,
> Didn't want my Lula loving no nigger man,
> I then grabbed that woman just to scare her a bit,
> The way that wench did holler, well you'd tho't she had a fit,
> Up jump'd the other nigger and I grabbed at his arm,
> When he drew his steel I knew he meant to do me harm,
> I felt myself a-going and I didn't know no more,
> 'Till I found myself a-bleeding just outside my Lula's door.

This episode is no doubt less fact than fiction, yet it introduces a quasi-realistically violent scenario with tongue-in-cheek.

Cook's poetry is somewhat irregular. Even though the stanzas are written with four couplets rhyming aa,bb,cc,dd, the rhymes are not always exact. For example, "clock" and "locked" in the first stanza and "stand" and "man" in the second. The two-stanza poetry is generally written in iambic feet either as iambic pentameter, iambic hexameter, or iambic heptameter. There are

Example 4.3 "We're Marching On," mm. 32–37.

Example 4.4 "Love Is the Tend'rest of Themes," chorus (Will Marion Cook [New York: Howley, Haviland, 1896]).

frequent violations of the basic iambic pattern, and the last line includes fifteen syllables, which is one more than the iambic heptameter. Given the crude language of Cook's verse, the irregular metrical pattern may be intentional, further creating the coon song milieu. (This kind of metrical freedom is also prevalent in the 2x2 beat framework of contemporary rap.)

"Love Is the Tend'rest of Themes" (1896), on the other hand, portrays Cook's romanticism, transcending racial specificity. The centralized poetic waltz admonishes:

> Love is the tend'rest of themes,
> Love is the sweetest of dreams,
> And it comes to the heart all forgot and forlorn,
> Like the glorious dawn of the sunlit morn,
> Love speaks of joys yet unknown,
> Love claims the soul for its home,
> And its passion sublime will be your's [sic] and be mine,
> Love is my all, my own.

This text is set in a melodic style suggestive of Franz Lehar's "Merry Widow Waltz." It can be seen as a precursor to "Society," from *In Dahomey* (ex. 4.4).

Whatever Will Marion Cook's compositional efforts prior to his time at the conservatory, by 1896 he had begun a compositional career in earnest. The above three songs, all in different styles, were published by an independent New Englander, George W. Broome,[15] and two New York firms—George W. Broome, Spaulding and Gray, and Howley, Haviland and Company. Their themes of nationalism, commercialism, and transcendence represent underlying motives that are present in Cook's entire output. The "home" motif is introduced in "We're Marching On" through its nostalgic reference to the African homeland. On the other hand, "Love Is the Tend'rest of Themes" reveals a more existential belief that: "Love claims the soul for its home."

Cook had also found a new love that seemed to offer more opportunity for creativity—namely, musical theater.

Chapter 5

"BROADWAY, HERE I COME!"

The American musical is considered by many to be this country's most significant contribution to world theatre.

Hollis Alpert

As musical productions were being created and perfected during the 1890s, a theater known as Worth's Museum in Manhattan served as the dramatic training center for black performers entering the profession. It also was instrumental in initiating Will Marion Cook to this genre, as he revealed in his unfinished autobiography:

> Worth's Museum, on Thirtieth Street and Sixth Avenue, was the place where I first got any real experience in Negro show business. On this corner was a small theater where the best performers—Ben Hunn, Tom Brown and Bob Cole—often put on afterpieces and shared in the proceeds with the proprietor. I lived on Thirty-second Street near there. When Bob Cole told me he was to run the show for a week and asked me to be musical director, I jumped at the chance.[1]

Cole organized a revue with an "All Star Stock Company" of fifteen young black vaudevillians during the early 1890s: Billy and Willie Farrel (the cakewalk dancers), Tom Brown, Fred Pifer, Mamie Flowers, Billy Johnson, Mattie Wilkes, Gussie L. Davis, Will Proctor, and Stella Wiley, among others. The Museum offered "dramatic training" to the company, with the multitalented Bob Cole serving as director, playwright, and stage manager.[2]

Cook soon realized that his European musical training was worlds apart from the demands of black musical theater. He confessed:

> To have studied orchestration; to have slept with petite editions of the Beethoven Symphonies and Overtures; to have gone night after night to the Academy of Music (where Burleigh and I were admitted free for copying music); to have heard a large orchestra render Wagner's tempestuous, langorous, voluptuous, tumultuous, dynamic music, expressing every human and sometimes unearthly emotion; to have heard Emil Paul, von Bülow and other greats render von Weber and other outstanding composers with orchestras of 80 to 120 men—then to try to orchestrate a little song or dance for five, six, seven men at most, which one had to do as musical director at Worth's Museum was a problem. I didn't make out so good, No, I wasn't any ball of fire. At Monday's rehearsal, when Ben Hunn, a 270-pound genius, who was just as evil as he looked, handed me a drum part only and said: "Bub, play this for me," he meant that the rest of the orchestra should fake. That was when I really lost heart and interest. So, it was no wonder at the end of the week when Bob Cole said: "I've got $32; how much do you want?" I replied: "Give me the two bucks." But believe me, folks, I had learned a lot.[3]

Will Marion Cook could not have chosen a more gifted mentor than Bob Cole to teach him the tricks of the theatrical trade. Cole was the creative genius behind many of the black musical productions of the day, including "Black Patti's Troubadours," which featured the gifted soprano Sissieretta Jones. She was able to exploit her New England Conservatory training by appearing in the finale, performing arias and operatic selections with the chorus.

The black musical theater being forged in Manhattan was a far cry from the caricatured imagery typical of minstrelsy. Notable composers, entertainers, and writers spent hours discussing the course blacks in theater should pursue. These meetings were held at Jimmie Marshall's four-story brownstone hotel on West 53rd Street, which became New York's center for Negro artists. On Sunday evenings, dinner was so popular that tables were booked days in advance, and an excellent four-piece orchestra provided the musical entertainment. The Johnson brothers, James Weldon and J. Rosamond, moved into the large back room on the second floor, added a piano, and began to write musicals. In the evenings their room was the scene of many conversations, usually centered on "the manner and means of raising the status of the Negro as a writer, composer, and performer in the New York theater and world of music."[4] Bob Cole, the other partner in their professional trio, lived two doors from the Marshall, providing an ideal working and living arrangement. The vaudevillian team of Bert Williams and George Walker also lived in the vicinity. Their flat soon became the headquarters of many artists, including Cook, Will Accooe, Harry T. Burleigh, and Paul Laurence Dunbar. The Marshall's "importance as the radiant point of the forces that cleared the way for the Negro on the New York stage cannot be overestimated."[5] In many ways it helped to shape the black musical theater that developed and flourished in Manhattan during the late 1890s and into the early 1900s.

The black musical sketch known as *Clorindy—The Origin of the Cakewalk* was originally conceived as a vehicle for the celebrated comedians Bert Williams and George Walker, although when the production was actually staged, a prior booking with Koster and Bial's music hall circuit prevented them from performing. Will Marion Cook got to know the comedians when he lived in New York. He outlined to them his idea of a musical whose plot revolved around the genesis of the cakewalk in Louisiana during the 1880s. After the idea was slightly refined, Williams and Walker introduced Cook to their manager, Will McConnell, who would provide a ten-dollar loan for Cook to return home to Washington, where he would write the piece. Cook was ready for a new venture. Luckily, he was able to persuade Paul Laurence Dunbar, the poet who had taken part in the Colored American Day program at the Chicago World's Fair, to join him. It was their first collaboration, and it occurred right after Dunbar completed writing his first novel, *The Uncalled.* Cook and Dunbar signed contracts with Witmark to publish *Clorindy* as early as 1895 but did not get around to writing it until three years later.[6]

Frederick Douglass had first introduced Cook to Dunbar at the Haitian Building during that famous 1893 Fair. Cook's notes offer a portrait of Dunbar as quite debonair:

[I]n his rusty black suit (in which you could see your face and figure) was a sight to behold. Of less than medium height—perfectly formed, and smooth black skin he inherited from his mother (also a beautiful black)— a brow noble in proportions—and eyes that were soft, glowing, [and] eloquent . . .. toothpick shoes (Dunbar had the feet of an aristocrat). [He had a] hat, cane and gloves to match and all the trimmings. He was a mess— I mean a mess of a good looking [fellow] except the mouth . . . the mouth which was ugly—uglier than mine—and that's a record. His teeth were perfect—and so white that they threw into bas-relief his glossy black skin and hair. He was a picture of the finest Kaffir type. And I don't believe any of his women ancestors had even looked at a white man much less stop to idle away a few moments.

Like all Negro geniuses, Dunbar had many white female admirers! . . . Dunbar always (as he aptly phrased it) stuck to his "corn beef and cabbage"—(Brown Skins). . . . He loved 'em all colors: thin and full figures—tall and short—and [what] he begged for—was a drop or two of African Sun, to make them respond and glow—to be ready for his mating call—and to love life—and joy. "He could spread some joy."

And he could write quicker, more beautifully and with less erasures than any body I've seen. . . . Lyrics of all kinds poured from his soul and pen in a coloring of beautiful melody.[7]

Their creative endeavor began in John Cook's Sixth Street home basement, just below Howard University.

> The three gathered . . . around the big piano. John thumped out the rhythm with musician's magic as Will hummed the tune. Paul walked back and forth, composing out loud. Sometimes a rhyme wouldn't come, or a balky phrase refused to fit the meter.
>
> "Here," Will said. "Have another beer." Refreshed, Paul began dictating again. Will scribbled down the words beneath the notes and jumped up to do an impromptu dance. A cakewalk. "Clorindy's" subtitle was "The Origin of the Cakewalk." Will read off the names of their songs: "Darktown Is Out Tonight," "The Hottest Coon in Dixie," "Love in a Cottage Is Best," "Dance Creole," "Who Dat Say Chicken in Dis Crowd?" "Jump Back, Honey."
>
> "We've got a hit show," Will said, slapping Paul enthusiastically on the back.[8]

The Cook brothers and Dunbar stayed up all night composing *Clorindy* with the aid of two dozen bottles of beer, a quart of whiskey, and a raw porterhouse steak, cut up with onions and red peppers. With no further use of the piano, merely the kitchen table, they finished the songs, the libretto, and all but a few measures of the ensembles.[9]

If there's any truth to Dunbar's story, each song was created in four hours, without accounting for the libretto in between. Cook was known for exaggeration. But given Dunbar's skill in writing swiftly, the story might be in fact true.

Some time afterwards Williams' and Walker's tour came through Washington with the Hyde and Behman show. Their manager was convinced that Witmark could be persuaded to produce *Clorindy*. Cook recounts a subsequent meeting with his publisher in New York:

> I am not now and never have been a great pianist, and I could sing only a little bit, but for forty minutes I struggled to give this man some idea of the songs and ensembles. At last, starting for the door of his private office, he interrupted me long enough to say that he thought I must be crazy to believe that any Broadway audience would listen to Negroes singing Negro opera.[10]

To nearly all prospective producers, opera was too cultured, highbrow, and sophisticated for persons of color, who were not equal under the law.

Disappointed, disheartened, and destitute, Cook walked to the 23rd Street ferry, where he happened upon Sol Johnson, a friend who worked as a porter on the Washington train. His friend locked him in a closed dining car and admonished him not to make a sound, and thus hidden, he returned to Washington without having to purchase a ticket.

For several months Cook plunged into a depression. His brother John, who worked at the pension office, refused to loan him money, insisting that he seek gainful employment. Predictably, Cook borrowed another ten dollars, this time from Bill Higgins, his brother's former Howard University classmate.

Another train ride to New York was now required, this time with Cook as a regular passenger: porter Johnson charged him two dollars fare. Many theatrical rejections later, Will Marion received a lead from George Archer, chief usher of the Casino Roof Garden, to contact Ed Rice, the producer of summer attractions.

Meanwhile, Cook assembled a genius aggregation of black talent and began rehearsing the show. For weeks he gathered three or four prospective cast members and taught them *Clorindy's* score, with and without the piano, sometimes singing or attempting to sing the choral parts himself. At the Greasy Front Club he met Ernest Hogan, a leading comedian and song-writer of the controversial "All Coons Look Alike to Me." Cook played "Who Dat Say Chicken" in the back room, and Hogan was impressed by the tune's catchy strains. That very evening, Hogan learned "Who Dat Say Chicken" as well as "Hottes' Coon in Dixie."

Daily trips to Ed Rice's office proved futile, however. Cook was asked, "Who are you, and what do you want?" for thirty straight days. On the thirty-first day he overheard Rice tell another group to return for a Monday audition. He immediately rushed to the Greasy Front Club, where some of the *Clorindy* cast congregated. "I told them a most wonderful and welcome story; we were booked at the Casino Roof! And I sent them to contact all the others. Everybody was notified to be at the Casino Roof Garden on Monday at eleven a.m. . . . . That was probably the most beautiful lie I ever told."[11]

Luckily, Ed Rice was not present where the audition began the following Monday. Instead, English conductor John Braham first viewed several smaller acts. Cook then impressed him by revealing his musical training with both Joachim and Dvořák and explained that he would present his "Negro operetta." Braham gestured for the score, whereupon Cook explained that his singers responded best to his conducting style, no doubt assuming that the theater orchestra would better execute the syncopated, swinging rhythms. Cook was then given the unprecedented honor to conduct an all-white theater orchestra. The twenty-six black singer-dancers envisioning work and steady pay sang "Darktown Is Out Tonight" as never before.

Just then, Ed Rice showed up and, hearing the syncopated sounds as he approached the theater, he shouted to Braham, "No nigger can conduct my orchestra on Broadway!" Braham—God bless him!—said, "Ed, go back to your little cubby-hole"—Rice had a little pagoda at one end of the roof, where he 'entertained' attractive women after the night show—"Go back to your little cubby-hole and keep quiet! That boy's a genius and has something great!"[12] Braham was so enthusiastic that he convinced Rice to allow a trial run to begin the following Monday as part of a larger variety show.

Rain the following Monday, however, caused a cancellation of *Clorindy* on the Casino Roof Garden. The cast was sent home disillusioned and heartbroken, Cook considered himself a failure. Ernest Hogan, on the other hand, took the situation in stride. He capitalized on the delay in order to eliminate Dunbar's dialogue, which had suffered because of acoustical limitations, enhanced the staging with sensational dance numbers, and refined the cakewalking scene.

The trial run began a week later on July 5, 1898. The performance marked Broadway's first black musical-comedy sketch—albeit on a rooftop.[13] The hour-long entertainment occurred just before midnight in the open summer air with action-filled songs and dances. *Clorindy* was preceded by a wide range of miscellaneous acts: Millie Stoller, Signor Ettore Negrini, and Adelina Routtino singing high-class vocal music; Signor Ricci with his violin and Eddie French with his virtuosic banjo; Alma Doerge, Mattie Phillips, and *Clorindy's* own stars Belle Davis and Ernest Hogan contributing renditions of popular songs. Six petite girls in colorful costumes tripped through two ballets, followed by Alice Atherton and George Fuller Golden featuring their specialty act; Catherina Bartho in her unusual dances; and finally Maude Courtney taking the audience by storm with her medley of familiar patriotic American songs[14]. Despite the strong roster of attractions, it was *Clorindy's* opening that created a sensation. Conductor Will Marion was attired in Charles W. Anderson's full dress coat (Anderson weighed 200 pounds; Cook, 126), Harry T. Burleigh's vest (he was very short; Cook, quite tall) and his own out-at-the seat, frayed-at-the-cuffs light pants, and the same feet-mostly-on-the-ground shoes, clean shirt, and tie.

Immediately I struck up the introduction and opening chorus. When I entered the orchestra pit, there were only about fifty people on the Roof. When we finished the opening chorus, the house was packed to suffocation. What had happened was that the show downstairs in the Casino Theatre was just letting out. The big audience heard those heavenly Negro voices and took to the elevators. At the finish of the opening chorus, the applause and cheering were so tumultuous that I simply stood there transfixed, my hand in the air, unable to move until Hogan rushed down to the footlights and shouted: "What's the matter, son? Let's go!"

So I started his strut song, which began and ended with an ensemble, "Hottes' Coon." . . . The rest of the performance kept them at the same pitch, especially "Who Dat Say Chicken in Dis Crowd?" This number . . . had to be repeated ten times before Hogan could leave the stage, and there were encores galore when Belle Davis sang "Jump Back, Honey, Jump Back!"

The Darktown finale was of complicated rhythm and bold harmonies, and very taxing on the voice. My chorus sang like Russians, dancing meanwhile like Negroes, and cakewalking like angels, black angels! When the last note was sounded, the audience stood and cheered for at least ten minutes.[15]

"Darktown" was provocative in several ways. It used confrontational jabs as verbal weapons and at white audience members. Prior to the cakewalking chorus came a proclamation:

> White fo'ks yo'
> Got no sho'!
> Dis huh's Darktown night.

Cook's lyrics proclaimed the overall uninhibited behavior of black life. In a society where African Americans were seeking social equality, on stage they felt at liberty to flaunt their mastery of sound, movement, timing, and the spoken word. The theatrical stage became a safe venue where they could feel equal, if not somewhat superior to mainstream Americans.

The second night of *Clorindy*'s performance, Cook got carried away by his new wardrobe:

> I get to the theatre about ten o'clock, full of everything that goes to make a man happy. A good bath, some decent underclothes, a hand-me-down dress suit, given or loaned me by one of the chorus men till I can get a real dress suit, and a pair of new shoes, a gift from George Archer. (And they hurt my feet for weeks; I was in no condition for a sudden pair of new shoes.)[16]

Cook was not alone in experiencing something new. James Weldon Johnson asserted that "*Clorindy* was the talk of New York." Cook's breathtaking ensemble numbers and finales, sung by a lusty chorus, were complete novelties. "Broadway had something entirely new."[17]

The New York Dramatic Mirror offered more restrained praise: "The music, while it is of the coon song order, is of a much higher class than the average rag-time ditty, and the orchestration is full of effects seldom heard outside of grand opera. . . . The chorus was well trained and sang the concerted numbers with excellent effect."[18]

In Cook's musical description:

> Rhythms very syncopated, peculiar chords, a bit contrapuntal and worst of all, 'twas all in Dunbar dialect.
> Here's a paradox! When speaking, these singers most of them with little or no education used a dialect that even Dunbar (the Master) could have listened, learned and transcribed. In fact, he did!
> But when they sang, that was different. They used a more perfect English than did Harvard or Yale.[19]

Conversely, one of the singing/dancing stars, Belle Davis, "a long, lean but voluptuous mulatto" from Texas, slowly drawled out funny songs that made you want "to laugh and cry at the same time. A small voice, but the timbre was exquisite." Cook believed in her vocal talent even when producer Ed

Rice judged it as too soft for the roof. She was an instantaneous success, however, in the thirty-minute song miscellany that preceded *Clorindy*. Since only two songs were rehearsed, they were repeated several times.[20]

Similarly, star performer Ernest Hogan favorably impressed New Yorkers and contributed greatly to the success of the show. "His enunciation was so distinct and his manner was so original and amusing that the audience gave him an ovation."[21] He and Belle Davis led the inimitable cakewalk finale.

The House of Witmark published Cook's hit songs from the production "Darktown Is Out Tonight," "Who Dat Say Chicken in Dis Crowd?" "The Hottest Coon in Dixie," "Jump Back," and "Creole Dance." The first four were among Isidore Witmark and Isaac Goldberg's list of twenty-two "song successes" for 1898.[22] Cook himself understood the power of the moment and declared that "Negroes were at last on Broadway, and there to stay."[23]

"Darktown Is Out Tonight" was the opening as well as the cakewalking finale. It represents one of the few coon songs that Will Marion published. His vernacular lyrics revealed stereotypical views of blacks as prancing, dancing, and fighting:

> Warm coons a-prancin',
> Swell coons a-dancin',
> Tough coons who'll want to fight;
> So bring 'long yo' blazahs,
> Fetch out yo' razahs,
> Darktown is out tonight![24]

The melody progresses from a declamatory verse style with patter-like repetitions to a more lyrically varied chorus. There are infectious iambic rhythmic patterns throughout, initially in the verse, then broadening in the chorus. The latter rhythm lends itself to the highstepping of the cakewalk, as does the predominantly disjunct melodic chorus line (ex. 5.1). A syncopated rhythmic spark complements the tension created between the voice and the accompaniment during the verses (ex. 5.2).

In this song and a few others of the same ilk, Cook adheres to the ragtime conventions of the day. The melody displays a lively syncopation while the bass proceeds in an um-pah manner. The lyrics, though hardly acceptable to modern-day taste, were considered "relatively refined ragtime" at the time. Ridiculing most ethnic minorities was customary:there were comic impersonations of Chinese, Germans, Italians, and Jews. Ragtime scholar Edward

Warm coons a - pran-cin', Swell coons a - dan-cin', Tough coons who'll want to fight;

Example 5.1 "Darktown Is Out Tonight," chorus (Will Marion Cook [New York: M. Witmark, 1898]).

Example 5.2 "Darktown Is Out Tonight," mm. 6–9 *The score indicates an inaccuracy; the sixteenth rest should be an eighth rest.

Berlin acknowledges that "The performance of coon songs by African Americans was not merely a reluctant adherence to a convention expected by the dominant culture. Rather, it was felt that a bit of mockery, even self-mockery, was 'good fun.'"[25]

"Who Dat Say Chicken in Dis Crowd?" parodies the Negro's preoccupation with chicken in song lyrics at the turn of the twentieth century. The chicken represents a dominant stereotype for which blacks presumably had a hopeless addiction.[26] The chorus also has an affinity with the chorus of "Darktown Is Out Tonight." The intervallic distances between the first five notes in the chorus of each song are identical. Moreover, the rhythms are the same in their opening measures (exx. 5.3 and 5.4).

By contrast, "Hottest Coon in Dixie" begins in a lilting, storytelling manner, describing the scene of a strolling gentleman—immaculately dressed (or overdressed) with gloves and cane. It portrays the city slicker (a Zip Coon carryover from the minstrel stage). The 6/8-metered verse shifts to a 2/4-metered chorus, accompanying a strutting dance. The "hot" song repertory was a popular contemporary staple. These songs exploited the connection between sexuality, body heat, and uninhibited black fun. "A Hot Time in the Old Town" of 1896 is another example.[27]

As the end of the summer of 1898 approached, *Clorindy* was transformed and renamed *Senegambian Carnival,* becoming a musical potpourri with a tinge of African identification (several sequels follow this practice). A prominent solicitation ad soon appeared in *The Colored American*:

> Colored girls with good voices, handsome faces and forms, who wish to join an opera company, to consult with Will M. Cook, Casino Roof Garden, New York City. Send photograph, correspondence strictly private.[28]

Presumably, responders would appear in this production. A new theatrical promoter, George W. Lederer, sent the cast on a tour of first-class theaters, opening at the Boston Theatre on September 5, 1898. To enhance its longevity, a month later *Senegambian Carnival* was reorganized yet again to be

Example 5.3 "Who Dat Say Chicken in Dis Crowd?" chorus (music, Will Marion Cook; lyrics, Paul Laurence Dunbar [New York: M. Witmark, 1898]).

presented in cheaper houses. By the end of October the two comedians for whom Cook had originally envisioned his show, Bert Williams and George Walker, were starring in *Senegambian Carnival* at Koster and Bial's in New York.[29] In the loose plot of *Senegambian Carnival*, Bert Williams won $30,000 in a lottery and was being fleeced out of it by George Walker. This production was referred to as a "rag-time craze receiving another boom," a black comedy in three scenes with the most elaborate sets ever used for a production of its kind. Regarding the two artists, Cook declared that "the Negro god of comedy and drama must have opened his thick lips and wide mouth and laughed loud, long, [and] raucously!"[30]

The first scene was set on a steamboat pier in Louisiana, the second on a New York street, and the third in a grand ballroom, with a stairway reaching into the skies. A profusion of red incandescent and calcium lights with a splashing fountain helped to make the final scene even more spectacular. The entire company walked down the staircase, creating a dazzling effect.[31]

Critics deemed the entertainment excellent, if a bit too lengthy and with a little too much idle dialogue. Williams and Walker were as humorous as

Example 5.4 "Darktown Is Out Tonight," chorus.

ever, Goggin and Davis introduced amusing acrobatics, while Hodges and Launchmere added to the general variety. Champion buck dancer Henry Williams displayed fancy steps, and a grand cakewalk by the entire company of forty concluded the performance, staged by Frank Mallory and conducted by Harry T. Burleigh.[32]

The early criticism of the show's length apparently was taken seriously, for a month later another review noted that "Williams and Walker's entertainment now moves with great briskness and is consequently very enjoyable."[33] It was further "brightened up" with added songs by new composers, but by mid-December their six-week engagement at Koster and Bial's had concluded.[34]

Cook appears to have had little to do with the Koster and Bial performances, since he was apparently touring with a separate road production of the same show. By November 1898 Harry T. Burleigh was directing the New York production.[35] Cook's collaboration with Williams and Walker, however, was just beginning. The continuously evolving *Senegambian Carnival* soon developed into a burlesque vehicle for the comedians under the name *A Lucky Coon* (which would itself soon mutate into Cook's *The Policy Players*).[36]

Williams and Walker's popularity heightened under Hurtig and Seamon's management. The crowd outnumbered the seating capacity at the January opening of *A Lucky Coon* at the Olympic in Providence. From there, Williams and Walker toured Philadelphia, New York, Dayton, Chicago, and Milwaukee.

However many changes the production underwent, it was the original *Clorindy* that proved essential in Cook's acquisition of two crucial career assets—namely, a wife and a publisher.

Will Marion's beloved was Abbie Mitchell, a young schoolgirl from Baltimore who was vacationing in Manhattan with her aunt as *Clorindy* was being cast. Some twelve years earlier, in New York, she had been born on East Third Street to a musically inclined African-American mother and a German-Jewish father. Tragically, her mother died during childbirth, leaving Abbie to be reared in Maryland by her mother's oldest sister, Alice, along with her father, grandmother, and Aunt Josephine.[37] Yet within six months of her arrival in New York, death had again robbed her: this time of both father and grandmother. These two had doted on Abbie throughout her childhood: her father had built a dollhouse and hand-crafted her shoes; while her chubby-faced, smiling grandmother met her each day at the corner after school, with an apple, orange, or homemade cookies. Grandmother further spoiled her by lying in bed beside her each night until she fell asleep. It's no wonder that Abbie became stricken with "unspeakable grief" after losing these devoted relatives. The family physician, a Doctor Horn, urged Abbie's aunts to provide her with a change of scenery so that she could leave behind her painful memories of Baltimore for the exhilarating sights and sounds of New York City.

Aunt Josephine and Abbie arrived in June 1898. They settled into a small Manhattan apartment on 33rd Street and soon became absorbed in elevated trains, the zoo, the theater, and the museum. Every morning at about 7:30 Abbie made her way to the fire escape "playground," where she sang to herself mostly "Ave Marias" from her church-choir repertory. The immediate neighborhood, instead of complaining, applauded, requesting the little "mockingbird" to sing more.

As fate would have it, the dark dapper comedian Billy English was living in the same complex. He heard Abbie serenading from the fire escape and told her that the chorus of the hit production of *Clorindy* needed more singers. Aunt Josephine protested that Abbie "was only a child and nice girls didn't go on the stage!" Billy English laughed and pointed out, "That child's voice has money in it—she'd earn easily fifty bucks—go see Cook."

So [I] dressed in my polka dot challis dress, my best ribbon on my hair, which was long, thick, bushy, hence was always in two braids down my back. We went to the Casino Theatre Roof Garden. What a lovely day! The sun shone brightly, it was warm, the sky was so blue, not a cloud. One would think it was a sign that life would be wonderful, that destiny was opening a path of beauty for me—thus I walked to my fate. Up we climbed to the roof. To me it was beautiful palm trees, ferns, boxes of flowers, rows of tables, chairs piled up in the air; the women were cleaning. Warm as it was in the street, up here it was coolly pleasant. There was a bare stage except for a piano, one electric lamp and three men standing in the middle. One was Will Marion Cook, tall, slender, with great burning eyes, a little mustache, hat on the side of his head.

Another was Harry T. Burleigh, not so tall as Cook nor so thin, with gray eyes and brown mustache. The third was Paul Laurence Dunbar, tall, black, homely, but with kindly eyes and gentle expression. These men were already famous . . . .

"Are you Mr. Cook?" I asked.

"Yes," he said. "What do you want, little girl?"

"Mr. Billy English sent me to sing for you. May I?"

"Yes. Where's your music? What do you sing? Do you know any Negro songs?"

"No," I replied quite pertly. "I'm a nice girl. I only sing classics." He laughed and pulled his hat further down over his eyes.

When Burleigh spoke in a reassuring voice:

"Come here, little girl, sing a scale for me . . . ."

I sang several scales that took in the entire compass of my voice, from middle C to the D in alt. With Mr. Burleigh accompanying me, I sang C. B. Hawley's "Because I Love You, Dear"—the composer himself had taught me that number—and an "Ave Maria" by Millard. Was I honored by Mr. Burleigh? No, who was he in my young life? All this time Paul Laurence Dunbar and Mr. Cook had remained silent. Then Mr. Cook said coldly: "You have a glorious voice, plenty of fire, but you can't sing a damn thing!" I was very insulted. The idea! I couldn't sing! *I*, who had thrilled my audiences from the fire escape! *I*, who felt that there was but one singer superior to me: Black Patti! Who was Cook to criticize me?

Mr. Cook sat down and played two of his own compositions: "Love in a Cottage" and "Darktown Is Out Tonight." When he had finished, he saw that I was deeply moved, for my soul was in my eyes, in my heart, in my voice, as I remained almost too affected to speak coherently. To think that this gruff man could create anything so wonderful! As dumb as I was, I knew that God had given him a great gift.

"That's the kind of music you should sing," he said: "that's Negro music and you're ashamed of it!" I tried to defend myself by explaining that decent colored girls did not sing coon songs or ragtime, as it was then called.[38]

After the audition, Abbie was offered $35 a week to join the *Clorindy* cast. "I was to see the show that night, rehearse the next morning to learn the songs by ear, for I did not know how to read music."[39] One of the first Negro songs she sang in the show was "Jump Back Honey, Jump Back." Surprisingly, it became a hit. Abbie admits that her extreme youth (she was only 12 years old) made the audience sympathetic: "to them I was a child with talent."

When September came, Abbie returned to school in Baltimore. "Mr. Cook expressed being sorry to lose me, for my voice had been of service; it could have been the way I tried to out sing the entire group—[he] added if I ever needed a friend just send a card or telegram, he'd respond immediately."

At school, however, Abbie's "fame" caused her to be ostracized by her peers. "I really had committed the unforgivable crime, I'd been on the stage, hence I'd become a lewd-girl at thirteen." (She had turned thirteen on September 25.) She was deeply wounded, ashamed, yet convinced "that I was really a good girl. Fate was working out my problem unknown to me, for Mr. Cook suddenly appeared at my home in Baltimore."

Clorindy was now on tour and urgently needed singers. Cook persuaded Abbie's family to allow her to rejoin the cast. Promises were made to continue her schooling while she was on the road and in the care of Mrs. M, the mother of two daughters in the show. The arrangement was sealed and Abbie returned more committed to a career on the stage.

The production successfully opened at Nerth's Boston Theatre with Abbie in the chorus observing everything everyone in the stellar part did. They toured other cities before arriving in Chicago, where Mrs. M. decided to remove her daughters and Abbie in order to advance their careers with Black Patti. Abbie should have been euphoric about performing with her idol, Sissieretta Jones, and laughing at the extraordinary humor of comedian Ernest Hogan. Instead, she felt betrayed by Mrs. M. Without consulting her, she wrote Mr. Cook and requested permission to rejoin the cast. He was in dire need of her talent, having had two leading ladies depart. Will Marion Cook wired consent and Abbie joined the touring company at the Great Northern Theatre in Milwaukee. Soon thereafter, she had aspirations of playing the title role. Ed Rice convinced Cook to audition her. "Fortunately," wrote Abbie, "I had learned every line, every dance step, everything and I went thru with colors flying in spite of my super awkwardness as a dancer."[40] She did become the leading lady in *Clorindy*, earning $75 weekly. "Thanks to Mr. Cook," Abbie acknowledged, "I was singing *his* [Cook's] music with proper phrasing, gestures and feeling notwithstanding."[41]

Abbie Mitchell soon became a major presence in Will Marion Cook's life, and within less than a year they became romantically and physically involved. It's no wonder the two were attracted to each other, given the similarity of their backgrounds. Both encountered death at an early age—he at 10 when his father died, she losing her mother at birth and her father and grandmother when she was 12. Mr. Cook (as Abbie addressed him) became a father figure, replacing the one she lost. Will and Abbie eventually married two years later in New York on October 21, 1900.[42]

As important as his new love was, Will Marion Cook enjoyed a new status as published composer through the House of Witmark:

It was in July 9 [1898] that a new star, one of the earliest of the gifted American colored composers, rose on Broadway. He rose, too, on the Witmark list, only to make, through no fault of his music, a sudden descent. The story of Will Marion Cook belongs to the short but definite catalogue of men who wronged Isidore Witmark and were never forgiven. . . .

About a month before the night of July 5, Isidore had had a call from the composer. The Witmarks were publishing many of the Negro song hits of that time, particularly "All Coons Look Alike to Me." Isidore was impressed with the Will Marion Cook score and felt it had the right stuff in it for success.

Cook was anxious to get a production for it and made him a proposition. He said, "If you will get me a production of this skit, I will give you the publication rights and all the royalties accruing."

Isidore replied, "I will do my best to get you a production, and publish the score, but I will not accept your royalties. You shall enjoy those yourself."[43]

When Cook received his first royalty statement, he was convinced that he had been cheated. With a lawyer by his side, he confronted the Witmarks; however, even the attorney became convinced of the publisher's integrity. Cook's confrontational approach ended hopes of any future publications with this firm.

Witmark's release of *Clorindy's* songs heralded Cook's theatrical entrée and ensured his popularity with the public. He made a meteoric ascent with his Broadway debut at the age of 29. This was an exceptional start for a uniquely talented black man, who began as a violinist and aspired to compose art music. The rigidity of the racial climate as well as his stiff violin fingers had caused Will Marion Cook to shift to the theatrical stage, where he found his niche broadening the imagery, rhythms, and harmonic palette for Broadway and beyond.

Cook's next theatrical involvement was as musical director of *The Policy Players* by Jesse A. Shipp, an outgrowth of the *Senegambian Carnival*, which became *A Lucky Coon*, as was mentioned earlier, or *4-11-44*, and was eventually renamed *The Policy Players*.[44] According to the contemporary entertainer Tom Fletcher:

> Policy was a game in those days. The winning numbers were picked after the turn of a wheel, patterned after a roulette wheel. Three spins of the wheel the winning digits were picked. Like this: 3-6-9, or like this: 3-11-33, or 19-29-39. If you had any of those digits on your slip you played, you were a winner. You were paid four dollars for [betting] five cents."[45]

Playing the numbers was an equal opportunity people's game, a community pastime in which old and young, literate and illiterate, the neediest folk and the well-to-do, all participated. The black community perpetually sought lucky numbers. "House numbers, car numbers, letters, telegrams, laundry, suits, shoes, hats, every conceivable object could carry a lucky number."[46] The experience of gambling could produce an addictive high and a dramatic low.

The *Policy Players'* plot centers on lottery fiend Bert Williams, who eventually wins a sizable sum of money, presumably by playing the numbers 4-11-44 ($4 + 7 = 11 \times 4 = 44$). He is destined for high society, a goal that his boon companion George Walker engineers very successfully.[47] A reviewer observed:

> The musical farce-comedy has little or nothing to do with policy playing, but serves [as] an excellent means to present Williams and Walker, about whom are surrounded a large company who indulge in solos, duets, acrobatic feats, yarn spinning, and negro eccentricities. The dancing of Williams Murray in the first act and of Aida Overton and Grace Holliday in the second, the solo of Mattie Wilkes, the gun-spinning of Fred Douglas and Arthur and Ollie Reese, and the Chinese impersonations of George Catlin were amusing.[48]

Another reviewer characterized the entertainment as "ambitious in a musical way" primarily because it featured an attractive chorus of thirty trained young women who helped to swell the volume of sound.[49]

The musical probably received its warmest reception in Lawrence, Kansas, the hometown of George Walker, who was given a silver cup for the prominence his career brought the city. On the other hand, *Policy Players* encountered its most racially tense reception in Cook's hometown of Washington, D.C., where a dispute arose over who was to conduct the house orchestra. "A compromise was made wherein Cook led the orchestra during vocal sections and the regular (white) conductor led the orchestra during the instrumental sections."[50] The tour ended by the summer of 1900, having had only limited success.

Between musical productions, Abbie and Will Marion sailed to London for two weeks. During their voyage, a storm caused seasickness in nearly everyone. Although Cook wasn't ill, he remained in bed for fear of the possibility. Abbie strolled on the deck as often as the steward would allow and ate heartily. When they disembarked, she toured the Tower of London, walked multiple times around Buckingham Palace, and shopped on Regent Street. She frequented the theater, seeing such plays as *The Bell of New York, Dante,* and *Shylock,* as well as the opera at Covent Garden. One day as Abbie was window-shopping on Regent Street, she saw:

> heads popping out of windows, people standing on the curb waving their hats and bowing, I too rushed to look and what met my eyes but a little plumb lady sitting in an open carriage with a little bonnet on her head (like my grandmother used to wear) only a hundred times more expensive—a small parasol over her head smiling and bowing, coachmen and footmen in fine livery. Was I happy to see her! She was so little, I thought, to be a queen, not pretty at all, I wasn't disappointed strange to tell. I waved to her and ran as far as I could so as to see her as long as possible. I had at last seen the Queen.

Since Abbie's formal education had been abruptly aborted, these cultural experiences contributed significantly to her professional development. When she and Cook returned to the United States, much attention was devoted to grooming Abbie artistically for a career on stage. Will Marion purchased season's tickets to the Metropolitan Opera; the Aborn English Opera (playing at the American Theatre), and the Henry Irving Repertory at the old Knickerbocker Theatre. Abbie studied piano nonchalantly. She never became the pianist that Will had hoped she would become. On the other hand, she memorized a Shakespearean scene every day and recited the lines every night to her lover. Sundays were spent viewing exhibits at the museum.

Will Marion Cook was then commissioned to write the musical *Casino Girl*, starring Mabel Gilman, Virginia Earle, and Sam Bernard. He composed such songs as "By-Gone Days Are Best," "Romance," "Whatever the Hue of Your Eyes," and "Down de Lover's Lane." Virginia Earle's performance of the Negro love song "Lover's Lane" was not exemplary, even after vocal coaching from Abbie Mitchell (then six months pregnant). Earle resented Cook for insisting that a "Nigger" teach her how to interpret the song.[51] Furthermore, the musical director asked Cook to modify his score, since the orchestral players found his writing too intricate and not commercial enough to be popular.

"If you'll let me direct the orchestra, there won't be any difficulty," Cook insisted. But to allow an African American to conduct an all-white Broadway show in 1900 would have jeopardized its success; consequently, he was instructed to "write in the style of the white composers who were successful."

Abbie remembered that Cook wrote beautiful music for the play, but after opening night (March 19, 1900), he argued with the manager, lost control of his temper, then walked down into the orchestra pit, took all the music, and destroyed it. He stormed out of the theater, returned home, and fell into a fit of melancholia. A white replacement rewrote *The Casino Girl*. Such demonstrations of rage caused his sometime producer Lederer to characterize Cook as "the greatest constructive and the greatest destructive genius in the American theatre."

At this crucial time, Abbie and Will Marion's firstborn arrived. It was on March 22, 1900, so, in Abbie's words, "I couldn't be near him to help calm him." Abbie was barely 14 and, to make matters worse, her pregnancy was threatened by complications. She was rushed to Sloan's Maternity Hospital, where after convalescing she gave birth to a twelve- pound baby girl, Marion Abigail (the namesake of both father and mother). Abbie's recovery required complete bed rest and a surgical procedure; so the couple took up residence at Will's brother's home at 2294 Sixth Street, NW, in Washington.

Will Marion's class-conscious family was disappointed that he was settling down with a mere chorus girl almost twenty years his junior as well as a "child of miscegenation." During their first night in the family home, Abbie overheard a conversation between Willie's mother, aunt, brother, and sister-in-law: "She [Abbie] hasn't even a high school education. And she was reared by two aunts who work as domestics!" Her unmarried status at the time of becoming a mother probably also disappointed her in-laws.[52]

Infuriated, Abbie determined to move out immediately. Will Marion relocated his young family to the home of Louise Lamprey, a white friend who was on the editorial staff of the *Washington Star* and a sometime song lyricist for Cook. She nursed Abbie while Will returned to New York in search of fame and fortune. He rented a room with Mrs. Reid, the mother of dancer Aida Overton Walker, on 6th Avenue near 29th Street. Abbie and their newborn later joined him.

Blacks were migrating further uptown into Harlem and populations were rapidly shifting. Miss Lamprey advised the Cooks to secure a home in New York City without delay. Finally a four-room flat at 10 1/2 West 99th Street opened to its first colored tenants. Abbie made a $5 deposit, then contacted her generous benefactress Miss Lamprey, who wired $175 and sent sheets, bedspreads, silver, dishes, and most essentials; two brass beds were to follow. When all was arranged, Abbie surprised Mr. Cook with the keys to their new home.

Cook, however, confided in a letter to Alain Locke:

Keep it quiet—I refused to marry her until long afterward [giving birth]. And even then twas a mistake. I'm no family man. Shall never 'stay put' even after I'm dead.

Will Marion felt dreadful after *The Casino Girl* debacle and was encouraged to explore a new Williams and Walker show. Reluctantly, he journeyed to Chicago to solidify the partnership with the two comedians. The relationship would last a decade, but for the moment, money matters with management forced them to postpone any involvement with Cook, and his spirits continued to plunge. "When he had serious disappointments, he'd go into a state of melancholia from which it was difficult to be around him. He'd remain in bed, smoke his pipe and read madly."[53]

In desperation, Abbie recalled Harry Burleigh's booking agents Brooks and Denton. She used Cook's name as an entrée, auditioned, and three days later sang for Mrs. Salomon Son on Fifth Avenue (a few doors from the Astors). The compensation was $35 for three songs, or more for additional numbers. She hadn't performed for several months, since the birth of Marion Abigail, yet she was able to make a sizable sum for an evening. "It took just that little encouragement to lift my husband out of his melancholia. We went home and celebrated: he with a cheese sandwich and a bottle of beer, and I with ice cream; we were so happy." From then on Abbie regularly sang for the likes of the Astors, Belmonts, Morgans, and Vanderbilts, as Will Marion accompanied her at the piano.

Composer Cook was not just stewing in a depression after *The Casino Girl* fiasco, however. He had again turned to Paul Laurence Dunbar as a collaborator. By the summer of 1900, the one-act Cook–Dunbar production of *Jes Lak White Fo'ks* opened at the New York Winter Garden. Ernest Hogan was otherwise engaged, so Irving Jones played the comedic role, assisted by

Abbie Mitchell. This work epitomized Cook's personal philosophy that African Americans should no longer imitate, but rather adhere to their own cultural mores.

James Weldon Johnson confirmed that "the book and lyrics were not so good, nor was the cast, and naturally, the music was not such a startling novelty."[54] *The New York Times,* on the other hand, hailed its opening as "a big success."[55] Over time, augmentations were made to the show's cast and content.

Cook's sole extant song is "Down de Lover's Lane." Here Dunbar's folk speech depicts picturesque natural imagery, a personified animal and bush, capped with humor, intersecting at "lover's lane." The male subject muses over whether or not heaven will have a lover's lane. A melodic monotonous lane winds through a series of verse sequences (ex. 5.5). This call-and-response form is also in Dunbar's "Jump Back" lyrics. Harmonic interest is sparked by a strategically and unique use of an augmented sixth chord dividing the verse from the chorus. A wordless chorus resonates to the moan, cry, or blues pathos of the African-American sensibility.[56] This plantation croon is characterized by a disjunct melodic line of slow-moving, slurred,

Example 5.5 "Down De Lover's Lane," mm. 8–16 (music, Will Marion Cook; lyrics, Paul Laurence Dunbar [New York: Jos. W. Stern, 1900]).

and syncopated motives which flaunt the voice over unusual pre-jazz augmented sixth-chord harmonies.

On August 12, 1900, during the summer run of *Jes Lak White Fo'ks*, a racially charged riot erupted in New York City. African-American Arthur Harris entered a shop at Eighth Avenue and 41st Street to buy a cigar, leaving his wife outside. She was assaulted by a white man, who then clubbed Harris when he intervened. Harris defended himself, fatally wounding his assailant with a pocket knife.[57] The incident led to an outbreak of random violence against men of color on New York streets; many were badly beaten. Among the victims were Ernest Hogan and George Walker. The two men had agreed to meet after their respective shows and were caught in the melee. Hogan was forced to leave the cast because of injuries caused by the mob, but Walker escaped to a cellar and hid throughout the night.

The racial climate in this explosive summer of 1900 could not have benefited the black musical *Jes Lak White Folks*. A work whose underlying theme mocked the pretension of whites would not have pleased the predominantly white audiences. The act of ridicule aroused superior sentiments on the part of the black joke-tellers.[58] In a society where African Americans were merely thirty-five years beyond slavery, this musical's message no doubt helped to assuage their feeling of inferior social standing.

Chapter 6

IN DAHOMEY

What is Africa to me?
Countee Cullen

In 1902, nearly two months before the winter 1903 Broadway début of the musical *In Dahomey*, Abbie Mitchell urged Mr. Cook to invite Williams and Walker's managers, Hurtig and Seamon, to their home for Christmas dinner to talk about recreating the musical with Abbie singing and Will Marion integrating the story line. "I didn't make a pretty picture singing in my condition," Abbie said. She was in fact six months pregnant with the Cooks' second child, and somewhat self-conscious. Still, "it gave them an idea of the music."[1]

Hurtig and Seamon heard the tale of Lightfoot losing a silver casket and hiring detectives Shylock Homestead and Rareback Pinkerton to search for the missing treasure. Their hunt leads them to Dahomey in West Africa, where the two are made governors of a province. They receive an honor for assisting in the liberation of the colonists and to confirm "There's No Place Like Home."[2] The plot symbolized the cultural affinity between blacks in their American homeland and their African motherland.

After hearing the songs and the story, the guests enjoyed Abbie's cuisine. "It was delicious even if I do admit it myself, they ate and drank their fill," she boasted. "The proof of the pudding is in the eating." After the meal, the men retired to the parlor for a smoke and a business agenda. In the end they completed the contractual terms to produce the musical.[3]

In Dahomey had evolved from the comic "opera" *The Cannibal King*, which Cook began as early as 1896. (His song "Love Is the Tend'rest of Themes" from that work was published the same year.) *Cannibal King* represented the collaborative efforts of lyricist James Weldon Johnson, librettist Bob Cole,

56

and composer Will Marion Cook, assisted by pianist/composer J. Rosamond Johnson. Because of discord between Cole and Cook, *Cannibal King* remained unfinished. Entertainer George Walker then became interested in performing the musical without Cole's libretto, and Jesse Shipp came on board to write a new script. The new musical, however, retained songs both from Cook's *Cannibal King* and *Jes Lak White Fo'ks*.[4]

The trial musical run of *In Dahomey* began in Stamford, Connecticut, and progressed through New York's off-Broadway Grand Opera House and more than a dozen midwestern venues during the late fall of 1902–1903 before arriving at Times Square's New York Theater in mid-February 1903. Its opening marked the historic arrival of a full-length black musical *inside* rather than on the rooftop of a Broadway venue.[5] The show's protagonists were Bert Williams and George Walker with their respective wives, Lottie Williams and Aida Overton Walker, along with Hattie McIntosh in a principal role. Jesse Shipp wrote, staged, and acted while Paul Laurence Dunbar created the lyrics, and Will Marion Cook composed most of the music. Although the Manhattan run was only fifty-three performances, *In Dahomey* represented a watershed for blacks on the musical stage.

Arrival at the long-denied "Promised Land" had come as no easy feat, Bert Williams reflected:

> The way we've aimed for Broadway and just missed it in the past seven years would make you cry. We'd get our bearings, take a good running start and—land in a Third Avenue theater. Then we'd measure the distance again and think we'd struck the right avenue at last—only to be stalled in a West Thirty-fourth Street music hall with the whole stunt to do all over again. We'd get near enough to hear the Broadway audiences applaud sometimes, but it was someone else they were applauding. I used to be tempted to beg for a fifteen dollar job in a chorus just for one week so as to be able to say I'd been on Broadway once.[6]

The idea of featuring a black musical in a legitimate theatrical hall was so novel and repugnant to some whites that *The New York Times* reported there had been talk that its opening might result in a race war. The article ended with relief when "all went merrily" on opening night.[7]

Another critic concluded that "the musical's composer has succeeded in lifting Negro music above the plane of the so-called 'Coon' song without destroying the characteristics of the melodies and he has provided a score which is likewise unusually diversified."[8] It encompassed syncopated songs, sentimental ballads, operatic choruses, waltz songs, as well as pseudo-African numbers.

In Dahomey's libretto gained less praise than did its music; in fact, reviewer Sylvester Russell believed its very title to be a misnomer, since most of the musical did not take place "in Dahomey," but rather in Boston or in Florida (probably, not coincidentally, the home state of the Johnson brothers).[9] It was further problematic to stage, as was evidenced by its many alterations and revisions necessary before solutions were found that worked for the theater-going public.[10]

The creators of *In Dahomey* had never been to Africa, so they dramatized the imaginings of their ancestral home through pseudo-Africanisms[11] derived from both contemporary media references and historical accounts of the Benin region of West Africa.[12] "Caboceers Entrance," for example, is based on actual cultural practices,[13] depicted with a chorus of African chiefs, soldiers, natives, and female dancers, accompanied by drum-like open fifths. Vocalists hum a nasal pentatonic melody and proclaim their status as the king's subjects. Such interpolated songs as John H. Cook's "Evah Dahkey Is a King" and J. Leubrie Hill's "My Dahomian Queen" conjured up more African associations with royalty.

The "musical farce," as it was billed, has a rather flimsy plot, although *The New York Herald* credited it with having more continuity than the average Broadway "musical comedy."[14] The detective roles of Bert Williams and George Walker provided the plot's centerpiece. The exotic African coast also presented an opportunity to expand beyond minstrel norms.[15]

Inspiration for the musical in all probability came from Dahomeans, who had lived in a reconstructed village at the Chicago World's Fair and later traveled to San Francisco's Midwinter Fair in January 1894.[16] Africans from Dahomey who were scheduled to appear were late in arriving for the fair's opening; so various black Americans, including Williams and Walker, had been hired to masquerade temporarily as Dahomeans. Once the natives arrived, the American entertainers closely scrutinized them. No wonder Williams and Walker were subsequently excited about a theatrical production that featured African-inspired content while still appealing to American audiences. Walker believed that the use of African subject matter would be liberating:[17]

> Many of the themes from which some of our best lyrics come are purely African. We were the first to introduce the Americanized African songs: for instance, "My Zulu Babe," "My Castle on the Nile," "My Dahomian Queen." From the time we commenced to feature such songs, not only the popularity of Williams and Walker, but that of the colored performer in general has been on the increase. I have no hesitation in stating that the departure from what was popularly known as the American "darky" ragtime limitations to native African characteristics has helped greatly to increase the value of the black performer on the American stage.[18]

The production received high marks more for style than for substance. Bert Williams scrutinized his craft as any other actor would. Born in the West Indies to a white woman and "a fair man with red hair" reared in San Francisco, he talked and behaved quite unlike the southern darky stage persona he portrayed.[19] Williams was a master of "slow and grotesquely awkward" motion. He could hold his face for minutes at a time, so that the least alteration would cause outburst of laughter. Williams bucked his eyes, used a stammering speech pattern, and sang wry comedy songs while developing a laughter-through-tears style of humor. The song from the musical in which he gained the most accolades was Alex Rogers's "I'm a Jonah Man," which received seven encores after one performance alone.[20] Its minor strains began:

> My hard luck started when I was born,
>   Least, so the old folks say;
> Dat same hard luck's been my best friend
>   Up to dis very day.
> When I was young my mamma's friends
>   To find a name they tried,
> They named me after papa,
>   And the same day papa died.[21]

This burnt-cork-faced unlucky man resigned himself to the weight of his misfortunes and exuded a tremendous human feeling of self-pity that transcended color. Williams confessed:

Nearly all of my successful songs have been based on the idea that I am getting the worst of it. I am the "Jonah Man," the man who, even if it rained soup, would be found with a fork in his hand and no spoon in sight, the man whose fighting relatives come to visit him and whose head is always dented by the furniture they throw at each other. There are endless variations of this idea, fortunately, but if you sift them, you will find the principle of human nature at the bottom of them all.[22]

Despite his masked, light-skinned face, Bert Williams's acting ability consistently enabled him to transform minstrel caricatures into intensely human elements.[23]

Williams's partner, Walker, meanwhile, was an expert in stage timing and comedy, making him a master craftsman for setting up Williams's punch lines. He played the flamboyantly overdressed city slicker, who would con the country bumpkin Williams out of his last dollar. "George Walker was highly amusing in his work, and his funny little laugh, his ludicrous explanations to his friend Shylock, his nimble dancing and clever all-round comedy work made him a prime favorite with all," wrote one reviewer.[24] Walker's contributions were most notable in his colored-dandy dressing and extraordinary agile dancing. His interpolated rendition of "When Sousa Comes to Coontown" received repeated accolades.

On April 23, 1903, *In Dahomey*'s cast embarked upon the S. S. Urania for a London engagement at the Shaftesbury Theatre. Though Abbie Mitchell and her newborn son were also on board despite the fact that she had just given birth three weeks earlier (on the March 30) to her second child, Will

Mercer. All of New York's black elite gathered at the port to bid the company *adieux* with gifts of candy, fruit, and flowers. Williams and Walker were somewhat reluctant to return to London because of their lukewarm reception six years earlier. Despite their hesitancy, they joined the male travelers who wore heavy overcoats, even in the warm weather, and carried binoculars over their shoulders. Golf caps were the prominent headwear, and nearly everyone carried a steamer chair. During the goodbyes, the ship slowly sailed from land, as feverish waving and envious tears flowed from loved ones left behind.[25] The passengers, after being delayed several days by a storm, finally docked on the May 7.

Cook sailed with the cast and personally conducted the rehearsals after arriving in London. One critic characterized him as "earnest in his manner and evidently impresses the people he teaches. Singing with them almost all the time, he constantly takes his hands from the piano, stands up, and beating time finishes without accompaniment. He finds them intelligent pupils, and they certainly appear to give the keenest attention to his instructions."[26]

Many last-minute revisions were debated in order to ensure a receptive audience. The final act, for example, became the introduction.[27] The performers, who assumed the cakewalk was passé, initially dropped it from the show, but critics who complained of its absence prompted its reintroduction within a week of the musical's debut. A more rousing conclusion was tacked on, since otherwise no one would be sure the end had been reached until the orchestra started the traditional rendition of "God Save the King."[28]

London audiences "had nothing so good of its kind before on so large a scale," one reviewer confessed.[29] On the day before opening night, Bert Williams was warned of certain disaster if he chose his usual blackened facade. It was predicted that his theatrical makeup would puzzle English theatergoers. Williams admitted, "For about ten minutes they had me going, but all of a sudden I got sort of bullish myself and stopped listening to suggestions. I wore cork, just as I had done [many times before]."[30]

Apparently the predictions about Williams's blackface were misguided, since one of the first reviewers of the Shaftesbury performance reported: "by far the best thing of the evening was an impersonation by Mr. Bert Williams of [a] long, lanky, awkward, despondent giant, who does everything at the wrong time with real charm."[31] "He had blackened his face, . . . but it was remarkably expressive, and his suggestion of character as a lazy, luckless, gloomy, persistent fellow was exceedingly entertaining."[32]

Cook always maintained that: Even though "the purpose of this piece" was primarily "to amuse . . . many of the lyrics have considerable value."[33] One such song lyric, and the only text written by Will Marion Cook, was titled "Swing Along." In an undated letter to his son, Cook disclosed:

> In the development and the *Andante* I sensed the [social] struggles—the difficulties—the drawbacks and finally the rushing ultimate triumphant end. We were going to swing along and it is best not to mention anything

in the road would be swept aside. "Swing Along" meant even more to me racially than personally.[34]

Cook was prompted to compose this song while sitting in a London hotel room, somewhat homesick, while watching the *In Dahomey* cast walk up and down Shaftesbury Avenue cleverly advertising the show.[35] The triumphal end to the struggles of his people was conveyed through the lyrics:

> Well-a, swing along, yes-a swing along,
>   An'-a lif'—a yo' heads up high,
> Wif pride an' gladness beamin' from yo' eye!
>   Well-a swing along, yes-a swing along,
> From a early morn till night,
>   Lif' yo' head an' yo' heels mighty high,
> An' a swing bof lef' an' right.[36]

That first night the curtain was delayed for twenty minutes while Jesse Shipp and others made a last attempt to dissuade him from presenting this number. "It's too long; it'll kill the show," they argued, but to no avail. "Either *that* opening chorus or nothing!" Cook insisted.[37] Its effect was tremendous. "Swing Along" became a standard work performed by every first-class college glee club in the United States for at least fifty years.[38]

Much of *In Dahomey*'s favorable reception was due to the music, which was "vigorous, tuneful, original, and throughout obviously the work of a cultured student."[39] *The Globe*'s critic wrote: "a considerable degree of musicianship was evident in the choral numbers and in the orchestration especially. . . . Mr. Marion Cook is an artist as well as a melodist of undoubted faculty and skill." Regarding his musical style, the *London Star* wrote: "His melodies are pleasantly original. Mr. Cook conducted on Saturday night, and his method of getting every ounce out of the orchestra is certainly effective, if somewhat unconventional." *The Standard* further noted:

Mr. Will Marion Cook is the composer, as also the conductor, and it might be said one of the principal vocalists, for as he faces the audience to direct the overture he sings all the airs, and, so far as could be observed, warbles or hums throughout the score. In fact, Mr. Cook is rather disturbingly in evidence; but he is a musician, most of his songs are pleasantly melodious, they are cleverly orchestrated, and he has perfect command over his instrumentalists.[40]

One "pleasantly melodious" Cook song of racial pride and popularity is "On Emancipation Day." Its introduction opens and ends the overture with syncopation and chromaticism, both characteristic elements of Cook's compositional style. The "Caboceers Entrance" begins the medley, "On Emancipation Day" follows, then "Brown-Skin Baby Mine," "The Czar," "Society," and finally a return of "On Emancipation Day." This song's significance is further stressed by its use as the climax of the second act, with an instrumental cakewalking march and two-step.

Clearly, the song had particular personal meaning for the composer. Washingtonians had held their first Emancipation Day celebration after Abraham Lincoln's signing of the Proclamation liberating African-American slaves in 1863. The practice continued during Cook's childhood, with the festivities distinguished by brass band parades and speeches by such dignitaries as Frederick Douglass and John Mercer Langston.[41] "On Emancipation Day" was undoubtedly inspired by Cook's memories of that historic day. Notably, in the British script, the song is sung just before the detectives sail for Africa, on the "grandest day of the year."[42] The song also represents one of the four collaborations between Dunbar and Cook, published by Harry von Tilzer in 1902, one of the most creative years of von Tilzer's long and brilliant career.[43]

A hallmark ballad from *In Dahomey* was "Brownskin Baby Mine," popularized by Abbie Mitchell. She received critical acclaim for having a charming and well-trained voice and rendering the song with much feeling.[44] The London reviewer from *The Times* (May 18, 1903) observed: "Abbie Mitchell, whose voice, though exceedingly small in volume, is of great charm . . . She is supported by a choir who sings with an amount of tone that is really tremendous." In light of Abbie's recent childbirth, and her hiatus from performing during the previous year, her small voice was easily understandable. *The St. James Gazette* noted, however, "that the orchestra was too loud, which handicapped Abbie Mitchell—who has a voice of excellent quality and a really refined method of production."[45] Cook later contributed to his wife's technical advancement by supporting her vocal training with Jean de Reszke, an excellent Parisian teacher.

Reviewers not only wrote of Abbie's vocal talent, but also of Cook's compositional gift. *The Boston Transcript* of March 21, 1905, reported that: "Musical comedies with *real* [emphasis mine] music are rarities, but this is one. The numbers all have merit and the ensembles are especially creditable pieces of work." Another critic wrote that "the music has a good swing, some of the airs being of the sort that will be whistled in the course of time. There is one chorus in the second act that is especially good and has a sort of grand opera flavor, which is in direct contrast to the rest of the music, which is of the light, fantastic and rag-time order."[46] "In several of the concerted pieces in his score his music displays true dramatic perception," concluded one London critic. Will Marion Cook "is a most promising musician, who should shed a luster on his race by work of a more solid and enduring character than is to be found in such a light and frankly frivolous production as *In Dahomey*."[47]

"The terrible difficulty that composers of my race have to deal with," responded Mr. Cook, "is the refusal of American people [and others] to accept serious things from us. That prejudice will be educated away one day I hope."[48] He further admitted that "in the musical *In Dahomey*, I have not strayed beyond themes that are light and amusing, and only here and there do I give glimpses of higher possibilities."[49] It is apparent, however, that "I mean to rise to the height of grand opera. My effort may not be a success, but I shall have paved the way for someone who will come after me."[50]

One of the prominent second act numbers in which a flavor of grand opera emerges is "Society," with lyrics by Paul Dunbar and music by Will Cook and Will Accooe, a composer who directed the earlier productions of *Octoroons* and *A Trip to Coontown*. Its opening dialogue by Cicero exclaims:

> Ladies and gentleman, allow me to introduce my friends, Dr. Straight, Mr. Reeder, and Mr. Hustler. Cecily, dey is high society gentlemen from the North wid great reputations.[51]

"Society," with its grandiose multi sectionalism, is musically indicative of a varied range of social status. (See ex. 6.1.) The song's uniquely extended form features solos, duets, recitatives, and choral ensembles. The melody, harmony, tonality, and range progress from a minor mode, quasi-pentatonic low melody, to a major mode, full-harmonic texture and high tessitura that mirrors the text. All prerequisites for attaining social status—wealth, reputation, ostentation, and royalty—are addressed, these attributes presented in a patter-like syllabic style with choral reiterative responses. This and other significant choruses symbolize the communal participation central to the African worldview, a perspective that is holistic and interconnected.

A change in key, meter, and mood occurs as the song transitions toward the end into a tuneful waltz. The waltz, typical of the most popular nineteenth-century European ballroom dance, represents a heightened level of artistic cultivation. The amorous duet admonishes that "love is the king" and is therefore oblivious to one's social position or material well-being. This axiom is reinforced with full chorus at the song's conclusion.

> Love looks not at estate . . .
> The humble cot becomes a throne
> Whose dwelling place love makes his own
> So all man's heart and being sing
> Love is the King! Love is the King!

On a personal level, the romantic theme might also represent Will Cook and Abbie Mitchell's relationship, which presumably had in it more love than money.

Adoration for "The Czar," a southern black leader, is expressed through another extended song form. The lyrics to this song were written by Alex Rogers; the music is by John H. and Will Marion Cook.[52] The song structure is the reversal of "Society"; the piece's essence is presented in the initial part—the greatness of this Dixie Czar. The verse, which appears only during the second half, elaborates on the multiple roles the Czar performs: "He's the

Example 6.1 "Society," mm. 115–129 (music, Will Marion Cook and Will Accooe; lyrics, Paul Laurence Dunbar [London: Keith, Prowse & Co., 1902]).

President, the Mayor and the Governor," by far the brightest star among the black leaders.

A female counterpart to "The Czar" is glorified in the "Leader of the Colored Aristocracy," with text by James Weldon Johnson and music by Will Marion Cook. This traditional 32-bar verse-chorus is altered by an eight-bar "intermezzo-like" solo which metrically fluctuates from 2/4 to 4/4, featuring a stride piano accompaniment. The heroine being celebrated is not unlike the protagonist in Scott Joplin's operatic *Treemonisha*—a symbol of the "new" Negro of freedom who prepares to lead her people to education, self-advancement, and social improvement. The chorus returns to a syncopated 2/4 dance-like ambiance as the feminist articulator signifies:

> And then I'll drill these darkies till,
> They're up in high so-ci-e-ty's hy-poc-ra-cy. . . .

Predictably, the melodic line is inclined to rise, then gives way with a sudden fall (ex. 6.2).

In Dahomey's cast was granted entrée into aristocratic society on the afternoon of June 23, 1903, when they performed at Buckingham Palace.

Example 6.2 "Leader of the Colored Aristocracy," chorus (music, Will Marion Cook; lyrics, James W. Johnson [London: Keith, Prowse, & Co., 1902]).

King Edward VII invited the repertory company to the ninth birthday celebration of Prince Edward of Wales (later to become Edward VIII, the British king who vacated his throne in 1936 to marry American Wallis Warfield Simpson). A production of this ilk had never before been performed before a royal audience.[53] More than 150 children attended the garden party on the palace grounds. Scenery, sets, props, musical instruments, and costumes were transported for the occasion. The Shaftesbury Theatre's full orchestra was seated to the right of the outdoor stage and was "conducted by Mr. Will Marion Cook, the talented coloured composer." The performers attempted to exclude Abbie Mitchell from the performance, assuming that the fifteen-year-old was too young to be missed, but the prince, amazingly, did notice her absence and sent his coach to retrieve her from the hotel.[54]

Upon obtaining the royal family's seal of approval, *In Dahomey* was assured an extended European run. Many audience members delighted in the added cakewalking finale, which included a prize competition for the dancing couples, in which a "huge cake over six feet in height, and illuminated by one-hundred electric lights" was presented, along with an actual cash prize equivalent to fifty U.S. dollars (a sizable sum in those days).[55]

According to *The Weekly Dispatch* (June 7, 1903), the entertainers were often asked to perform after the show in the homes of the rich and famous. Chief among the dance instructors was Aida Overton Walker, a leading lady and an extraordinary cakewalker. She gave an extensive exposé on "how to" execute the dance in *The Tattler* of July 1, 1903:

> It is difficult . . . to call the steps of the cake-walk by name. In the walk you follow the music, and as you keep time with it in what is best defined as a march you improvise. Gestures, evolutions, poses, will come to you as you go through the dance. The partners may develop steps which they think will impress the judges. Every muscle must be in perfect control. The step of the cake-walk is light and elastic; after it has been learned fancy steps may be practiced. Some are very intricate; but the success of cake-walking depends largely on temperament, and as far as the actual steps are concerned the pupils may pass their instructors in time. The faces must be interested and joyous, and as the cake-walk is characteristic of a cheerful race, to be properly appreciated it must be danced in the proper spirit—it is a gala dance.
>
> In dancing, all the muscles of the body are brought into play, any effort or fatigue is concealed, the shoulders thrown well back, the back curved, and the knees bent with suppleness. The swing, all jauntiness and graceful poise, must come from the shoulders, and the toes must turn well out. The *tempo* is between that of the two-step and the march six-eight time. The Negro melodies which may be played for the dancers are without number. In the quicker number the women should be careful to manage their long skirts gracefully, an art which requires a good deal of practice, and beginners do well to wear the shorter skirts.
>
> The cake-walk may be danced by any number of couples. A tall couple leads off, holding up the hands as in a barn dance. A cake is placed in the

center of the room on a pedestal, the opening bars of the music are played, and the dancers march around. The walk over, with its various features, its impromptu steps, and gaiety coming to an end, the question arises, "Who takes the cake?" The couples now march round in all solemnity and bow to the cake *en passant.* A halt at command when every couple has passed by. Then the master of the ceremonies names the winners. The cake is carried before them by the master or one of the guests, two lines are formed of the dancers, and the happy couple dance between the lines to general handclapping. So ends the cake-dance.

This fast-stepping syncopated cakewalk and its principal performers helped to popularize the dance in the United States to the extent that at one White House party, President Theodore Roosevelt led a cakewalk promenade down to the East Room. Scholars Henry Louis Gates and Cornel West have asserted that with the cakewalk: The first black music and the first black dance "crossed over" into mainstream America, initiating an unstoppable cultural process.[56]

In Dahomey and its aftereffects were not inconsequential. From 1902 through 1905 the production ran in national theaters, on Broadway, and in London and the British provinces for eight months. A new company was even formed, starring Avery and Hart, with James Vaughn conducting. *In Dahomey* played more than a thousand times and was published in a full piano score by Keith, Prowse of London (a first for a black musical).

Even though it was highly successful, not everyone was satisfied with the income acquired from its production. Williams and Walker charged in a ten-page letter to Booker T. Washington that Hurtig and Seamon were defrauding them.[57] Abbie also recalls that Cook "had an altercation with the managers and made them pay him a sizeable sum for permission to use his music." Apparently, Mr. Cook received a $10,000 check for the rights to his music. Abbie Mitchell tied it around his neck for safekeeping, since he was inclined to give much of it away.

In spite of such problems, *In Dahomey* is a legendary musical, symbolic of a people's history. Its title suggests a return to the Motherland, for Dahomey was at the center of the West African slave trade. The genre of nineteenth-century minstrelsy is represented through the banjo, blackface, and stump speeches interwoven with bleaching cream and hair straightener references. The overture and finale focus on the liberation theme of emancipation.

Will Marion Cook's musical styles include a diverse range of pseudo-Africanisms, a nostalgic plantation song, tender ballads, waltzes, recitatives, and operatic ensembles. At 34 he was at the pinnacle of his career. Never again would he reach the heights of *In Dahomey.*

Chapter 7

THE "STUDENTS" AND THE STAGE

Black people create, interpret, and experience music out of an African frame of reference—one that shapes musical sound, interpretation, and behavior.

Portia K. Maultsby

During the years of Will Marion Cook's theatrical work, he was also intermittently conducting various ensembles. As early as 1901 he proposed to Booker T. Washington, the president of Tuskegee Institute, to organize an octet of "Tuskegee's Real Negro Singers'."[1] The idea was no doubt inspired by the Fisk Jubilee Singers from a generation earlier. At the age of three Will heard this ensemble perform such Negro spirituals as "Steal Away," "Roll Jordan Roll," and "Deep River." He longed to recreate the more "authentic" sound of the original Jubilee Singers. Cook wrote:

> 'Tis pitiful to hear Negro songs in the Southern colleges of today, and the Negroes of the North burlesque this undying heritage of our suffering, our agony, and our death, yes, even of our Freedom! ("John Brown's Body"). [While listening to the Jubilee Singers, you experienced:] "Roll Jordan"—and you heard Jordan River rise, rise to a Niagara in cataracts of sound, and you saw it fall so that the weary pilgrim might cross over. "Steal Away" I shall not attempt to describe. . . . Lest you heard them, you'll never know; it is gone forever. Our bodies, our minds, our desires, our lives have gone 'White.' We have lost something that can never return: we have no pride of race.[2]

Cook wanted to demonstrate the extent to which African Americans had been able to develop plantation melodies. He proposed to Washington a concert program of twelve numbers: four traditional slave songs such as

68

"Swing Low, Sweet Chariot"; four simply arranged melodies by Samuel Coleridge-Taylor, Harry T. Burleigh, and himself; and four more ambitious numbers which would display the range of voice and musical cultivation of the singers. As he wrote to Booker T. Washington:

> The fact would be proved that there is an abundance of musical material in the themes of the Southern Negro capable of thorough development and may form a basis for the growth of a music which shall be called truly American; further—the compositions of the three Negroes mentioned may be taken to show that the Negro himself is to play some part in the development of this music (a fact not hitherto conceded); and lastly, the Negro voice loses none of its tenderness and sweetness when carefully cultivated.[3]

The influence of Cook's former teacher Antonín Dvořák is apparent in the way he justified his idea.

There is no evidence that Booker T. Washington ever agreed to Cook's proposal, probably because there was already a singing quartet touring on behalf of Tuskegee Institute at that time. Furthermore, one wonders how long Cook, who was mentored by the racially outspoken Frederick Douglass, would have been able to work for the racially accommodating Booker T. Washington.

Cook did eventually become active with a musical ensemble known as the "Memphis Students" (sometimes called Nashville Students), a group that was neither of students nor of musicians from Memphis or Nashville. This playing-singing-dancing orchestra was organized in New York City in 1905 by Ernest Hogan in Jimmie Marshall's café.[4]

As was discussed earlier, in the early 1900s Marshall's cafe and hotel on West 53rd Street between Sixth and Seventh Avenues lay at the heart of New York's black bohemian life. Not only did the "who's who" of black society congregate there, but many white actors, Broadway stars, and musicians frequented Marshall's for an evening of delicious dining, energizing music, and spirited conversation. The group that called themselves the "Memphis Students" found this atmosphere artistically exhilarating. They became the first ensemble to perform syncopated music on a public concert stage, a radical departure from the previous dance halls or theater orchestra pits. The group numbered about twenty and performed predominantly on banjos, mandolins, guitars, saxophones, and drums, along with a violin, a few brass, and a double bass instrument. Will Marion Cook rehearsed them for their debut at the Proctor Twenty-third Street Theater early in the spring of 1905. Other artists performing with them besides the group's leader, the famed comedian Ernest Hogan, were Abbie Mitchell, and the dancer Ida Forsyne, who later became the cakewalking toast of Russia. Will H. Dixon's choreography was full of novelty:

> All through a number he would keep his men together by dancing out the rhythm, generally in graceful, sometimes in grotesque, steps. Often an easy

shuffle would take him across the whole front of the band. This style of directing not only got the fullest possible response from the men but kept them in just the right humour for the sort of music they were playing.[5]

Although Dixon was the conductor viewed by the public, apparently the training and directing of Will Marion Cook was behind the scenes. The rhythmic energy was dramatized by the innovative stick-juggling artistry of the drummer, Buddy Gilmore, who has been called "the first jazz drummer" in the modern sense of the word;[6] moreover, he incorporated the use of other noisemaking devices in order to enhance the rhythmic effect. All of the players, except for the wind players, simultaneously sang parts of the songs in four-part harmony. The result: a playing-singing-dancing orchestra. An advertisement for performers in *The Freeman* read:

- First Tenor Singers who play first mandolin;
- Second Tenor singers who play second mandolin;
- Barytone [sic] singers who play guitar; and
- Bass singers who play banjo and cello.
- And additionally, each must be able to read music at sight.[7]

The Students' Proctor engagement was so successful that they were booked at Hammerstein's Victoria Theater during the day and on the roof-garden at night. What began as a two-week engagement eventually became five months, including more than 150 performances.[8]

In the fall of 1905 Will Marion Cook stole The Students from their organizer, Ernest Hogan, and took them on a European tour for several months. Hogan unsuccessfully attempted to serve a court injunction on the group while they were en route to Europe.[9] For this trip their name was changed from the Memphis or Nashville Students to the Tennessee Students, on the theory that Europeans would be more familiar with the American state than with its principal city. Their performances took them to Brussels, Berlin, Vienna, St. Petersburg, Paris, and London. The musicians and entertainers on this tour included Abbie Mitchell, Will H. Dixon, Ida Forsyne, Jo Gray, Bobby Kemp (the principal comedian), Charles Wilson, and Henry Williams (the noted buck and wing dancer). Among the attractions were Mlle. De Dio's Japanese pantomime act and dances; Madame Juliette's Sea Lions; 'Moonshine,' a singing and dancing act; Wilson Hallett, mimic of child characters; and Belle Davis and her famous pickininnies.[10]

The ragtime pianist and composer Joe Jordan helped to organize, direct, and compose much of the music for the original Students. In 1908 he revived and directed the group's second edition with Tom Fletcher. The revised Memphis Students also featured Abbie Mitchell and three dancing girls: Edith Harrison, Esmeralda Statum, and Isola Ringold. "The act played Proctor's 125th Street Theater and the Orpheum in Brooklyn, and it was such a success that it was booked for the summer season at Hammerstein's Roof Garden at Broadway and 42nd Street."[11] This novel group paved the way for the syncopated song-and-dance music presented on the concert stage nearly a generation later by the likes of Paul Whiteman and Duke Ellington.

Meanwhile, Cook's attention was absorbed by another African-inspired musical that opened at New York's Majestic Theatre on February 20, 1906. *In Abyssinia* represented the most elaborate efforts to date of Jesse A. Shipp, Alex Rogers, Bert Williams, and Will Marion Cook. It ran for 31 performances and featured an unsubstantial plot that consisted mostly of loosely connected musical numbers or comedy scenes. What drama there was revolved around the adventures of Jasmine Jenkins (Bert Williams) and Rastus Johnson (George Walker), who had decided to visit the land of their ancestors—presumably Abyssinia (modern-day Ethiopia). The plot was fueled by surprise situations resulting from their ignorance of African customs and laws. Jenkins was found guilty of stealing a small vase from a street vendor. Though the crime seemed minor, the penalty was major— amputation of the offending anatomical part, in this case his hand. A suspenseful sentencing scene ensued at Ruler Menelik's palace. The punishment was determined by the ringing of a gong: three rings signified that the sentence would be imposed; four rings meant a pardon would be issued. Of course, the tension mounted between the third and fourth gongs.[12]

Much was made in the production of the difference in speech between Africans and African Americans. The Africans spoke a King's English in a stilted parody of a dialogue.

> Soldiers of the King are we,
> We bow to his supremacy,
> We know naught of disloyalty,
> Hence can not spare an enemy.

The black Americans, on the other hand, spoke in a happy-go-lucky minstrel mode:

JASMINE: And you's a philosophy?

RASTUS: Philosopher

JASMINE: What's the duty of a philosophiloso—
(Finally add *pede*) [The humorous mispronunciation of the word *philosopher.*]

RASTUS: To look on the bright side of other people's troubles when you haven't any of your own.[13]

The lavish staging effects included a mountain pass with an actual background waterfall, a colorful marketplace, and live camels; contortionists and acrobats were costumed to imitate other jungle animals.[14]

In Abyssinia also became a vehicle for Bert Williams's famous musical hit "Nobody," performed by the actor-singer with his original music and lyrics by Alex Rogers. First sung in 1905, this signature song would serve as Williams's for the next seventeen years, until his death in 1922; rarely could he leave the stage without performing it. "Nobody" helped to establish the hard-luck character trademark that was attached to him for the remainder of his theatrical career. His rendition was described in one biography as follows:

> Season after season he was obliged to sing this song, by insistent demand. He used to deliver his newest efforts and finally after repeated encores, reached for the little red memorandum book in his upper right hand pocket and the audience would sit back.
> The stanzas of this song were short, but for some unknown reason Bert had a terrible time learning them; so he wrote the cue words into the little book. He "mugged" the situation and worked it up so cleverly that the audience never realized why the book came to be a part of "Nobody.". . .
> Then he sang with a noisy wail,

> I ain't never done nothin' to nobody,
> I ain't never got nothin' from nobody, no time.
> Until I get somethin' from somebody, some time,
> I'll never do nothin' for nobody, no time. . . .[15]

Even though *Abyssinia* was viewed by some as Williams and Walker's "most ambitious effort,"[16] at least one reviewer declared that "The book and lyrics followed too closely the lines of Yankee comic opera to give the added attraction of novelty, and the proceedings in themselves were tame."[17]

According to *The Freeman*, little of the public ever saw *Abyssinia* in its original form, "because after the first week, a cruel manager had ordered it chopped to pieces."[18] Perhaps, this manager was reacting to one of the early reviewers, who advised that whether "too many cooks (meaning Shipp-Rogers-Cook-and-Williams) spoiled the broth or the very meaning of the word Abyssinia, 'Habesh, a mixture,' got into the composition, the whole affair is a hopeless jumble and the pruning knife, to be effective, must be an axe."[19]

After several months, on August 18, 1906, the revised musical returned to New York, where it reopened at the Grand Opera House. Singer Aida Overton Walker joined the cast with an extensive new repertoire; she proved to be a popular favorite. Cook served as the show's musical director, but it did not feature any of his compositions. The show was expected to travel to Europe, but that tour never occurred.

During his compositional heyday, Cook was not satisfied to see his songs published by such leading publishers as G. Schirmer, M. Witmark, and Harry von Tilzer; he also satisfied a desire for self-sufficiency through his role in the development of Gotham-Attucks Music Company. This New York firm, a merger of his black-owned enterprises, enjoyed a brief but brilliant career publishing popular music during the early 1900s. Cook may have been instrumental in founding the original Gotham Company, as his works were among their first publications. By 1901 he was also in charge of the firm's Sherman House branch in Chicago.

The New York Age ran advertisements for the Marion School of Vocal Music for several months. The offices of Gotham-Attucks at 136 W. 37th Street were directed by Cook and were also used as the home address of the school. Harry T. Burleigh was the vocal instructor. The advertisement read: "Wanted: Young men and women of pleasing appearance" who were to be "thoroughly taught concert, dramatic and ensemble singing, as well as dance—positions will be secured for those who are successful."[20] Cook was to give free instruction in sight reading, choral singing, and beginning harmony. No one knows to what extent this ad drew students or what clientele it may have yielded.

When Cook was not absorbed in publishing, teaching, developing Manhattan musical productions, or touring the United States and abroad, he was composing and conducting stage shows at the Pekin Theatre in Chicago. In the summer of 1904 Robert Motts opened a small music hall and vaudeville theater on Chicago's South Side at 27th and State Streets. Motts advertised the Pekin as "The only theatre in America playing colored artists exclusively."[21] He is credited with establishing the first legitimate black theater in the United States. The *Chicago Daily Journal* reported: "In all the world there is but one theatre owned and managed by colored folk, and for which the plays are written, the music composed, the costumes designed and made, and the properties built by colored folk."[22] Damages incurred from a fire in 1904 caused Motts to enlarge the stage and add a balcony, and the "New Pekin" opened in the spring of 1905.

The theater induced many talented performers to become members of its Negro Stock Company of composers and musicians, actors and singers, writers and directors. Their emphasis on musical plays attracted an impressive array of musicians such as Joe Jordan, Tim Brymn, Shelton Brooks, H. Lawrence Freeman, and Will Dixon. Will Marion Cook was described as "a great favorite of the Pekin patrons."[23] He, along with Joe Jordan and Lawrence Freeman, conducted the orchestra. Cakewalks were performed, and ragtime was interspersed between waltzes, sentimental ballads, and coon songs of the nineties. The dominant elements of the Pekin plays were comedy, dance, and music. Their librettos were loosely knit with "a few situations and plots in which the hero or heroine blundered about until his or her final extrication. But in and out of this array of predicaments, 'retort dialogue,' and roguish whimsicality ran catchy strains that somehow managed to keep things together. There was no scene so bad that it could not be rescued by a catchy song, and the Pekin composer managed to write plenty of them."[24]

New shows opened every two weeks, and ten performances were presented weekly. While much of the material may have been borrowed, the new shows were conceived, written, orchestrated, rehearsed, and staged while the ongoing show was still playing. J. Ed Green was responsible for casting and directing the new comedies. One writer acknowledged:

> His success thus far has been marvelous, when one considers that this man has taken farce comedies that were written for and by white people and so arranged the text and situations as to make them dovetail in and suit an all-colored cast.[25]

The productions were played before full houses of mixed audiences, with white patrons generally occupying the boxed seats.[26] Reactions of black audience members were noted by a perceptive white observer:

> No quip of the comedian, no expressive sentimental song, no touch of humor goes without prompt reward in applause. Like children, they enter into the fun of the hour. Many a sly jest at the frailties of the race is received in the blandest good humor. Many a satirical thrust, intolerable from a white man, is met with indulgent shrieks when delivered by their own comedians. It is evident they understand their own weaknesses and limitations, and the satire of their theatre is an evidence of their sincere efforts to rise above them. As a kindly satirist of his own race, J. Ed Green is inimitable. Each week he picks out some foible of the Negro to turn to ridicule. His childishness in a bargain, his love of games of chance, his vanity in dress, his adoration of tinsel and titles, all these are turned to gentle absurdity before the negro's eyes. In this way, the theatre has become a new school for the colored man, in which he may view himself in his struggle for social emancipation.[27]

The Pekin was responsible for the early development of many singers and actors who later won national fame. These included Charles H. Gilpin, Charles (Bass) Foster, Lawrence Chenault, Harrison Stewart, Leona Marshall, Lottie Grady, Flournoy E. Miller, Aubrey Lyles, Irvin C. Miller, and Quintard Miller. Miller and Lyles's 1905 Pekin success in *The Mayor of Dixie* became the basis of their 1921 Broadway phenomenon *Shuffle Along*.

Cook's wife, Abbie, accepted an invitation to join the Pekin stock company and Will himself became a composing conductor in November 1906.[28] *My Friend from Georgia* was his first Pekin show to feature Abbie. He hurriedly wrote two songs, which he considered among his most outstanding—"Wid de Moon, Moon, Moon" and "Ghost Ship."[29] (The latter work is based on the Middle Passage of the slave trade.) He contributed to another show, *In Zululand,* and his song "Red, Red Rose" was interpolated by Mitchell in *The Man from Bam.* Cook also wrote a musical production called *Swing Along,* starring Lizzie Hart. He collaborated with Joe Jordan in writing the "Pekin Rag," better known as "Sweetie Dear."

On December 4, 1906, the Pekin sponsored a concert of Afro-British composer Samuel Coleridge-Taylor's music performed by Joe Jordan and the

Pekin Orchestra, along with Harry T. Burleigh, William H. Tyers, Will Marion Cook, N. Clark Smith, and Irene Howard, as well as composer Coleridge-Taylor himself.[30]

It is not known to what extent Cook's songs were performed at the Pekin, though he conducted there periodically. Animosity between him and Jordan led to Cook's dismissal.

> I also conducted a part of the show. This, to my great surprise, was not so acceptable to Joe Jordan, the regular conductor. Petty little arguments began to be so annoying that after the third or fourth show I commenced to lose the enthusiasm without which I cannot happily work. To this day I cannot understand what actuated Jordan's peculiar actions, except that he thought I desired his job. Nothing was further from my mind. I began to refuse to go into the orchestra pit, and even lost my zest for composition. Motts, the owner, argued with me once or twice, but since there was no proof of my suspicions (although Ed Green agreed with me), I failed to tell Motts why I had lost interest in the Pekin shows. So he threw me out, even refusing to give me my return fare to New York.[31]

The famous playwright and producer Jesse A. Shipp was later hired to assist in producing musical comedies at the Pekin. He preferred big shows that would enjoy a long run, while Motts opted for frequent turnovers of new productions. Motts's ideal proved unattainable, and eventually the Stock Company had to close. The theater returned to vaudeville billings. Motts's subsequent illness and untimely death in July 1911 virtually terminated an important era in black theatrical history.

What proved to be the last of the Shipp-Rogers-Cook collaborations was the three-act "chocolate colored" comedy *In Bandanna Land* that opened on February 3, 1908, again at New York's Majestic Theatre, for an eleven-week engagement. Scenes set in a North Georgia city centered around the ventures of Skunton Bowser (Bert Williams) and his guardian, Buck Jenkins (George Walker). For nearly a year before the show's opening, Williams and Walker studied black people in various parts of the South, in order to depict them with true and natural effect. Critic Lester Walton appreciated the authenticity this preparation achieved:

> In the first act when Bert Williams produces an old pocket Bible his mother has given him years ago to keep, and George Walker looks at it and states that his mother also gave him one which he kept in his trunk, this sentiment was strictly Negro. . . . Then, in another act when George Walker names the property in question "Bandanna Land," after a bandanna handkerchief which he sees and causes him to grow reminiscent and recall the days when his dear old mother wore just such a handkerchief [,] there was displayed another bit of sentiment that should have been appreciated by many in the house.[32]

"With all its savor of a minstrel performance, the piece comes very close to being opera comique," one reviewer opined. "There is a plot and most of the songs relate to it; the comedy is a natural outcome of the story, and the music—some of it, at least—is far above the ordinary."[33] The *Boston Globe* described *Bandanna Land* as "decidedly the best of the many Williams and Walker shows."[34] The music was "quite as good as is found in the average musical comedy—some of it is very much better—and the choral numbers are sung by voices of surpassing richness and power."[35] Cook conducted the orchestra and wrote numbers which he considered to have been some of his best musical efforts. One such piece, peppered with folk humor, was "Rain-Song," as performed by lyricist Alex Rogers with a male chorus.[36] Hypothetical rainfall predictions are detailed in a quasi-recitative minor mode:

> An-y time you hear de cheers an' ta-bles crack
> An' de folks wid rheu-mat-ics dey jints is on de rack
> Look out fu' rain, rain, rain![37]

Prevalent syncopation is a key element to the song's success. The "rain" ambiance in the accompaniment includes well-positioned grace notes in bass chords against tremolo treble passages for heightened drama.

The refrain picturesquely counters why there will *not* be rain today, in a major mode:

> Kase de su't ain' fall-in' an' de dogs ain' sleep,
> An' you ain' seen no spi-ders from dere cob-webs creep;
> Las' night de sun went bright to bed,
> An' de moon ain' nev-ah once been seen to hang her head.

The song "Late Hours" performed by Bert Williams as well as his famous pantomime poker game became hallmarks of the show.[38] Williams once told Tom Fletcher the genesis of this routine, which was inspired through the observation of a hospital patient:

Evidently his mental illness was due to gambling, playing poker. In his room was a table and a chair. He was there all alone, talking to himself and acting as though he were in a poker game for he would go through the motions of having a drink, looking around the table and smiling at the other players. He would reach in his imaginary pile of chips and throw in his ante, looking around to see if everybody was in, then smile again. He would shuffle and begin to deal around and after he finished dealing, he would pick up his imaginary hand and look at each player after they had discarded, to see how many cards they wanted. All this time he would have a smile on his face as if he believed he had the best hand, and as each player asked for cards his smile would get broader. As each imaginary player would ask for cards he would put up fingers to show he understood how many. Then, when one of the imaginary players stood pat, his smile would suddenly begin to vanish. When the deal was all over, the betting would start. Each player would call or pass. When it was up to him he would look at his hand, put it down, pour a little drink from his imaginary bottle and look again. Then he would push in the last of his chips and call.

After the showdown he had the second best hand. He would stand up, brush off his pants and go back to his bunk, place his elbows on his knees and leaning on his hands, shake his head slowly.[39]

One of the more lighthearted numbers was "Bon Bon Buddy," the story of George Walker's pride-filled grandmother, who always called him "choc'late drop."[40] The first phrase of its melodious chorus survives in Louis Armstrong's 1931 classic performance of Ford Dabney's *Shine* (1924). There is also a strong resemblance to "Swing Along." (Examples 7.1–2) Cook employed a syncopated chromatic melodic pattern both in the verse and at the midpoint of the chorus, creating a subtle continuity.

The nostalgic "Any Old Place in Yankee Land Is Good Enough for Me" was written collaboratively by Alex Rogers, Chris Smith, and Will Marion Cook. Apparently inspired by George M. Cohan's hit "The Yankee Doodle Boy" (1904), this song predictably begins with an excerpt from the American Revolutionary War song "Yankee Doodle." An interlude quotes Dan Emmett's "Dixie," and the "Yankee Doodle" refrain returns at the final verse.

The ragtime title song "In Bandanna Land" was probably sung and danced by the full Williams and Walker Company during the finale of the second act. Its melody is immediately reminiscent of "Darktown Barbecue" from *The Southerners* and "On Emancipation Day" from *In Dahomey*. The introductory material in all three songs is virtually the same. (Examples 7.3–5) Moreover, this motif is used as a transition to the choruses of "Bandanna Land" and "Darktown Barbecue." Cook may have borrowed from his earlier "Barbecue," since both songs have culinary content. "Mord" Allen's lyrics describe *Bandanna Land* as a grand utopian place for the darker race: "Fixed so he'll for-get his color[,] his hair[,] en his race…"

This musical enjoyed a successful traveling tour to such locations as Atlantic City, Boston, and Louisville, with revival performances in Manhattan and Brooklyn. Aida Overton Walker (George Walker's wife) introduced a "Salome" dance, which was the rage in New York, after Isadora Duncan and Marie Madeline created a European sensation.[41] She received mixed reviews, especially outside of New York.[42] No entertainment was considered complete without a "Salome" dance, and *Bandanna Land* was no exception.

George Walker was suffering from paresis, advanced syphilis, and his condition worsened as the performing season progressed. He experienced all of the normal symptoms: memory loss, tantrums, voice alterations, stuttering, and unsteadiness. February 1909 marked his final appearance, and for the remaining performances Aida Overton Walker (dressed as a male) assumed her husband's role as "Bon Bon Buddy." The famed Williams and

Swing a - long chil-lun, swing   a - long de lane;   Lif' yo' head and yo' heels might - y high.

Example 7.1 "Swing Along," mm. 1–4 (Will Marion Cook [New York: G. Schirmer, 1912]).

Bon - Bon Bud - dy   the   choc - o - late drop,___   Dat's   me,____

Example 7.2 "Bon Bon Buddy," chorus (music, Will Marion Cook; lyrics, Alex Rogers [New York: Gotham-Attucks, 1904]).

Example 7.3 "Darktown Barbecue," mm. 1–4 (Will Marion Cook [New York: John H. Cook, 1904]).

Example 7.4 "In Bandanna Land," mm. 1–4 (music, Will Marion Cook; lyrics, Mord Allen [New York: Gotham-Attucks, 1907]).

Example 7.5 "On Emancipation Day," mm. 1–4 (music, Will Marion Cook; lyrics, Paul Laurence Dunbar [New York: Harry Von Tilzer, 1902]).

Walker comedic duo that had dazzled audiences for nearly two decades was history.

The black musical stage suffered a devastating triple blow in the years 1909 to 1911. Ernest Hogan died on May 20, 1909, George Walker died at the age of 38 on January 6, 1911, and, finally, Bob Cole died on August 2, 1911. This series of losses virtually ended the golden age of black musical comedies.

Chapter 8

REMOVING THE "MINSTREL MASK"

Minstrelsy's portrayals of slavery and blacks, reveal the evolution and functioning of American racial stereotypes better than any other source.

Robert C. Toll

Many turn-of-the-century artists were preoccupied with transforming the black stereotypic images on the stage. Since the early 1830s, African Americans had been portrayed as comic figures, first by whites who painted their faces black, and then by blacks who painted theirs still blacker in the popular entertainment tradition known as minstrelsy. The instrumentalists Tambo and Bones, the ragged Southern plantation darky, and the overdressed Northern city dandy were all masked characters perpetuating stereotypic imaginings of the black American. Childlike grins with pearly teeth, eyes rounded like saucers, rollicking laughter with overindulging appetites for watermelon and chicken, razor fights, and coon dialect were only a few of the caricatures reflected in the theater. The music was expected to be light and cheery, and the dialogue gay and frivolous. These contradictions between the stage representations of African Americans and the grim realities of racism were poignantly addressed in Paul Laurence Dunbar's famous poem "We Wear the Mask."

> We wear the mask that grins and lies,
> It hides our cheeks and shades our eyes,—
> This debt we pay to human guile;
> With torn and bleeding hearts we smile,
> And mouth with myriad subtleties.

Why should the world be overwise,
In counting all our tears and sighs?
Nay, let them only see us, while
We wear the mask. . . .[1]

How to elevate the content, form, and style of the Negro as theatrical writer, composer, and performer was one of the most important questions confronting black contemporary intellectuals. This prominent group of black artists included the entertainer/lyricist Bob Cole, the collaborators James Weldon and J. Rosamond Johnson, librettist and vaudeville entertainer Jesse A. Shipp, vocalist/composer Harry Burleigh, composer Willis Accooe, and multitalented vaudevillian Billy Johnson, who toured with and wrote for John Isham's Octoroons Company as well as Black Patti's Troubadours.[2] Will Marion Cook was among the group who held serious conversations at Marshall's Hotel in Manhattan in an attempt to determine how the image of the Negro as a writer, composer, and performer could be elevated.[3] The musical artists frequented Marshall's for an evening of Southern food, syncopated music, and stimulating dialogue regarding how, in effect, to change the derogatory images of minstrelsy on the stage.

Upon his arrival to Broadway, Cook proclaimed that "Gone was the uff-dah of the minstrel! Gone the Massa Linkum stuff! We were artists and we were going a long, long way."[4]

How far did Cook go? Several songs from his musicals offer an analytical perspective on the complexities surrounding African-American theater at this crucial juncture in its history. Underneath the surface of the genre, the metaphor of the "minstrel mask" is at work, producing its mixture of accommodations and strategies that give Cook's work its peculiar energy.

Clorindy exemplifies the play of ambiguities involved. On the one hand, despite Cook's claim, in reality the "uff-dah" of minstrelsy was still evident in any number of *Clorindy's* songs, such as "Darktown Is Out Tonight," "Who Dat Say Chicken in Dis Crowd?" and "The Hottest Coon in Dixie." In the last-named coon song, Cook confessed that "[t]his was hardly Dunbar's finest lyric, but the chorus, the dances, and the inimitable Ernest Hogan made that Broadway audience think that it was."[5]

Yet Dunbar himself was unnerved by *Clorindy*. On its opening night he sat in a special box seat reserved for authors and their guests. As he "listened to the lyrics that he had helped to write, he felt a sense of embarrassment. The musical was in the worst of the minstrel tradition. Not only were black people laughing at themselves, they were also performing on stage, offering themselves as objects for the laughter of others. . . . [Dunbar] vowed that he would never write lyrics for another show. . . . *Clorindy* would be his last "coon show."[6]

Whatever Dunbar's embarrassment about some songs, a closer examination of others in this musical suggest a more complicated reaction. Among *Clorindy's* extant musical numbers is "A Negro Love Song." Dunbar wrote this poem while he was employed as a waiter in a Chicago hotel during the World's Fair of 1893. He observed that as some of the waiters congregated near the kitchen door recounting their romantic escapades, working waiters coming through the swinging doors would say, "Jump back, honey, jump back."[7] As Dunbar listened to the song on opening night, however, it sounded more ridiculous than humorous.

Nevertheless, there was more opposition in the song than might be suspected at first hearing. The mere fact that blacks were describing a *realistic* courtship scene in song, rather than a burlesqued, unrealistic encounter, signaled the slipping of the minstrel mask:

> Put my ahm around huh weys,
>> Jump back, honey, jump back.
> Raised huh lips an' took a tase'
>> Jump back, honey, jump back.
> Love me, honey, love me true?
>> Love me well ez I love you?
> An' she answe'd, "Cose I do"—
>> Jump back, honey, jump back.

Another method Cook and Dunbar employed to remove the minstrel mask was the use of confrontational jabs or signifiers as verbal weapons aimed at the white audience members. Prior to the cakewalking chorus of "Darktown Is Out Tonight" was the proclamation, "White fo'ks yo' / Got no sho'! / Dis huh's Darktown night." These lyrics celebrate the overall uninhibited pride in black life.

In a society where African Americans were seeking social equality, on stage they were at liberty to flaunt their mastery of sound, movement, timing, and the spoken word. In many ways the entertainment venue offered a safe haven where blacks could feel somewhat superior, instead of inferior, to mainstream Americans.

One example is "On Emancipation Day," from Cook and Dunbar's later collaboration, *In Dahomey.* "On Emancipation Day" stands out as one of Cook's most crafted and successful "ragtime" compositions. It excels in its development of a small musical idea, its rhythmic energy, its artfully crafted climactic structure, and its use of harmonies just beyond the ordinary. Moreover, Dunbar's lyrics aim their most profound barbs at whites (see ex. 8.1):

> On E-manci-pa-tion day,
> All you white folks clear de way . . .
> When dey hear dem ragtime tunes
> White fo'ks try to pass fo' coons
> On E-man-ci-pa-tion day.

Here was a clear, perhaps even prophetic statement about the appropriation of African-American culture that would characterize the emergent

Example 8.1 "On Emancipation Day," chorus; in Thomas Riis, *Music and Scripts "In Dahomey,"* 117–118),

popular music industry in subsequent decades. Dunbar's observation had deep roots in antebellum social history.

Black Americans were well aware that whites had been enthralled by their singing and dancing styles since the days of slavery. "After dinner Ol' Marster would give us a little tap wid de switch. He say he was settling our dinner. Den he'd let us play and he'd set on de big porch and watch." Whites constantly watched. "Ef de fiel wuk wuz up, us didn't wuk Saddy ebenin," recounted a former Alabama slave; "en we could hab er banjo dance nearly ebery Saddy night. Lots er times, Ole Mistis en her company come ter our dances en looked on." Many an ex-slave recalled similar situations:

> Our Mistress would cum down sometime, early ter watch us dance. Marse Bannett would call all us little niggers up to de big house to dance for him, and us sho would cut de pigeon wing, den us would sing "reels" for him.
>
> Miss Jane Massingale wud cum to de slave quarters wid her young com'ny an' j'ine in wid de slaves.[8]

The white racialized gaze became a theme that resounded in some of the monuments of African-American intellectual achievement. The fact that

African Americans were self-conscious about the watchfulness of whites resulted in a dual perspective that was brilliantly articulated in W. E. B. Du Bois's classic *Souls of Black Folk*:

> [T]he Negro is sort of a seventh son born with a veil, and gifted with a second sight in this American world—a world which yields him no true self-consciousness, but only lets him see himself through the revelation of the other world. It is a peculiar sensation, this double consciousness, this sense of always looking at one's self through the eyes of others, of measuring one's soul by the tape of a world that looks on in amused contempt and pity.[9]

Such profound insights could echo in music as well. The double-conscious watchfulness of whites is further revealed in one of Cook's most popular songs, "Swing Along," also from *In Dahomey* (see ex. 8.2):

> Come along Mandy,
> Come along Sue,
> White fo'ks a-watch-in'
> An' seein' what you do,
> White fo'ks jeal-ous when you'se walkin' two by two
> So Swing along chil-lun
> Swing a-long.[10]

(These lyrics were also sexually suggestive of what the Algerian psychiatrist Frantz Fanon and the American Studies scholar Eric Lott infer as black penis envy,[11] concluding with a defiant message for blacks to swing their sexual prowess along.) The overriding message of this song conveyed racial pride and optimism in the pursuit of social justice. Will Marion Cook wrote in an undated letter to his son that "'Swing Along' came almost all at once . . . and when I sat at the piano to work it out I made very little if any change. I felt as if 'Swing Along' was exactly what we were to do—no obstacles—nothing could stop us."

Cook's musicals exemplified not only double consciousness, but also a sense of dual identity. Du Bois further describes this latter phenomenon: "One ever feels his twoness—an American, a Negro; two souls, two thoughts, two unreconciled strivings; two warring ideals in one dark body, whose dogged strength alone keeps it from being torn asunder."[12] The black middle class in America largely accepted and aspired to European standards of taste and behavior. They sought to dissociate themselves from the stereotypical image of common black folks, thinking this tactic would hasten their acceptance into mainstream society.[13]

One of the significant ways that the minstrel mask was further removed in musicals was by transforming dialect into standard English and removing coonlike images. Cook adopted his European-American identity wherein he wrote what he called "white songs."[14] Sometimes he even created a black

Example 8.2 "Swing Along," mm. 13–20 (Will Marion Cook; in Riis, *Music and Scripts "In Dahomey,"* 156).

and a white version of the same song. For example, "The Little Gypsy Maid," with changes in lyrics, became "Brown-Skin Baby Mine." "Gypsy Maid's" chorus reads:

> She is no tulip rare—
> In colors bright arrayed
> She's just a wild flow'r
> Of the forest shade,
> This little gypsy maid.[15]

Compare this with the chorus of "Brown-Skin Baby Mine" which concludes:

> She ain't no tulip rare
> Nor mornin' glory fine'
> But mongst de flowers fair
> Kaint none compare
> Wid brownskin baby mine.[16]

Cook may have simply adapted a composition written for a white musical to fit the conventions of a black genre. He wrote the tune used for both maiden songs, but the standard English lyrics were written by Harry B. Smith and Cecil Mack; the dialect lyrics by Cook and Cecil Mack. We don't know which text was created first.

This song with a double lyric was a favorite in both black and white theaters. Irene Bentley (the wife of Harry B. Smith) made "The Little Gypsy Maid" a hit in George Lederer's production *The Wild Rose.*[17] Similarly, Abbie Mitchell (the wife of Will Marion Cook) popularized "Brown-Skin Baby Mine" in Bert Williams and George Walker's production of *In Dahomey.* That this piece also conveyed a positive message regarding a person of color was extraordinary for the stage at this time.

Another work of sentimental uplift came into evidence in Cook's last theatrical venture of note, *Darkydom* (1915). One of the most favorably reviewed songs from this show was "Mammy," which predated Al Jolson's similar blackface song of the same name by five years.[18] During the last half of the verse, a poignant passage in Cook's song briefly shifts from A-flat major to its parallel minor as the text reveals nostalgia for home and mother:

> I long to be back home a-gain
> Before your last good-bye,
> And hear you croon some sad, slave tune
> "Bout char-i-ots in the sky."[19]

As the final poetic line is sung, the melody ascends and the key returns to A-flat major.

The "crooned slave tune" refers to the sorrow song known as "Swing Low, Sweet Chariot." Longing to hear *this* slave song sends a cloaked double message, conveyed through maternal moans and revolutionary lyrics:

Swing Low, Sweet Chariot,
Coming for to carry me home.
Swing Low, Sweet Chariot,
Coming for to carry me home.

To the outsider in pre–Civil War America, "home" referred to heaven; but to the informed insider, "home" symbolized the North, Canada, and freedom! It was an "alerting" song used as a preparatory signal for slaves to escape by means of the Underground Railroad.[20] This and other spirituals, such as "Steal Away to Jesus," "Good News, de Chariot's Coming," and "Oh, Sinner, You'd Better Get Ready," provide numerous examples of veiled protests.[21] Cook's suggestion of "Swing Low" evokes a powerful image of an unassuming mother who is singing a pregnant heritage song of resistance.

During its heartrending conclusion, "Mammy" portrays deeply felt emotions with well-timed fermatas: "And I know we'll meet again some day, Mammy." At the crucial word "again," Cook launches the vocal line to the song's highest note (see ex. 8.3). "Mammy" was entered in a songwriter's

Example 8.3 "Mammy," mm. 30–34 (music, Will Marion Cook; lyrics, Lester A. Walton (New York: Artmusic, 1906]).

contest, with Abbie Mitchell singing and Will Cook at the piano. It received the prize, which, to Cook's dismay, was a mere ten-dollar bill.[22]

This song was performed frequently as a vocal as well as an instrumental solo. The well-known tenor Roland Hayes acknowledged: "I sang it last night at a concert where a good-sized crowd of both white and colored people gathered, and it took like wild fire; so vociferous was the applause that I had to repeat it the second time. It is truly a very beautiful song and one with a sentiment which does not fail in its appeal. I shall use it on all my programs."[23]

The universality of idealized motherhood—a particularly common theme in the early twentieth century—was crucial to "Mammy's" popularity, which quite likely crossed racial boundaries. Cook's collaborator, Paul Laurence Dunbar, best known for his dialect, once voiced the desire "[t]o be able to interpret his own people through song and story, and to prove that after all we are more human than African."[24] The eminent sociologist E. Franklin Frazier, writing on the black bourgeoisie, inferred that "The desire to aspire, to be educated, to be affluent is not to be white—it is to be human."[25] In this same vein, certain songs in Will Marion Cook's musicals were written on more general humanistic themes rather than race-specific ones.

One such song is "Red, Red Rose," featured by Abbie Mitchell in the 1908 black musical *Bandanna Land*.[26] It is Cook's most popular art song and has a universally appealing subject. Alex Rogers's lyrics poetically search for the red rose that holds love's secret:

> If you are not my love O! red, red rose
> Then won't you tell me just which red rose knows.

Love is romantically tied to nature, as in the questioning scenario, "Does she love me or love me not, love me or love me not" while petals are torn off until the remaining one reveals the secret. Cook's piano accompaniment partners with the voice, sharing equally in supporting and intensifying the poetic meaning. A dramatic metric change occurs from simple 4/4 to compound 12/8 meter as the refrain approaches. This transformation enhances the textual intensity, broadening its pace and sentimentality. The top voice assumes the melodic line as the accompaniment continues with triplet figurations (see ex. 8.4) lyrically inquiring:

> Are you my love O! red rose speak to me?
> Tell me red rose that I may cling to thee,
> Breathe just one word that I may know 'tis thee.

When the last line is sung, Cook suddenly modulates from B-flat major to D-flat major for a brief moment to heighten the listener's expectations. "That I may love thee thro' eternity" follows, which reverts to the home key of B-flat major.

Example 8.4 "Red, Red Rose," mm. 20–24 (music, Will Marion Cook; lyrics, Alex Rogers [New York: Maurice Shapiro, 1909]).

The musical style is not unlike that of the favorite 1892 sacred song, "The Holy City," by Stephen Adams.[27] Many of the accompanimental procedures are identical, including the use of triplet devices to magnify the intention and a dynamic use of bass octaves to enhance the drama. Similarly, both songs are in B-flat major with a D major section in "The Holy City" and a D-flat major segment in "Red, Red Rose." Cook considered this song one of his most successful.[28]

Will Marion Cook made use of compositional techniques that were employed by both black and white contemporary composers. He utilized the African themes, ethnic humor, and coon variety stereotypes that were prevalent among black songwriters, but he also wrote songs about love, women, patriotism, nostalgia, and themes affecting Everyperson that were also common in songs by whites. The movement to remove the minstrel mask from the musical stage included:

- The use of realism as opposed to myth when portraying African-American life and culture, with realistic courtship and love subject matter rather than burlesqued illusions.

- Exploiting of confrontational jabs as verbal weapons aimed at white audience members, who had no knowledge of their full meaning. This practice had its roots in African memory through the trickster tradition—there were power implications in these situations for the socially less powerful.
- The ability to see themselves and others from multiple perspectives.
- The use of universal themes such as nature, home, and mother; on occasion, however, they were used with a twist of veiled protest.

Ironically, many of Cook's musicals featured Bert Williams and George Walker billed as "Two *Real* Coons." Williams lived a rather "schizophrenic" existence in which, offstage, he was an urbane, fair-skinned, and intelligent black man whereas onstage he portrayed a rural, blacked-up, slow-talking buffoon. The blackface mask actually distanced him enough so that truths could be expressed that would have been unacceptable or socially dangerous if presented in a more serious context.

The ultimate purpose of masking was for deception, which for blacks was a method of coping with their dual role in a multiracial society. As is revealed in the lore of the folk:

> Got one mind for white folk to see
> 'Nother for what I know is me.[29]

In unmasking the musicals of Will Marion Cook, African Americans came closer to revealing the truth about themselves and others in their pursuit of social justice and equality.

PHOTOS

Will Marion Cook (Photographs and Prints Division, Schomburg Center for Research in Black Culture, The New York Public Library, Astor, Lenox and Tilden Foundations)

Abbie Mitchell (Photographs and Prints Division, Moorland-Spingarn Research Center, Howard University)

Bert Williams (Photographs and Prints Division, Schomburg Center for Research in Black Culture, The New York Public Library, Astor, Lenox and Tilden Foundations)

George W. Walker (Photographs and Prints Division, Schomburg Center for Research in Black Culture, The New York
Public Library, Astor, Lenox and Tilden Foundations)

Bert Williams and George Walker (Photographs and Prints Division, Schomburg Center for Research in Black Culture, The New York Public Library, Astor, Lenox and Tilden Foundations)

Aida Overton Walker and George Walker (Photographs and Prints Division, Schomburg Center for Research in Black Culture. The New York Public Library, Astor, Lenox and Tilden Foundations)

Bob Cole, James Johnson, and J. Rosamond Johnson (Photographs and Prints Division, Schomburg Center for Research in Black Culture, The New York Public Library, Astor, Lenox and Tilden Foundations)

Chapter 9

THE CLEF CLUB, *DARKYDOM*,
AND WORLD WAR I

We must strike out for ourselves, we must develop our own ideas,
and conceive an orchestration adapted to our own abilities
and instincts.

James Reese Europe

Will Marion Cook's life was checkered with melancholia and bizarre behavior. His good friend and vaudevillian partner, George Walker, once confessed that "If Will Marion Cook was a white man I reckon he would pass as eccentric, but, being as he's a negro, he's sure enough plumb crazy." This assertion was made after Abbie found her stage clothes cut up and her golden slippers slashed with a razor. It was 3:00 P.M. and the curtain was to rise on the matinee performance of the Memphis Students' act at 4:26. Stage hands witnessed Will Marion go into her dressing room beforehand. Fortunately, Abbie was able to purchase a new outfit from a downtown Manhattan department store just in time for the afternoon curtain call.[1]

In August 1905 Will and Abbie's marital difficulties led her to move herself, her five-year-old daughter, two-year-old son, mother, and mother-in-law into an apartment at 20 West 99th Street in Manhattan. At least some of their trouble resulted from Will's instructing Abbie to give $40 of her earnings from *The Southerners* to his brother John. She resented this demand and resisted. When she performed with Ernest Hogan and the Memphis Students, she gave Will half of her $25 weekly salary. After their success, she purchased a tailor-made dress.

Will was mad at this, and he struck me several times. We were married in Washington when I was very young and he always treated me like a baby. Now, I am a woman and refuse to be bullied.[2]

Abbie divorced Will Marion in August 1908. The couple settled custody of the children out of court.[3] In the spring of the following year, however, Abbie was in New York's West Side Court pleading with Magistrate Breene for protection from her divorced husband. "He haunts my life with a gun, Your Honor," she squeaked. Lawyer Wheaton, Abbie's counsel, explained that the previous August she had secured a divorce and was to receive $40 a week in alimony. Cook countered that she owed him $160. Abbie described how

> last night, while she was in bed, he entered her room and demanded $25, at the same time saying that the balance would have to be paid within four days. He also emphasized his demand by looking, significantly at his pocket, where, it is believed, he always has a gun concealed.

Abbie promised to pay the money as soon as she could, provided the court would prevent Cook from "haunting her life with a gun." Cook agreed and left the court looking greatly relieved.[4]

Will's social relationships soured on many fronts, from publishers to personal friends. As was discussed earlier, he falsely accused Witmark of cheating him on royalties from *"Clorindy:* The Origin of the Cakewalk." This confrontation curtailed future contracts with this influential publishing firm.[5]

In 1906, while assisting Eubie Blake in publishing his first rag, Cook took Blake to Schirmer's Music Company. Blake played his work on the piano for the arranger Kurt Schindler, who liked what he heard and bought it for $100. Before scoring it, however, Schindler asked politely, "Mr. Blake, why do you change keys without modulation?"

> Will Marion Cook flared up and said, "What right have you to question my protégé? How long have you been a Negro?"
>
> "I'm only asking a question," Schindler said.
>
> "Well, you've no right to ask it. We write differently from other people."
>
> "Good day, gentlemen," said Schindler, and all bets were off.[6]

Blake was finally able to publish his first rag more than a decade later with Witmark, no thanks to Cook. Its original title was changed from "Sounds of Africa" (Cook's title) to "Charleston Rag" (Blake's title).

Will Marion Cook's notoriety as an eccentric went hand in hand with his reputation as a brilliant musician. James Weldon Johnson once justified Cook's behavior: "He has many of those personal peculiarities and eccentricities which we, no doubt, ought to expect and excuse in original geniuses."[7] He was hot-tempered, and argumentative; he would often belittle the entertainer and playwright Bob Cole regarding Cole's limitations in musical and general education; he would even sneer at him after a mispronunciation. Cole was particularly sensitive, and Cook's taunts both humiliated and maddened him.[8]

During Will Cook's years of concertizing, he was also a contributing member of the group known as the Clef Club, which probably evolved from the Memphis Students. One of the original "Students" was James Reese Europe (1881–1919),[9] born in Mobile, Alabama, Europe's mother taught him piano and his father encouraged him to improvise on the banjo and fiddle. Although he was twelve years younger than Will Marion Cook, they led parallel lives in several significant ways. When James was nine, the Europe family moved to Washington, D.C., where he studied violin with Joseph Douglass (the grandson of Frederick Douglass) and Enrico Hurlei (the assistant director of the United States Marine Band). James Reese and Will Marion both spent much of their youth in the District of Columbia, studied the violin, moved to New York, conducted black musical comedies, and syncopated orchestral concerts. Cook is credited with placing the baton in Europe's hand and showing him how to indicate time.[10] Europe directed *The Shoofly Regiment* and *Mr. Lode of Koal,* among other musical productions. Most important, he was instrumental in dramatically altering the status of black musicians in New York for the next decade as founder and first president of the famous black musicians' ensemble known as the Clef Club, organized April 11, 1910.[11] He arranged bookings and negotiated contracts for social affairs in parlors, drawing rooms, yachts, private railroad cars, exclusive millionaires' clubs, swanky hotels, and fashionable resorts.

Working conditions improved for black performers during Jim Europe's tenure as Clef Club president. Until then, black musicians had been paid not as musicians but as hired help who performed menial tasks. They would provide entertainment between other duties and afterward sing and stroll among the guests, soliciting tips. Jim Europe made sure that musicians were given a salary for entertainment only, as well as transportation, and room and board when required.[12] Membership in this extraordinary club afforded many unique and diverse experiences. Distinguished club member Noble Sissle describes the club members' activities: "They played and sang in the home of the Vanderbilts, the Goulds, the Wanamakers in Philadelphia one day, and in Pittsburgh for Mrs. Stotesbury the next, then the day after that in Washington for Mrs. Evelyn McLean, or on the private yacht for a cruise with their small organ and drums with the Astors."[13] Their talents led them to entertain the white American elite.

Ironically, the group was named for a symbol used in musical notation, even though it consisted largely of men who played only by ear; apparently "two-thirds of them could not read a note when they first joined the organization."[14] Furthermore, they were available for practice only during odd hours, since many were employed as barbers, elevator boys, porters, waiters, and the like. Clef Club members later purchased a brownstone directly across from the Marshall Hotel at 134 West 53rd Street. This facility functioned as a clubhouse, booking office, and another venue where African-American musicians fraternized.

Jim Europe was also instrumental in organizing the Clef Club Symphony Orchestra, a group that included well over a hundred musicians who integrated vocal, instrumental, and dance music. On many occasions Cook served as one of its conductors. A "Musical Melange and Dancefest" was held at the Manhattan Casino on 155th Street and Eighth Avenue on May 27, 1910, in honor of the club's formation. It was to become a semiannual event for the next four years. The orchestra's unconventional instrumentation consisted of mandolins, violins, banjos, harp-guitars, cellos, trap drums and timpani, complemented by eleven pianos. The orchestra performed marches, dances, operatic medleys, and popular songs. Composer Olly Wilson contends that the Clef Club's unique instrumentation was simply the result of combining the entire membership of the Clef Club into one ensemble. He believes that Europe was too smart a showman to reveal this reality to intrigued music critics.[15]

The Clef Club Orchestra aspired to gain respectability by adhering to a strict dress code: tuxedos for advance bookings, and dark suits, white shirts, and bow ties for pickup engagements. Their desire for racial uplift was also evident in their removal of the minstrel format in segments of their performances.[16] Interestingly, however, Maurice Peress has viewed a dancefest photograph from May 11, 1911, under a magnifying glass and discovered a band on stage (behind the Clef Club) fronted by a minstrel line with several wearing blackface. "Jim Europe was not about to cut off the generation of musicians who carried the torch from minstrelsy. He simply brought them along."[17]

On May 2, 1912, a historic first Clef Club concert was held as a benefit for the Music School Settlement for Colored People—an institution providing a rare opportunity for talented black youth to become musically educated at nominal fees. Carnegie Hall was secured for this occasion largely through the efforts of one of the school's founders, David Mannes, who himself had been inspired and instructed by the black violinist Joseph Douglass. Mannes served as the concertmaster of the New York Symphony Orchestra and later founded the Mannes School of Music. The Music School Settlement promoted the encouragement, development, and preservation of the Negro's music. The Carnegie Hall concert featured black artists singing and playing compositions primarily by African Americans before an integrated audience.[18]

Soon the orchestra of the Clef Club had grown to 145 players consisting of 47 mandolins and bandores, 27 harp-guitars, 11 banjos, 8 violins, 1 saxophone, 1 tuba, 13 cellos, 2 clarinets, 2 baritones, 8 trombones, 7 cornets, 1 set of timpani, 5 trap drums, 2 double basses, and 10 pianos. These instruments were used in a rather unusual manner: For example, first violins instead of second violins, accompanied the mandolins and banjos, producing a peculiar, steady strumming accompaniment. Two clarinets were used in place of an oboe (because they had not yet been able to find a good oboist). Two baritone horns substituted for the French horn and were added to no less than eight trombones and seven cornets.

James Reese Europe, who in many ways emulated Will Marion Cook, favored this unorthodox instrumentation because he believed it was futile to imitate the methods and organization of a white orchestra. In an interview in *The New York Evening Post*, Europe argued, "[As blacks,] we must strike out for ourselves, we must develop our own ideas, and conceive an orchestration adapted to our own abilities and instincts."[19] Likewise, Will Marion "believed that the Negro in music and on the stage ought to be a Negro, a genuine Negro; he declared that the Negro should eschew 'white' patterns, and not employ his efforts in doing what 'the white artist could always do as well, generally better.'"[20]

Besides the Clef Club Orchestra, a 40-voice male choir from St. Philip's Church sang at the Carnegie Hall concert. Contralto Elizabeth Payne also performed; J. Rosamond Johnson sang one of his works and played a piano solo; and the Royal Poinciana Quartette and the Versatile Entertainers' Quintet interpreted popular contemporary songs. There was also a large chorus of 150 voices trained by Will Marion Cook for the occasion. This group sang "Swing Along," which was exceptionally well received. In fact, it was sung three times before the enthusiastic audience was satisfied. "The artistic way in which [*Swing Along*] was rendered bore out the statement often made that classical music is not the only kind that requires preparation and intelligent interpretation."[21] Another Cook and Rogers's popular choice, "The Rain Song," from *Bandanna Land*, also "struck the fancy of the audience."[22] Cook was so affected by the audience's overwhelming reaction to his music that he was visibly moved to tears.[23]

Will Marion Cook's name (after that of James Europe and songwriter William Tyers) appeared as second assistant conductor of the Clef Club Orchestra. Cook had been invited to guest conduct his songs for the auspicious Carnegie Hall concert, but instead he opted to play violin with the orchestra. (Obviously, his fingers were no longer stiff and his instrument no longer in the pawn shop.) According to Noble Sissle, Cook was initially opposed to this concert and "raved all over town about Jim not knowing anything about conducting and what right did he have going to Carnegie Hall with his inexperience? Cook claimed that Jim would set the Negro race back fifty years, and many of those remarks he even made in Jim's hearing."[24] These comments may have been signs of envy. After all, Europe was younger than Cook, and largely self-taught. Certainly he had not matriculated at prestigious music schools in Oberlin, Berlin, and New York as Cook had. The tears on Carnegie Hall's stage must have been a combination of embarrassment, guilt, joy, and regret, considering his previous resistance to the engagement.

After receiving a euphoric reception in 1912, Clef Club concerts were continued at Carnegie Hall for the next two years. These performances were instrumental in popularizing Cook's "Swing Along," "Rain Song," and "Exhortation." In the 1914 concert, the repertoire and personnel were broadened to include the newly formed Afro-American Folk Song Singers, led by Will Marion Cook and featuring vocalists Abbie Mitchell, Harry T. Burleigh, and J. Rosamond Johnson.[25]

Cook also conducted the 25-member Washington Conservatory of Music Folk Singers in a program on October 26, 1913, featuring his recent compositions and spiritual arrangements, as a part of New York's National Emancipation Exposition celebration. The concert was well appreciated, and on the final night of the Exposition both Cook and Europe, along with pianist-composer J. Rosamond Johnson, pianist Raymond A. Lawson, and entertainer Bert Williams, were among the "100 distinguished freedmen" who received a gold medal for their achievements.[26]

James Reese Europe also had a hand in Will Cook's last major musical production, the 1915 *Darkydom*. This musical comedy, accurately billed as a "medley of mirth, melody and measured motions,"[27] proved to be "the biggest and best colored attraction," after a six-year hiatus.[28] The major mirth-makers were the blackface Miller and Lyles team, perceived as successors to Williams and Walker.[29] The principal melody-makers were Will Marion Cook and James Reese Europe, with lyricist Henry S. Creamer. The show was produced by Lester Walton, staged by Jesse Shipp, and written by Henry Troy. "Measured motions" were created by the dancer Ida Forsyne. Other principal artists were Abbie Mitchell, Will A. Cook [no relation to Will Marion], Allie Gilliam, Henry Troy, Opal Cooper, and Fannie Wise. This list of prominent writers and performers was once described as "the most representative group of theatrical geniuses of which the Negro race . . . can boast."[30]

The threadbare plot that connected comedy situations and musical numbers took place in the all-black city of Mound Bayou, Mississippi. The story concerned two tramps (Miller and Lyles) who were caught illegally riding a train; to eject them, it became necessary to switch tracks. While this train was on the other track, a freight train running without orders whizzed by on the main track. When the conductor realized that the hoboes had unwittingly saved many lives by preventing a collision, he commissioned the valet (Henry Troy) to find the two fellows and reward them with $500. The complications that arose from this pursuit of the tramps provided the fun and frolic of the production.

Reviewer R. W. Thompson noted that the singing was the best feature of the performance: "The music is tinctured with the characteristic Cook and Europe flavor and here and there are bars that are reminiscent of other famous compositions by those gifted artists. The solos are tuneful and the ensembles reach lofting heights at times." [31] Musical selections that received the most favorable mention included "My Lady's Lips" sung by Abbie Mitchell, "Mammy" performed by Opal Cooper, "The Ghost Ship" by Creighton Thompson, and "Rat-a-Tat" by Helen Baxter, featuring girl-drummers in drill formation. *Variety* reported that Cook wrote nineteen musical numbers for this musical.[32]

"My Lady's Lips" and "Mammy" were two songs that received critical acclaim,[33] and Schirmer published "My Lady's Lips Am Like de Honey" in 1915. This song; depicting romantic African Americans, transcended the burlesque and reached the universal. The female subject is given the genteel title "lady"—a revolutionary gesture for its time. James Weldon Johnson's lyrics passionately leap from nature to lovers:

> Honey in de rose, I s'pose, is
> Put dere fo' de bee
> Honey on her lips, I knows, is
> Put dere jes' fo' me.[34]

The song entitled "Mammy" was the combined creation of drama-music critic Lester A. Walton and composer Will Marion Cook for tenor Henry Troy. It was dedicated to John White, Cook's harmony and counterpoint teacher at the National Conservatory.[35] Nearly two decades later, "Mammy" was successfully featured on radio by the singer-actress Ethel Waters.[36]

Even though the critics praised *Darkydom*, revisions were still recommended. According to one review: "Much remains to be done in the way of strengthening the plot . . . . The dramatic element . . . is lacking and there should be a tightening up of the situations that are designed to lead up to climaxes. . . . Much trivial talk could be cut out."[37] Another said: "The appearance of the stars should be made sooner, and the first act ought to be shortened at least fifteen minutes. . . . A love theme should run through the piece, no matter how lightly touched, and at least one more good song could be added."[38]

Moreover, the title *Darkydom* proved to be offensive to many black patrons. *The Freeman* writer observed, "If the management consults the wishes of the masses of the colored patrons of the show, they will select a title that will convey the idea that it is a genuine Negro entertainment without using a term that is banned by polite society."[39] It was generally believed that *Darkydom* had Broadway possibilities, provided certain modifications were made. Significant capital backing was also crucial in order to maintain the considerable number of high-salaried performers. But whether the revisions were not made, or the funding not forthcoming, *Darkydom* proved to be short-lived.

Will Marion Cook's dynamic music had attracted the famous modern dance duo Vernon and Irene Castle, and their subsequent partnership proved mutually beneficial. Europe's music brought diversity to Castle's dances, and the Castles provided more exposure for Europe's energetic music.[40]

Vernon and Irene Castle became national idols with pace-setting trends that transcended the dance floor. Irene explains:

> The clothes I wore were practical for me and that is the reason I wore
> them. I could not dance in a hobble skirt (though I tried at the beginning),

therefore I wore simple flowing gowns that would leave my legs free. When we danced in Paris I could not afford jewelry to compete with the patrons so I went to the other extreme and wore none at all. I found that a frock with uncluttered lines and flowing sleeves was more comfortable for everyday wear. And soon I was surprised to find myself with a following.[41]

As the Castles' star continued to rise, so did that of James Reese Europe Soon professional jealousies mounted among Clef Club members, a circumstance that led to Europe's resignation as president and his decision to establish a splinter group called the Tempo Club. The membership of this ensemble grew to about two hundred, and it also became fashionable in the high society circles of New York, accompanying functions at the Astor, Biltmore, and Plaza Hotels, Delmonicos and Sherry's restaurants, and the Tuxedo Club.

In April 1914 the Castles embarked on a "Whirlwind Tour." Irene Castle acknowledged Jim Europe's musical appeal in a reminiscence: "As I look back over a very full dancing career I realize his music was the only music that completely made me forget the effort of the dance."[42] Europe described how his group achieved their extraordinary effects:

> With the brass instruments we put in mutes and make a whirling motion with the tongue, at the same time blowing full pressure. With wind instruments we pinch the mouthpiece and blow hard. This produces the peculiar sound which you all know. To us it is not discordant, as we play the music as it is written, only that we accent strongly in this manner the notes which originally would be without accent. It is natural for us to do this; it is, indeed, a racial musical characteristic. I have to call a daily rehearsal of my band to prevent the musicians from adding to their music more than I wish them to, whenever possible they all embroider their parts in order to produce new, peculiar sounds. Some of these effects are excellent and some are not, and I have to be continually on the lookout to cut out the results of my musicians's [sic] originality.[43]

These novel performance techniques were also characteristic of Will Marion Cook's ensembles and represent the African sensibilities as well as the aesthetic heritage of the Duke Ellington sound. The Clef Club continued to perform for several years assisted by Tim Brymn, Will Marion Cook, and Fred "Deacon" Johnson.

Cook, meanwhile, continued to be outspoken about racial prejudice his orchestra encountered in America. On one occasion while touring Marion, Ohio, with the Clef Club, he confronted his white audience about the hypocrisy of their enthusiastic ovation:

> We don't want your applause. We just want to fulfill our obligation here and leave. Early this morning this group of great musicians and myself arrived here. All day long we've sought places to sleep, to eat. Everywhere we went we were turned down because we're Negroes.

The only rest we've had was the little we could get on trunks and boxes backstage. Our only food has been sandwiches made from cold meat we bought in shops along the avenue.

Then you come here tonight and have the audacity to applaud our singing. It's hypocracy[sic] and we don't appreciate it.[44]

The local newspaper editor, state senator, and future United States president Warren G. Harding responded from the audience, appointing a committee to see that the orchestra members were housed in the homes of the city's "best." Ironically, Cook was omitted from their list; presumably everyone assumed that someone else was housing him, or so they said.

By the time the United States entered World War I in 1917, the Europe-Castle team had dissolved, after a four-year alliance. Jim Europe enlisted in New York's volunteer black 15th Infantry Regiment and organized a band comparable to the Clef Club ensembles. Since New York musicians were well compensated, Europe was able to enlist only one of them, recruiting others from across the country and Puerto Rico. He secured the Harlem dancer Bill "Bojangles" Robinson to strut as drum major. The band members all became fighters as well as musicians and were tagged the Hell Fighters. They not only provided a marching unit, but also divided into dance orchestras versus theater bands.[45]

The 15th Infantry Regiment was well respected on the European continent and traveled 2,000 miles throughout France between February 12 and March 29, 1918. They were "the first American Negro combat unit to set foot upon French soil."[46] Before their travels abroad, they were distinguished as a good band. Between military warfare, opportunities continued with musical programs of the Clef Club variety, comprising overtures, vocal selections from a male quartet, plantation melodies, "The Memphis Blues," and a conspicuous Sousa march.[47] Once overseas, the division was attached to the French Army as the 369th, "when the American military there officially rejected the idea of black combat troops. The regiment distinguished itself nonetheless, being the first Allied unit to reach the Rhine."[48]

Three months after the February 1919 armistice, the 369th Infantry returned home to New York and was greeted with a ticker tape parade from a victory arch at 25th Street up Fifth Avenue through Harlem, with Lieutenant James Europe and his Hell Fighters Band. Subsequently, the band was engaged in a nationwide concert tour which culminated in a performance in Boston on May 9. During the intermission, Jim Europe was attacked and killed by the crazed percussionist Herbert Wright, over what Wright considered an act of unfairness.[49]

Before his untimely death, James Reese Europe helped to pave the way for the emergence of jazz on the East Coast. Ragtime pianist-composer Eubie Blake characterized him as "our benefactor and inspiration. Even more, he was the Martin Luther King of music."[50] His influence was far-reaching—as one who unionized black musicians in New York through the creation of the Clef Club, increasing their work opportunities as well as their financial gain; he, along with Vernon and Irene Castle, contributed to the popularization of modern dancing to his unrivaled orchestral accompaniment; he was an effective advocate of the writing and performing of works in the African-American idiom; and was credited with having "produced an organization which all Americans swore, and some Frenchmen admitted, was the best military band in the world."[51]

Before and after Jim Europe left the Clef Club, Will Marion Cook continued to serve as its assistant conductor and chorus master. The group's concert appearances featured Cook as a violinist, conductor, and composer of the songs performed. This exposure led to critical acclaim for his talents and to major publications of his music. Cook's association with the Chef Club also introduced him to many of the men who would become players in his next musical group, the New York Syncopated Orchestra.

Chapter 10

THE SOUTHERN SYNCOPATED
ORCHESTRA

The SSO was as much concerned with proving to the public that black
musicians could attain high musical standards as with making converts,
to the music of their own community.

Albert McCarthy

Much of the spirit of the Jazz Age can be traced to African-
American music that countered the restraints and strait-
laced Victorian era. Influenced by Freud and the sexual revolution, the post-
war years were a time of defiant heavy drinking despite Prohibition, of a
liberating dance called the Charleston, and of syncopated music that traveled from the bordellos of New Orleans to the nightclubs of Chicago and
New York. African Americans became a symbol of that freedom from restraint which others longed to acquire.[1]

Such was the social backdrop for the rise of the Southern Syncopated
Orchestra—an all-black group of 50 formally attired men, with a few women,
who played and sang a diverse repertoire of light classics, popular songs,
ragtime, spirituals, and waltzes. Just two generations after slavery, the orchestra aimed to encourage, preserve, and uplift African-American culture
and to help obliterate racial discrimination by modeling democratic ideals
through instrumentation, personnel, and programming. It was hoped that
those who heard this fine, talented group perform works by such composers
as Johannes Brahms and Harry T. Burleigh would change their attitudes for
the better regarding black Americans.

Since Cook's advanced age of 50 made him ineligible for service in the
armed forces, he was available to fill the conducting void created by James
Reese Europe's death. The New York Syncopated Orchestra (which later

came to be known as the Southern Syncopated Orchestra) appears to have been a renaming of the Clef Club ensemble that toured the northeastern United States under Cook's baton in November 1918. Cook entered into a partnership with lawyer and businessman George Lattimore, who provided the necessary contacts, allowing Cook to concentrate on directing, composing, and providing artistic arrangements.

Two months later the New York Syncopated Orchestra embarked upon its first, five-week tour of the Eastern and Midwestern states, performing in such venues as Orchestra Hall in Chicago, Pabst Theatre in Milwaukee, and Carnegie Hall in Pittsburgh. During the fall, winter, and spring they also entertained in exclusive homes in Boston, Cincinnati, Philadelphia, Pittsburgh, and Providence.[2]

This unusual performing group adopted the term "orchestra" as it was used in its earliest and broadest sense: a group of mixed instruments playing together, with more than one instrument on a single part. The 50 players and singers consisted of violins, saxophones, trombones, trumpets, mandolins, banjos, guitars, a bass horn, tympani, and drums, in addition to a double male quartet and a soprano soloist. The unorthodox instrumentation was no doubt a result of using the entire Clef Club membership of former musical comedy and minstrel musicians.[3]

Guest stars billed with the orchestra included Buddy Gilmore, the celebrated drummer of the Vernon Castle Dance Tours; Frank Withers, the trombonist featured in advertisements as having introduced the blues to New York; the female saxophonist Mazie Mullins; the original Lenwood Quartet of Ziegfeld's Midnight Frolics; the African-American baritone singer George Jones; and the exponents of syncopation known as the Exposition Jubilee Four. Tom Fletcher was also a member of the group for four months and served as assistant manager, stage manager, leading comedian, and sometimes advance agent.[4]

The SSO's concerts were similar to other nineteenth-century theatrical entertainments encompassing the full range from farce to tragedy, juggling to ballet, and minstrelsy to opera, all in one evening. The orchestra demonstrated versatility and flexibility by performing sacred and secular, art and folk, written and unwritten music with equal effectiveness and skill. The programs epitomized democracy in art. Their wide-ranging repertoire of classical waltzes, blues, marches, and spirituals included such popular songs as Will Marion Cook's "Exhortation," "Rain Song," and "Swing Along"; W. C. Handy's "Memphis Blues" and "St. Louis Blues"; and such spiritual arrangements as Nathaniel Dett's "Listen to the Lambs."

Early twentieth-century audiences remained proudly independent, insisting upon receiving what they had been promised, while judging openly what they had heard. It should come as no surprise then that the orchestra's repertoire was not always satisfying to its listeners. In Ohio the *Youngstown Daily Vindicator*'s headline read: "A Negro Orchestra, But Little

Negro Music." It continued: "The Colored music masters played at the Park Theatre last night to an audience that comfortably filled the house. But practically everyone was disappointed, because they had expected to hear jazz. While the artists were present who could jazz, they did little jazzing. Billed as the jazziest of jazz orchestras, it proved anything but that." When the orchestra returned to Ohio, their program was altered to be more appealing to the audience, incorporating a lighter fare and a noticeable trend toward syncopated numbers.[5] The orchestra often used the classics as a basis for improvisation, taking operatic excerpts and improvising around them. At a certain point, Cook would say, "Take it! And they'd cut loose!"[6]

The majority of the music was written out and arranged by Will Marion Cook, including slides, glissandos, and lip slurs.[7] The orchestra was also expected to transpose at a moment's notice. At one concert the pianos were given a low tuning during the audience's applause, Mr. Cook passed a quick word among the players for the encore to be played a tone lower — in the key of E-flat instead of F. Occasionally they were given the key changes and were expected to fill in the harmonies extemporaneously. They also made extensive use of call-and-response techniques (one instrumental phrase answered by another). The orchestra knew whether their harmonic renderings were acceptable or not by gauging Mr. Cook's facial expressions. Unfortunately, to date no manuscripts of these arrangements have come to light.

The American tour concluded with a week's engagement that began March 17, 1919, at Nora Bayes's Theatre on 44th Street in the heart of Broadway. Lester Walton of *The New York Age* described the group as "presenting an enjoyable entertainment of ragtime, jazz, syncopation and song."[8] It had been years since a black aggregation had been housed in a Broadway theater, and the presence of the New York Syncopated Orchestra was considered a happy omen. After this engagement, the orchestra was scheduled to leave on its second Western tour, which climaxed on Easter Sunday, April 20, with a return engagement to Chicago's Orchestra Hall. (See appendix 4 for itinerary.) The group's popularity had increased so much that it attracted an audience of more than 2,500 people, 25 percent of them Chicago Symphony subscribers. The Syncopated Orchestra was featured in yet a third appearance at Orchestra Hall, when the Russian Symphony Orchestra canceled for the following week.[9]

All these appearances prepared the ensemble for widened exposure abroad. In February 1919 London theater manager André Charlot arrived in New York to scout for unusual talent for European audiences. He was introduced to the New York Syncopated Orchestra and its conductor, Cook. Before long, a six-month engagement at London's Philharmonic Hall was negotiated for the orchestra.[10]

London was primed for the kind of entertainment that would provide release from the tensions brought on by World War I plus lingering unemployment and material shortages. Since the tour in the 1870s, the London public had shown an affinity for Southern sounds of the Fisk Jubilee Singers. The freely syncopated rhythms and sounds of the New York Syncopated Orchestra would more than meet the audience's expectations.

In June 1919, 25 members of the orchestra's personnel arrived in Liverpool. They sailed on two ships — the *Northland* from Philadelphia, which arrived on June 12, and the *Carmania* from New York City, which arrived on June 14.[11]

It was on this tour that the orchestra's name was changed from the New York Syncopated Orchestra to the American Southern Syncopated Orchestra. The SSO opened at Philharmonic Hall on July 4, 1919. The debut received almost no advance notice. "But the very high quality of playing and singing furnished by the 35 negroes under the efficient direction of Will Marion Cook was quickly whispered about town by the first night audience," noted *Variety*. [12]

So well received was the SSO that they gave over 300 consecutive performances, purportedly a new record in the concert world; and subsequently put on more than 1,200 performances in England, Scotland, and France. During the Philharmonic Hall engagement, the group performed nightly with two weekly matinees on Saturdays and Sundays. The program changed approximately every three weeks.[13]

The orchestra's personnel included trumpeter Arthur Briggs, clarinetist Sidney Bechet, and violinist Paul Wyer. Besides the dedicated singers, some instrumentalists doubled as vocalists. The group's core remained largely the same as that which had performed in the States, with a few replacements. Business manager George Lattimore, for example, recruited Haitian flautist Bertin Salnave while the latter was studying at the Paris Conservatory.[14]

One of those who frequently heard the orchestra was Swiss conductor Ernst-Alexandre Ansermet. He commented in the *Revue Romande*

> The first thing that strikes one about the Southern Syncopated Orchestra is the astonishing perfection, the superb taste, and the fervour of its playing. . . . The musician who directs them and to whom the constitution of the ensemble is due, Mr. Will Marion Cook, is moreover a master in every respect, and there is no orchestra leader I delight as much in seeing conduct.[15]

Ansermet further recognized the virtuosic genius of the clarinetist Sidney Bechet.

One of Cook's important legacies was his inclusion of Bechet, who is said to have introduced authentic blues to European audiences. Bechet's unusual talent helped to bring unique fame to the Southern Syncopated Orchestra. While on this London tour, Bechet made the transition from clarinet to straight soprano saxophone and became one of the few to master it.[16]

On August 9, members of the SSO were invited to perform at a private afternoon party for servants of the Royal Household and their families, given by King George V and Queen Mary. Cook took a quarter of the orchestral members as well as a quartet featuring Sidney Bechet as soloist. Other performers were cornetist Arthur Briggs, trombonist William Forrester, bandolinist Lawrence Morris, and drummer Robert Young. Carroll Morgan sang "I've Got a Robe," and Lottie Gee also performed "Mammy O' Mine." Other selections included "Jessamina," "Peaches Down in Georgia," "It's Me, O Lord," "Exhortation," and "Swing Along." The King enjoyed most Bechet's rendition of "Characteristic Blues.[17]

Not all of the Southern Syncopated Orchestra's experiences were amiable. In fact, considerable dissension had arisen among the members by the end of their Philharmonic performances on December 6, 1919.[18] Dissatisfaction after business manager George Lattimore failed to share his profits fairly with the orchestra led to litigation and a Cook–Lattimore split. Cook recruited local talent for his ensemble while Lattimore secured orchestral replacements from America for his group.[19] André Charlot was sued for breach of contract, and judgment was entered for $8,655 and court costs. After engaging the orchestra for the Folies Marigny in Paris at $15,000 for a month, Charlot repudiated the contract. There was dissatisfaction as to the amount of remuneration, and the orchestra also wanted Cook reinstated as conductor.

Mr. Lattimore decided to keep the settlement for *his* expenses, hence the dissolution of the orchestra into two distinct groups, one with Lattimore and the other with Cook. Abbie Mitchell, Cook's former wife, joined Cook's faction in London, breaking her contract with the Lafayette Players in New York.

This internal turmoil of distrust in late 1919 and throughout 1920 made Will Marion Cook's tenure as orchestral director a sporadic affair. As early as November 12, 1919, the SSO concert program lacked the name Will Marion Cook as musical director, instead listing trumpeter E. E. Thompson in that role. Cook did, however, conduct the orchestra during its appearance in Liverpool on April 15, 1920, and for at least two other engagements: at the London Coliseum on May 10–23 and June 21–July 4, 1920. A small ensemble known as Will Marion Cook's Syncopated Orchestra was featured from July 5 to September 18 in the Australian Pavilion at London's Crystal Palace. During the engagement on August 16, Will Cook and Abbie Mitchell joined the Colored Players (probably SSO members) and opened as a double act at the Olympia in Liverpool.[20]

Under lawyer and business manager Lattimore, the orchestra filed for bankruptcy in December 1920. Whatever the group's artistic success, the Southern Syncopated Orchestra — plagued by personnel disputes, a depression in theater going, a lack of capital, and players' strikes — had proved a financial failure.[21] Further disaster struck a year later when a large number of SSO members were drowned when the *S. S. Rowan* sank on October 9, 1921. They had just completed a two-month engagement at the Lyric Theatre in Glasgow and were scheduled to open at the Scala Theatre in

Dublin. The ship was rammed in a dense fog by the American steamer *West Camak*, then severed by the British steamer *Clan Malcolm* while it was attempting a rescue. More than thirty SSO members were on board;[22] reports of those missing or dead differed, ranging from eight to eighteen. In addition to the tragic loss of life, many musical instruments and scores were destroyed. The shipwreck, along with the bankruptcy, guaranteed the orchestra's demise, for no group performing under that name survived far into 1922, and the last ensembles using the name included no one from the original Southern Syncopated Orchestra.

By 1922, however, several spin-off groups emerged, including the Jazz Kings, the Royal Southern Singers, and the Rector's Red Devils. After the Southern Syncopated Orchestra's demise, ten former members remained in Europe much longer — including trumpeters, a clarinetist, drummers, pianists, and a banjo player. They contributed to the spread of African-American music throughout the continent. One such ensemble — which included Benny Peyton, Frank Withers, and Sidney Bechet — was reportedly the first jazz group to play in the Soviet Union.[23]

During these various reorganizations, a number of British musicians who later continued in the jazz arena performed with the group, including Tom Smith, Ted Heath, and Billy Mason. The racially integrated makeup of the SSO brought musical benefits to the players. White trombonist and trumpeter Ted Heath later revealed, for example, that African-American drummer Buddy Gilmore taught him different approaches and techniques essential to jazz.[24]

As the catalyst of the original Southern Syncopated Orchestra, Will Marion Cook played a notable role in extending the dissemination of African-American musical traditions to broader international audiences. In the SSO concerts, diverse groups were brought together for an evening featuring a new and vital popular music that offered a way out of many of the limitations of early twentieth-century society. The song lyrics contained themes of nature, love, hope, and freedom, as well as plantation images of cotton, banjos, Mammy, and home. In the United States their music provided vital entertainment for audiences coping with the transition from rural to urban life, and from slavery to freedom. Within the musical and social context of the Southern Syncopated Orchestra and its offshoots, there were no lines of demarcation between the sacred and the secular, between the highbrow and the lowbrow, between the instrumentalists and the vocalists, and between blacks and whites. This orchestra was trying to place the musical art of the African American in the sphere where it properly belonged. Their billing affirmed that "in the democracy of art, the prejudices of race must disappear."[25] And so they did within the context of the orchestra and its racially mixed audiences.

Chapter II

"A HELL OF A LIFE"

I'd like to be known as a person
Who never whined and rarely complained,
But often protested.

Maya Angelou

W ill Marion Cook had returned to the United States from Europe by March 1923 and was concertizing periodically with a 25-piece "Clef Club Orchestra," touring the South and performing at Baltimore's Douglass Theatre and Philadelphia's Dunbar Theater. The tour culminated in New York City, where they were featured at the Lafayette Theatre with a singing ensemble. Pianist Fletcher Henderson was a performing member of the group during these engagements.[1] Cook's mother had died of arteriosclerosis in Washington, D.C. on February 18, 1923, a month prior to his homecoming.[2] Heartbreak over this loss, plus the lack of funds, may have precipitated his return.

For the next several months Cook freelanced with his orchestra, but by late April his personnel had dwindled to twelve men. He must have found it impossible to meet the large payroll required for his ideal orchestra of 50 members.[3] On May 20 Cook's orchestra received $100 compensation for a concert to benefit the Delta Sigma Theta Sorority's Negro Scholarship Fund.[4] Two months later Abbie performed for a week at the Lafayette Theatre, assisted by Cook at the piano.[5] Because of popular demand, they were engaged for another week.[6]

In early 1924 Cook and other well-known artists presented The Negro Musical Nights, a series of Sunday concerts at the 44th Street Theater. Their sponsor was The Negro Folk Music and Drama Society, assisted by Edmund T. Jenkins, a product of London's Royal Academy of Music.[7]

During the summer of 1924 Cook was elected to the American Society of Composers, Authors, and Publishers (ASCAP), the distinguished society founded in 1914 to protect the copyrights and performing rights of artists. ASCAP provided a convenient "home" for him, to and from which correspondence could be easily forwarded.

In 1925 The Negro Folk Music and Drama Society sponsored "Virginia Nights," a program devoted to "all Negro-music," in a Greenwich Village theater.[8] These evenings provided a platform for the black aesthetic expressions in art, literature, and music that were part of the artistic flowering of the Harlem Renaissance. The next year Cook presented Negro music at the Ambassador Theatre in New York to benefit the proposed Art School he was to found. Also on the program were Abbie Mitchell, songwriter Henry Creamer, and others. He served as accompanist.[9]

Shock waves vibrated around the music world on November 1, 1927, after 32-year-old ballad singer Florence Mills died suddenly of appendicitis. More than 250,000 mourners lined the Harlem streets, with many fainting as the cortege passed. The "little black bird" had entertained audiences since appearing in 1898 in Bob Cole and Billy Johnson's *A Trip to Coontown;* a generation later she debuted on Broadway in *Shuffle Along* and attained international stardom. According to one article, "She was probably the most beloved performer of her race."[10] On December 3 a mammoth testimonial benefit was held in her memory at three Harlem theaters simultaneously. Will Marion Cook volunteered to appear as one of the conductors; his name, however, was not among those who actually performed.[11] Cook's activities during 1928 are still a mystery.

On February 17, 1929, Cook's daughter-in-law, Bernice Wilson Cook, a 25-year-old public school teacher in Greensboro, North Carolina, was killed in an automobile accident near Reidsville, North Carolina. She was married to Cook's son Mercer, then a professor at Howard University.[12]

The next month Cook was to participate in *Swinging Along* at the Lafayette; however, because Cook lacked a union card, Will Vodery directed the show. Several months later, in October, Cook trained the chorus for Vincent Youmans's *Great Day,* which opened at the Cosmopolitan Theatre for 36 performances (twelve days before the Stock Market crash). Subsequently, Cook assisted with Miller and Lyle's *Runnin' Wild,* which appeared at the Colonial Theatre.[13]

The next theatrical venture in which Cook was involved was *Dust and Dawn,* for which he assembled a company for the Lafayette Theatre. Among those also assisting were Duke Ellington, Jimmie Johnson, and Mercer Cook. The show experienced delayed rehearsals.[14]

From the early 1930s until the end of Cook's life, he suffered bouts of illness that affected his productivity. The prelude to these episodes began as early as April 1915, when he had a complete breakdown while staying at the YMCA in Chicago and was unable to make his scheduled appearance at Orchestra Hall. Instead he was sent to his mother's home in Washington to recover. In June of the same year he was diagnosed with tuberculosis. For six-teen years the disease remained in abeyance, but for the last decade of his life he was in and out of recuperational facilities in Asheville, North Carolina, and the Edgecombe Sanitarium in New York.[15] In February 1931 Cook was confined to New York's Edgecombe Sanitarium, where he was reported as improving and scheduled to leave soon for Asheville. In March, interestingly, he was to make a tour of the South, going as far as New Orleans, before returning to New York. A year later he wrote music for poet Sterling Brown's "Slim Greer," while still in Asheville.[16]

In late July of 1933 Cook returned to the Lafayette Theatre to accompany Abbie Mitchell at the piano.[17] The following month, on August 25, Will Cook and Eubie Blake were guest conductors on Black Achievement Evening at the Chicago World's Fair. It had been 40 years since Colored American Day at the Columbian Exposition.[18]

Early the next year Cook's "Mammy" (now almost two decades old) was successfully featured on radio by the singer-actress Ethel Waters.[19] As an incentive for his father to overcome his compositional drought, Cook's son Mercer wrote the lyrics for one of Cook's last publications, "A Little Bit of Heaven Called Home" (1934), an extension of the mammy subject. Cook's most charming refrains were transformed from homespun sentimentality to a jazzy sevenths style, syncopated rhythms, and ragged bass—no doubt a contemporaneous setting provided by a contemporary Schirmer arranger.

In August 1934 Cook returned to Chicago to be part of the "Musical Spectacle—O, Sing a New Song" at Soldiers Field, featuring a choir of 5,000 voices and 3,500 actors. They performed African-American repertoire including Cook's songs.[20]

More than a year later, in September 1935, The Negro Festival Chorus of America performed Cook's choral works at the Exposition held at Spreckel's Organ Amphitheatre in San Diego.[21] No other Cook performance involvements are known for that year. In May 1936, however, he visited Brainard Institute in Chester, South Carolina, a preparatory school established in 1868 by the Presbyterians to help build its programs. Two months later he candidly revealed in a letter to Alain Locke: "After many, many, many long months of illness, travail, money worries due to over helping my stranded 'children' in France and Italy and a weakened brain there from, I am at last, the old Cook."[22]

In October, six months later, Cook's songs were heard at Carnegie Hall in observance of the 25th anniversary of ASCAP.[23] The next August he was taking political issue with the notion of a third presidential term for Franklin Roosevelt. Cook was widely known as an advocate of Republican principles and an outspoken anti-New Dealer.[24]

By December 1943 Will Marion Cook's health had seriously deteriorated, prompting his son to move him to Port-au-Prince, Haiti, where Mercer Cook was serving as an ambassador and could better care for his father. In a short time, however, Cook was admitted to Saint Francois de Sales Hospital. His condition improved, but then took a turn for the worse, and he was returned to the States. Six months later, on June 21, 1944, Will Marion Cook was received at the Harlem Hospital, where for 29 days he battled the pain of pancreatic cancer and a heart condition. On July 24 Will Marion Cook succumbed at the age of 75.

Agitation and controversy followed Will Marion Cook his entire life. During the latter years he began to write his autobiography, *A Hell of a Life.* The title was indicative of how he perceived reality from the moment of his birth in January 1869:

> So it came about that I was born in the soldiers' barracks—in a storm— and it has been a rough, rocky, stormy way most of the time. . . . in the main, a hell of a life, with the downs usually obscuring the ups. . . . I had no place. I dreamed and I fought and I sought to reach the stars.
>
> My failure to gain the goal was not because of color; rather, because of uncontrolled passions, too violent a resentment against real or fancied wrongs; too large and too visible a chip on each shoulder and to be sure I missed nothing, another chip on my woolly head. . . .
>
> Many men have told the story of their lives and achievements. They were great and left to posterity a blaze of light to brighten the way. I have dreamed much and achieved little. My biography has nothing of personal greatness therein; but still leaves a valuable lesson to boys, especially my grandson, of the value of time, the importance of reserve and restraint, and self control without which no man ever became and remained really great.

This pithy Cook confession shows that he recognized that his shortcomings in life were due not to the color of his skin, but rather to his uncontrollable actions or reactions—from his own lack of reserve, restraint, and self-control—to the real or imagined wrongs. It appears that he may have naturally acquired his disposition from one or both grandfathers. In *A Hell of a Life* Cook sketches their profiles:

> Both grandfathers were interesting characters of many talents and strong personalities. Grandpa Lewis, born free, a wagon-maker and blacksmith by trade was highly respected. Domineering and cruel at times, he was possessed, in his better moods, of a heart of gold. . . .
>
> If I love trouble, excitement and danger, Grandfather Lewis is sponsor. From both I am at times moody, quick of temper, and ready for anything that comes. Even now at sixty-nine, feeble and almost ready to welcome the last, long, dreamless sleep, Trouble to me is sweet music, and I do love sweet music!

The beginning signs of trouble for William occurred during his youth, when, as he described himself, he was "undisciplined, 'spoiled,' given to violent temper tantrums, I was constantly embroiled in scrapes. I loved to fight—boys, girls, friends, strangers, anybody—and yet I usually came out the underdog."

These outbursts of violent temper continued into adulthood. Abbie Mitchell's memoirs reveal:

Notwithstanding his eccentricities—his erratic temperament which in later years caused him many disappointments, much poverty, loss of influential contacts and friends and a deep sorrow.[25]

She later admonished:

You're old, tired, disappointed, ill, perhaps, but the creative fire never dies—so Carry on![26]

Abbie began to take on the breadwinner's role by performing at high society parties. "I wanted to inspire Mr. Cook to continue writing his lovely songs," she acknowledged. " . . . It took just that little encouragement to lift my husband out of his melancholia."

The personal peculiarities and eccentricities of Will Marion Cook spawned many apocryphal stories that have taken on a life of their own. The one that appears most often explains why Cook did not pursue a career as a concert violinist. According to Duke Ellington:

When he first returned to New York [from studying in Germany] and did a concert at Carnegie Hall, he had a brilliant critique the next day in a newspaper. The reviewer said that Will Marion Cook was definitely "the world's greatest Negro violinist."

Dad Cook took his violin and went to see the reviewer at the newspaper office.

"Thank you very much for the favorable review," he said. "You wrote that I was the world's greatest Negro violinist."

"Yes, Mr. Cook," the man said, "and I meant it. You are definitely the world's greatest Negro violinist."

With that, Dad Cook took out his violin and smashed it across the reviewer's desk.

"I am not the world's greatest Negro violinist," he exclaimed. "I am the greatest violinist in the world!"

He turned and walked away from his splintered instrument, and he never picked up a violin again in his life.[27]

The truth of that story has yet to be determined. It seems to show an extraordinary willingness on Cook's part to give up the violin and a justification for doing so. Yet it is not clear whether or not Cook ever concertized at Carnegie Hall; to date, no record has been found to substantiate the claim. If he did ever perform there, it may have been in conjunction with the well-known operatic singer Sissieretta Jones (better known as Black Patti),[28] an example of the kind of stereotyping Cook was attempting to avoid.

Arthur Briggs, a trumpeter from the Southern Syncopated Orchestra, has recounted yet another version of the violin-smashing story:

> Will Marion Cook—was first violinist with the Boston Symphony—not the soloist but the first violin. Anyway, the soloist passed on, so Cook figured that he would automatically replace him. So the orchestra committee had a meeting and they told him, "From tomorrow you will sit in the first chair, the soloist's, but unfortunately we can't allow you to play the solos." This was because he was black. . . . So he took his fiddle and broke it. He stamped on it and walked out.[29]

Yet a third version of the story was told by the Southern Syncopated Orchestra's clarinetist, Sidney Bechet.

> [When Cook returned to America from Europe,] he went in for a contest, for a scholarship, playing violin. And when it was over one of the judges said to him that if he hadn't been coloured he would have won the scholarship for sure. Well, that burned him up, and he broke his violin and never played no more.[30]

A less dramatic recounting of the story is reported by the entertainer Tom Fletcher:

> Returning home [from Europe] he gave a concert at Carnegie Hall, in 1895. The next morning after his concert the critics proclaimed him as the greatest colored violinist in the world. Will was very tempermental [sic] and became enraged at this segregation. He laid his violin down and swore never to play it again in an orchestra.[31]

Although Cook discontinued his concertizing, he is known to have continually practiced his instrument and occasionally to have played during orchestral rehearsals for instructional purposes. Moreover, it is known that he performed with the strings in 1912 at the first Clef Club Concert at Carnegie Hall.

Whether there is any validity to the numerous Cook legends is almost insignificant. What is important is that these stories embody aspects of Cook's personality that he and others wanted to be known publicly—namely, his desire to be recognized on his own merit, his uncompromising racial pride, and his grievances, which evoked the unashamed expression of rage. He would rather break an instrument (the source of his livelihood) than bow to racial discrimination or stereotyping.

In yet another incident, Cook's erratic behavior was evident as he led the orchestra at a Broadway playhouse.

He had written all the music to the production, which was immensely popular. However, he took offense at something that had been done by the management and took every piece of music of the production with him. It is needless to state that on account of the actions the management was in a predicament, as the orchestra did not have a piece of music from which to play. A flag of truce was raised and the show was given.

Yet, regardless of his peculiarities, Will Marion Cook was a great musician, and he did more injury to himself because of his eccentricities than to anyone else.[32] In his autobiographical notes, Cook confessed:

> I pray every night to my dear departed mother; sometimes, not often to God, that these obsessions to destroy will forever leave me. These destructive rages are aroused by real or fancied wrongs which hurt my feelings or rather, my pride.[33]

This confession is revealing on several counts—the godlike prominence that his mother had in his life; the less prominent role of spirituality or organized religion; the awareness of his self-destructive behavior and his desire to eliminate it; the possibility that the impetus for his rages might be true or might be imagined; and finally, his cognizance of the role that pride played in his psyche. Cook further exposes his discontent with life in a published poem in *The Afro-American*.

> What matters the goal, though you
>   play a great part?
> What matters the genius that
>   straight like a dart—
> Soars upward and onward through
>   clouds to the sky;
> And there writes a message to
>   angels—on high.
> Writes bold and clear for all man-
>   kind forsooth,
> And men laugh to scorn your
>   message of truth.
> What matters the goal when you've
>   played the great part
> And then—you die of a broken heart.[34]

Cook's pessimism is also apparent in an open letter to writer and patron of the arts Carl Van Vechten: "I have lived a fairly long and judging by results, unsuccessful life. But, I am striving for myself, my race and perhaps for humanity."[35] Moreover, in a letter to a faithful friend, he candidly acknowledged, "You have tolerated me and my many sudden changes—my angry outbursts, my foolish denunciations for years—and I'm most grateful."[36]

These outbursts and denunciations had a long history, caused by a grief-stricken wound from his youth; when he was ten years old, his distinguished, even-tempered father died of tuberculosis and his family virtually disintegrated.

Cook's personality was ridden with extreme behavior. P. L. Prattis described:

> His faults, I learned, were so grand that they took on the nature of virtues. I had heard tell of his temper and his indulgence in the most violent profanity. I am quite willing to believe that the tales told were true. . . . He was extreme. He could throw his baton at an erring musician and damn the musician's soul.

Prattis continued:

> Abbie has told me of how he would stand her, his wife, in a corner and patiently make her sing over and over again some passage one hundred, three hundred times—until she got it right.[37]

Another who worked under Cook's baton with noteworthy results was the violinist and choral conductor Hall Johnson. A masterful arranger of Negro spirituals, he led the Hall Johnson Choir to the Broadway stage and Hollywood films. Johnson was so inspired by and indebted to Cook that upon Cook's death he penned this poetic portrait:

> You took us many miles o'er land and sea
> To show the people what a thing you'd found—
> A mind of God-sent music, welling up from eaves
> Whose unsuspected riches waited on your hand,
> The master-hand—to turn them into sound.
>
> You stood before us, humble and yet proud,
> And, at your call, old things took on new birth
> Old voices sang in new, the past awoke
> In present splendor, as we climbed with you
> To glorify the lowly of this earth.
>
> And when we sang to you! Oh, sometimes
> The fires of Heaven would light up in your frown
> And, in one look of satisfaction and of love,
> Proclaim your birthright, guarantee your throne—
> A king who knew his subjects and his crown.
>
> And, sometimes, there were flames, but not of Heaven;
> Your tortured soul would writhe and lash and beat
> Against the bars that held you from the full,
> Keen realization of your dreams awhile
> But could not sink you down in stark defeat.

Ah, master, we are blest that you were here
With us awhile, with thunder in your face,
You taught us how to sing—and to be proud of singing
The theme you sang and never tired of singing—
The rich, dark beauty of your rich, dark race.[38]

History is indebted to this troubled man of genius for his pioneering black musical comedies, syncopated orchestral achievements, and uncompromising fight for racial equality.

Chapter 12

A COMPOSER'S LEGACY

When I write something for a choir and it's jazzy and bluesy and spiritual
and Tchaikowsky all rolled into one, I laugh to myself, "That is
Will Marion Cook."

Margaret Bonds

A s a composer, Will Marion Cook was highly regarded among
his peers. Author-songwriter James Weldon Johnson described
him as "the most original genius among all the Negro musicians."[1] Music
critic Sylvester Russell ranked Cook as the leading "light music" composer
of his race.[2] In *The Freeman*, Carle Brown Cooke concluded, "As an instructor of choruses and soloists as well as a master in ensemble grouping and directing, Will Marion Cook is peerless."[3] Similarly, Lucien W. White, reviewing a Clef Club concert in *The New York Age*, reported, "As a composer and
cultivated musician Will Marion Cook is without a peer, and when he seriously and earnestly gives his mind to musical endeavor the result is always
beyond cavil."[4] Implied in this latter review is the notion that his output was
not always consistent but that his artistic capabilities were impressive.

Will Marion Cook's extant compositions date from 1896, when he was
nearly 30 years of age. His first three published songs were indicative of the
genres and motivations that fueled his originality throughout his career.
For all three works he wrote the lyrics and the music. This practice changed
after his first poetic collaboration with Paul Laurence Dunbar. "We're
Marching On," "That'll Be Alright," and "Love Is the Tend'rest of Themes"
represent Cook's writing in a colored American hymn, a coon song, and a

love ballad genre—indicative of his propensities for nationalism, commercialism, and transcendence, respectively.

Cook's style largely adheres to the popular songwriting practices at the turn of the twentieth century. There are brief introductions (one to ten measures) that characteristically anticipate motivic material. Verses are generally two stanzas, except in the case of Dunbar's poetry, when they may have three or four. Song forms include 32 bars (8 + 8 + 8 + 8) in the verse-chorus structure; 16-bar verses and 32-bar choruses (with some 16-bar repeated choruses); and a few with both 16-bar verses and choruses. Most of the remaining songs consist of various versions of extended lengths, particularly in the verse. The internal makeup of the verses range from 8-measure varied segments or exact repetitions, concluding with a contrasting segment (AA^1A^2B), to those in which the music is completely new or returns to that earlier presented AA^1BB^2, AA^1BC, or AA^1BA^1. In nearly half of his songs Cook prefers to present new material immediately after the opening eight bars, yielding an AB verse form.

A large number of the refrains present new material in the first eight bars, which is immediately varied in the next eight bars and often repeated. This structure contributed to melodic retention in the memory. Various forms consist of AA^1BA, or AA^1BC patterns; or refrains containing alternating sequences with contrasts $ABAB^2$ or ABA^1C. Other variants include $ABCC^1$ and $ABCA^1$.

In most instances, the refrains present melodic substance that is different from the verses. However, a few songs contain the same melodic form in the verses as in the refrains. The majority do not have the same melodious structure in both verses and refrains.

There are several examples of extended song forms in which Cook goes beyond any of the previous verse-chorus forms as just described. Scholar-composer John Graziano has coined this phenomenon "Beethovian length:" These may be found in "Swing Along," "Society," "The Czar," "Leader of the Colored Aristocracy," and "Exhortation."[5]

Cook's songs use keys with few sharps and flats in their signature. Almost half are in the keys of G and F major. There are the same number of songs in keys with flats—F, B-flat, and A-flat—as keys with sharps—G, D, and A, in order of prevalence. Most are written in major keys, although some begin in a minor mode and shift to their relative major or parallel major key. The alternation from minor to major usually coincides with changing circumstances or moods in the action. "Hurrah for Captain Kidd," for example, opens in c minor as it describes the seamy side of the subject, and the chorus's conclusion in E-flat major reveals how the captain's buried treasure is found.

The triadic harmonies used by Cook are built on the first, fourth, and fifth scale degrees, with occasional inclusion of secondary dominants, augmented sixths, and diminished seventh chords. One of his frequent stylistic traits is chromatic writing. This is evident in "Love Me with a Tiger Love," which was sung by Clara Palmer in the Broadway production *The Deacon and the Lady.* Addison Burkhardt's lyrics convey the sensual desires of a liberated woman of 1910 who wishes for more passion and less timidness. Cook reinforces the sentiment by expanding the boundary of the diatonic scale.

The majority of Cook's songs are written entirely in duple or quadruple meter. A few employ 3/4 waltz time or metric deviations at the refrain.

Will Marion Cook's songwriting career extended more than forty years, from 1893 to 1934. His most productive period was the decade from 1898 to 1908, while he was married to Abbie Mitchell. His extant songs (which number about sixty) encompass everything from art songs to coon songs and all that is in between. While songs of the coon variety are few, the art songs, ballads, nostalgia, and waltz songs are more numerous. Interestingly, Cook published only one Negro spiritual, "Troubled in Mind," with an original bluesy drag segment that juxtaposes sacred and secular sensibilities. His "Exhortation" is a quasi-religious piece set as a Negro folk sermon.

Following the Clef Club's Carnegie Hall concert on May 2, 1912, Cook began to receive more attention from the prestigious G. Schirmer firm. His notable works—"Swing Along," "Rain Song," and "Exhortation"—were performed on that auspicious occasion and subsequently published by Schirmer. In a promotional article, the music editor Kurt Schindler indicated:

> After the publication of these larger and more ambitious works of a colored musician, the attention of the musical world is sure to be focused upon a man of extraordinary talent who has been living in our midst for fifteen years unrecognized and unheeded. Not that Will Marion Cook was unknown, but because his melodies have been confined to the light opera and vaudeville stage, where although much enjoyed, few in the audiences were able to appreciate their true artistic value. Most of his larger works remained unprinted, and lacked the stamp of approval from authoritative critics, which would have raised them above the *niveau* of mediocrity in which they flowered.[6]

Will Marion Cook's legacy as a songwriter sets him apart from his black and white contemporaries in his use of highly syncopated, chromatic melodies and extended song forms. His ingenious melodic lines probably resulted from his training as a classical violinist, accustomed to playing beautiful melodies. The inclusion of operatic-like numbers in the musical-comedy ensembles probably has a similar origin. Not only were Cook's works featured in black productions with Bert Williams, George Walker, and Abbie Mitchell, but they were also interpolated into white stage productions with Irene Bentley, Marie Cahill, and Fannie Brice.

Will Marion Cook was also a lyricist who wrote words for about a dozen of his and other composers' songs. Three songs in the latter category were "Sweetie Dear," "Lovie Joe," and "I'm Coming Virginia." Joe Jordan composed the music for the first two, and Donald Heywood wrote the last.

In "Sweetie Dear," Cook describes the love of a man for a woman with poetic impressions of nature in folk speech. The verse reads:

> De poets sing of de daisies, de vi'lets sweet an' so fine
> De lover sighs 'bout beauty's eyes, longs fu' de summer time
> De roses yearn fu' de sunshine, de bird jes' pines fu' de tree
> All dese tho' fine, don't go fu' mine, kase Sweetie's de one fu' me.

Jordan's catchy chorus is the song's most memorable feature and survives well on its own merit. Although Cook's text is not extraordinary, it doesn't detract from the tune.

> Sweetie, dear, don't yo' hear what my heart is tryin' to say,
> Sweetie, dear, please draw near, whisper 'bout dat weddin' day,
> Say you'se mine all de time, wid' out love de day am drear,
> My heart's sad, make it glad, I'm jes' mad 'bout Sweetie dear.

A show stopper in the 1910 Ziegfeld's Follies was "Lovie Joe," popularized by Fannie Brice who received twelve encores on opening night.[7] Its text and tune are integrated into a lively syncopated whole. When the lyrics refer to a grand wedding march, predictably, Mendelssohn's "Wedding March" is quoted.

> An' when I hear the weddin' march so gran',
> I jes get myself a weddin' ban'.

The nostalgic "I'm Coming Virginia" is the best-known song associated with Cook's name. It is among the popular standards of the 1920s, but Heywood's tune is better known than Cook's lyrics. The sentimental text conveys a "Wish I Was in Dixie" proclivity for Virginia, a more contemporary version of James Bland's "Carry Me Back to Old Virginny" (1878). Interestingly, Virginia represented to Cook his own paternal roots. Throughout much of Cook's life and song career, an elusive "homeward-bound" motif prevails: its various guises include the ancestral Motherland of Africa, the nostalgic Dixieland of the South, and the existential homeland of the soul.

In *Lost Sounds* Tim Brooks chronicles and reissues Will Marion Cook's historic recordings, including one of Ethel Waters singing "I'm Comin' Virginia." This session was recorded with Columbia Phonograph Company in September 1926, with Cook leading a chorus promoted as "Ethel Waters and Her Singing Orchestra." The recording is prominently soloistic and the singing "orchestra" briefly enters at the finish. Numerous versions have been made of this jazz standard, featuring such artists as Paul Whiteman and his orchestra, Les Brown, Fats Waller, Artie Shaw, Art Tatum, Sidney Bechet, and Benny Goodman.

Lost Sounds also reissued "Swing Along," with Will Marion Cook conducting his Afro-American Folk Song Singers.[8] Their ensemble of about twenty was more or less evenly distributed among soprano, contralto, tenor, and bass voices. Because of technological limitations, however, they probably used a smaller group for this recording. The reissue is valuable historically for its insights into Cook's performance practices, especially his energetic syncopated lines, liberties in tempo, and prominent bass counterpoint. The climactic conclusion gradually builds with thematic variations and an artfully measured crescendo.

"The Rain Song" also appears on *Lost Sounds*, with Cook leading his male chorus.[9] The vocal articulation and technical clarity is far less than for "Swing Along." Nevertheless, Cook's harmonies, call-and-response, cadenza, and recitative-like stylistic treatment can be appreciated.

Will Marion Cook's compositional career was meteorically brief, yet innovative. He identified with the German Romantic tradition—that of Beethoven, heroism, liberty, equality, Wagner, nationalism, nature, wandering, unrequited love, and so forth. He found modern music unappealing and continued to recycle or modify the same musical style throughout his career. Contemporaries who once admired his genius became frustrated in the end by his lack of originality. Perhaps his greatest gift to musical history was to pave the path for Eubie Blake, Duke Ellington, Eva Jessye, and Hall Johnson.

Postlude

"SWING ALONG!"

I have been and still am a proud old soul: proud of my ancestry, proud of
my country which both loves and scorns my people. Proud that despite all
barriers, all bodily and mental ailments, I was able to wing it and swing it.

Will Marion Cook

The final rites for Will Marion Cook at the Rodney Dade Funeral
Home, 2332 Seventh Avenue in New York, were simple, as he requested. His former wife and lifetime companion, Abbie Mitchell,[1] made the
arrangements, since his son, Mercer, had to remain in Haiti—regrettably,
unable to attend. There is no mention of his daughter Marion's having attended. She had become a dancer and married dancer Louis Douglas; the
couple resided in Europe. The Reverend Willard Monroe officiated and
Cook's song "Mammy" was performed instrumentally, as Cook had instructed. He further requested that there be no eulogy. Immediately following the service, Abbie Mitchell accompanied Will Marion Cook's body by
train to Washington, D.C.,[2] where he was laid to rest in the family plot of the
century-old Woodlawn Cemetery.[3]

Through Cook's ups and downs, Abbie Mitchell never abandoned him
(even though she had two other brief marriages). She and Will Marion Cook
both died at the Harlem Hospital, sixteen years apart, and were symboli-
cally joined in death by performances of "Mammy" at both their funerals.
Abbie was the major promoter and disseminator of Will Marion's songs. It
is difficult to discern how often his music would have been performed or
generally known had it not been for the light, lyrical, and dramatically
articulate vocal flare of Abbie Mitchell. She had an impressive career as a
concert soprano vocalist and dramatic actress. In addition to appearing in

Cook's musical productions, Abbie performed with Black Patti's Trouba-dours, the Memphis Students, the Southern Syncopated Orchestra, the Pekin Theatre in Chicago, and the Lafayette Theatre in Harlem. She received accolades from such notables as Emma Calvé, Enrico Caruso, Maurice Ravel, and Jean de Reszke. In 1935 she played the original Clara in George Gershwin's *Porgy and Bess*. Other major roles were *In Abraham's Bosom* (1926), *Coquette* (1927), *Mulatto* (1937), and *The Little Foxes* (1939). Late in her career she accepted William Dawson's invitation to chair the voice department at Tuskegee Institute in Alabama. Cook encouraged Abbie's progress through artistic exposure, tutorials, and teachers.[4]

Will Marion Cook was admired by many whose careers he advanced. He served as father, mentor, teacher, and tutor to black and white artists alike. Those who benefited most directly were his pupils. Cook was the first violin and harmony teacher of the famous violinist Clarence Cameron White. White recalls a childhood incident which virtually ignited his musical career:

> One evening my mother took me to hear the pupils of Mrs. Alice Strange-Davis, the most renowned piano teacher in Washington at that time among our people. I was especially anxious to hear Will Marion Cook play the violin. He had just returned from European study and was to play a number toward the end of the program. As usual, a program by pupils is a rather long drawn-out affair, so by the time Cook's number came I had fallen asleep. I was awakened by the tremendous applause after his solo and when I was told that he had played, I burst out crying and made such a fuss that my mother had to hustle me out of the concert and home I went in disgrace.
>
> This rather unusual "carrying on" at the concert prompted Cook to inquire who the little boy was and when he discovered the cause of my great disappointment, he came to see my parents and offered to give me violin lessons during the coming summer vacation period. Every lesson was one of pure joy and it was during this period that I definitely made up my mind to be a violinist.[5]

Upon learning of Cook's death, White wrote, "His great genius will always be a guiding star to those of us who remain."[6]

Another who gained from Cook's tutelage was the jazz pianist, composer, and bandleader Duke Ellington, who acknowledged:

> Several times, after I had played some tune I had written but not really completed, I would say, "Now Dad, what is the logical way to develop this theme? What direction should I take?"
>
> "You know you should go to the conservatory," he would answer, "But since you won't, I'll tell you. First you find the logical way, and when you find it, avoid it, and let your inner self break through and guide you. Don't try to be anybody else but yourself." That time with him was one of the best semesters I ever had in music.[7]

The compositional formula Cook advanced to Ellington—"Don't be anyone but yourself"—also seems to have been Cook's personal mantra. There were also times when Cook would give Ellington composition "lessons" while riding around Central Park in a taxicab.

> I'd sing a melody in its simplest form and he'd stop me and say, "Reverse your figures." He was a brief but strong influence. His language had to be pretty straight for me to know what he was talking about. Some of the things he used to tell me I never got a chance to use until years later when I wrote "Black, Brown, and Beige."[8]

Musicologist Mark Tucker has indicated that Ellington's work was the culmination of a long-standing desire not only to write a large-scale composition, but to link such an ambitious piece to vital issues in African-American history.[9] It is believed that the original impetus for Ellington was to write a Negro opera "Black, Brown, and Beige," tracing the culture from the jungle to Harlem. The work's second section, "The Slave Ship," corresponds to Cook's earlier "Ghost Ship." Cook wanted African Americans to write large serious works, particularly operas, to gain more artistic respectability. Moreover, "Black, Brown, and Beige" focused on a central element in African-American life—color. Since Ellington began his career as a fine arts painter, color nuances were all too familiar to him. Social-historian W. E. B. Du Bois reminds us that "The problem of the twentieth century is the problem of the color line."[10] Similarly, Cook wrote "Brownskin Baby Mine," "Darktown Is Out Tonight," and "Leader of the Colored Aristocracy"—all songs that refer to color. Furthermore, Cook's best-known song, "Swing Along," parallels Ellington's "It Don't Mean a Thing If It Ain't Got That Swing." The ultimate sign of Ellington's admiration for Cook was his naming his son Mercer (after Will Marion's given name); similarly, Ellington's grandson is Paul Mercer, perpetuating the family tradition.[11]

Cook also mentored ragtime pianist-composer Eubie Blake. "Much of what he became," said Blake, "was owed to 'Pop' Cook."[12] "From their first meeting Cook liked Eubie, and constantly encouraged him to play better. 'Don't be lazy,' Cook would tell him. 'Work at your composing. Keep on writing. You learn by doing.'"[13]

Cook is further credited with masterminding several publications such as "Under the Bamboo Tree" (1902) by Bob Cole and the Johnson brothers, J. Rosamond and James Weldon.[14] He assisted Eva Jessye in printing a book of Negro spirituals put out by Robbins Publishing firm. She distinguished herself as the choral director of Virgil Thomson's *Four Saints in Three Acts* and George Gershwin's *Porgy and Bess*. Cook claimed Jessye as one of his "little protégés" and encouraged her to continue studying music. Jessye's initial contact with him was in 1907 when a Cook show played in her hometown, Coffeyville, Kansas. Although she was only twelve, she assisted in copying some of the orchestral scores.[15] Jessye later studied with Cook in New York City.[16]

W. C. Handy learned from Will Marion's conducting skills and observed that Cook

> set the tempo with the sway of his body and developed perfect crescendos without a baton by the use of his opened and extended palms, he, again was my ideal.[17]

Cook also mentored James Reese Europe as a conductor.[18]

The violinist, choral conductor, and arranger of Negro spirituals Hall Johnson wrote in a letter to Cook, "I am always telling somebody about you and that I learned more from you than from anybody I ever worked under."[19]

Trumpeter Arthur Briggs similarly admitted:

> "Dad Cook" was directly responsible for the success of my musical career. He gave me my first opportunity and surveyed my musical and instrumental studies. He was also "My Dad." The greatest real musician ever![20]

Will Marion did not maintain a traditional family lifestyle, but he had a large surrogate family. Many orchestral members and close friends called him "Dad" because of his paternal nature. Perhaps he was trying to be the father he lost to tuberculosis during his childhood. In fact Natalie Spencer, the white pianist who joined the SSO in Europe, revealed that Cook considered himself *in loco parentis* and criticized her severely for not wearing galoshes during inclement weather.[21]

Will Marion Cook persuaded many, such as Taylor Gordon, to pursue artistic careers. While Gordon was employed with the Ringling Brothers Circus, Cook recognized his musical talent and "told me to quit my job, that no man with a voice like mine should be a cook."[22] Gordon heeded the advice and became one of America's foremost interpreters of Negro spirituals.

Similarly, Will Marion encouraged songwriter Perry Bradford to follow his interest in the blues.[23] Bradford facilitated Mamie Smith's commercial blues recording, the first by a female artist. Her recording of "Crazy Blues," written by Bradford and accompanied by his Jazz Hounds Band, sold 3 million copies. This success not only saved the Okeh Recording Company from demise, but opened the market for Victor and Columbia to issue "Race Record" catalogues.[24]

Cook had a knack for recognizing talent and providing the appropriate channel for its development. He suggested to Caroline Dudley that Josephine Baker play the starring role in a Negro revue in Paris.[25] She had enjoyed some success as a chorus girl in the 1921 *Shuffle Along*, and the gamble of giving her a prominent part proved to be successful. Josephine Baker became one of France's great music-hall stars and an international sensation. Cook was also convinced of Ethel Waters's artistry and persuaded Otto Kahn to feature her in the Broadway *Africana* show.[26]

Cook's professional assistance in advancing other artists transcended racial boundaries. His encouragement of Harold Arlen, for example, led to the creation of Arlen's song "Get Happy." In 1929 Cook was the choral director of *Great Day*. During rehearsal breaks, Arlen once improvised on a "vamp" from a musical number at the piano. Cook was impressed and prompted him to develop it into a song.[27] Arlen followed through and collaborated with Ted Koehler on the lyrics to "Get Happy," producing his first hit song. "Stormy Weather" and "Over the Rainbow" are other popular favorites for which Arlen is known.

Will Marion Cook similarly claims responsibility for advancing Al Jolson's career. After seeing him perform in a third-rate vaudeville house, Cook apprised Hammerstein and Shubert of his exceptional talent.[28] The Shubert brothers cast Jolson for more than a decade in their Winter Garden shows on Broadway.[29]

Will Marion candidly admits in his memoirs

> I seem to have a gift for selecting talent, and most of the time those I help make a much greater success than I, partly because they seem to be more adaptable and have lots more common sense.[30]

The Chicago Defender described Cook as a man who was generous with his talent, his money, and his enthusiasm, yet completely lacking professional jealousy. When Florenz Ziegfeld invited him to arrange his "Negro numbers," Cook said, "Here's a man who can do it better than I," and introduced Will Vodery, who remained with him until Ziegfeld's death.[31]

Will Marion Cook embodies the essence of the Talented Tenth, a designation first coined in 1896 by Henry L. Morehouse, for whom the all-male black liberal arts college is named. It represents a class of highly educated and morally upright African Americans who were in the vanguard of the black masses. W. E. B. Du Bois later appropriated Morehouse's term to denote black "leaders of thought and missionaries of culture."[32] Significantly, Du Bois delivered a paper on "The Conservation of Races" at the American Negro Academy in the District of Columbia in 1897, the year that academy was founded. Although he recognized the physical differentiations with respect to race on that occasion, he also recognized attributes that went beyond those distinctions:

> While race differences have followed mainly physical race lines, yet no more physical distinctions would really define or explain the deeper differences—the cohesiveness and continuity of these groups. The deeper differences are spiritual, psychical, differences—undoubtedly based on the physical, but infinitely transcending them.

Du Bois concluded with a proposed Academy Creed which begins:

1. We believe that the Negro people, as a race, have a contribution to make to the civilization and humanity, which no other race can make.
2. We believe it the duty of the Americans of Negro descent, as a body, to maintain their race identity until this mission of the Negro people is accomplished, and the ideal of human brotherhood has become a practical possibility.[33]

No doubt these words were scrutinized by Paul Laurence Dunbar, as a founding member of the Academy. This historic event took place one year prior to Cook and Dunbar's Broadway debut.

Cook inspired and encouraged not only musicians, but writers too—especially Jean Toomer and Sterling Brown. When Toomer heard Cook's orchestra at the Howard Theatre in Washington, he was ecstatic. Instead of brass and blare, Cook created subtle contrasts, shadings, and authentic crescendos. Toomer was privileged not only to observe Cook's talents, but to experience his generosity:

> I have been to his rehearsals, and I have been on the stage at his concerts. Nothing here has so moved me. His gift is so pure and evident that I wanted to read him some of my stuff. I did. And tired and sick and harassed by the obligations of management and money matters as he is, his response came clear and true. Since then he has been unending in his enthusiasm much to the discomfort of the little fellows here who have kept me in the background, or tried to keep me there. And he has placed whatever he has at my disposal. Food and room in New York. Money whenever he has it.[34]

The poet Sterling Brown also characterized Cook as his mentor—as a man, as an artist, and as a dedicated person.[35]

Will Marion provided an important link to the Négritude movement through Sterling Brown, his son Mercer Cook, and other writers.[36] In an interview published in *West Africa* (August 30, 1919) Cook expressed a desire to visit his beloved African homeland. Even though he was unable to fulfill this wish during his lifetime, he visited Africa vicariously through the life and work of his son Mercer. A graduate of legendary Dunbar High School in Washington, D.C., Amherst College, the University of Paris, and Brown University, Mercer Cook had a distinguished career as teacher, author, translator, diplomat, and French scholar. He maintained the family ties to Howard University, serving as professor and chair of the department of Romance Languages for over forty years. Moreover, Dr. Cook nurtured a long friendship with President Leopold Senghor of Senegal (where he also served as ambassador) and provided an indispensable liaison between Senegal and the United States.

The accomplishments of major black thinkers and writers in the twenties were absorbed not only in America, but in Africa by young writers like Senghor. While speaking at Howard University in 1966 (with Mercer Cook translating), Senghor paid tribute to pioneering visionaries such as Alain Locke, W. E. B. Du Bois, Marcus Garvey, and Carter G. Woodson.[37] On the same occasion Senghor also rendered well-deserved homage to the poets whom Africans translated, recited, and emulated—including Claude McKay, Jean Toomer, Countee Cullen, James Weldon Johnson, Langston Hughes, and Sterling Brown. Significantly, two of these authors, Jean Toomer and Sterling Brown, identify Cook as their mentor. Thus, he provides an intergenerational, international connection to the Harlem Renaissance and to the Négritude Movement.

Will Marion Cook tried to foster and implement racial consciousness and pride through agitation. Once he solicited the assistance of Carl Van Vechten in this endeavor through a letter, in which he explained:

> Men like you can stop our habit of weak imitation. The fault is yours, not ours. You tell us that Anglo-Saxon civilization is the best, perhaps the only right one. You tell us that all white is good, all black, bad and evil. Then you expect us to be proud of and develop something that we have been taught is inferior. Help us to develop a race consciousness, a pride of things Negroid.[38]

Notably, Cook was looking outside himself and his culture for validation.

William Grant Still observed that Cook "was vigorous in his insistence on giving Negroes the credit that is rightfully due them for their innovations in the world of American music and drama."[39] This insistence took the form of protest in the press when *The New York Times* credited George White with creating the "Charleston" and "Black Bottom" dances.

> I have the greatest respect for Mr. White, his genius as an organizer and producer of reviews; but why do an injustice to the black folk of America by taking from them the credit of creating new and characteristic dances?[40]

Cook further reviewed the history of the two dances, which originated with blacks in the South.[41] He was doubtful that White had ever seen the Charleston prior to the final rehearsals of *Runnin' Wild*.

Cook was an outspoken critic of social inequities. In an editorial letter to *The New York Age*, for example, he articulated one of the discriminatory issues involving white music publishers:

> A recent experience with a music publishing concern inspires me to comment on the treatment colored composers and artists receive from some of these firms. As you know, for the past year all my songs have been published by the Harry Von Tilzer Publishing Co. Knowing this to be my

headquarters many well known colored writers, actors and singers have called on me at the Von Tilzer offices to consult about material either for use on the stage or in regard to having songs published.

The professional manager of the Von Tilzer Company, Max Winslow, after expressing disapproval of many of these visits by sour looks and evidences of lack of courtesy to my visitors, finally blankly informed me recently "that entirely too many spades came into the office."

Inasmuch as music of the day is to a great degree popularized by the colored performer and café singer, and inasmuch as the majority of music firms cater to the colored actor and singer when they have new songs, I feel that the color prejudice of Mr. Winslow should be widely known. I would suggest that since our singing of songs helps to popularize and increase the sale, that we seek those firms where our presence is not only welcomed but eagerly sought.[42]

It is not known what effect, if any, Cook's grievance had on black patronage of Tilzer's publishing firm. Certainly he went public in the hopes that some commercial loss would ensue.

Will Marion Cook used an agitation strategy like that recommended by W. E. B. Du Bois, who wrote in *The Crisis*:

Some good friends of the cause we represent fear agitation. They say: "Do not agitate—do not make a noise; work." They add, "Agitation is destructive or at best negative—What is wanted is positive constructive work."

Such honest critics mistake the function of agitation. A toothache is agitation. Is a toothache a good thing? No. Is it therefore useless? No. It is supremely useful, for it tells the body of decay, dyspepsia and death. Without it the body would suffer unknowingly. It would think all is well, when lo! Danger lurks.

The same is true of the social body. Agitation is a necessary evil to tell of the ills of the suffering. Without it, many a nation has been lulled to false security and preened itself with virtues it did not possess.

The function of this association [The National Association for the Advancement of Colored People] is to tell this nation the crying evil of race prejudice. It is a hard duty but a necessary one—a divine one. It is Pain; Pain is not good but Pain is necessary. Pain does not aggravate disease— Disease causes pain. Agitation does not mean Aggravation—aggravation calls for Agitation in order that Remedy may be found.[43]

Cook launched an important challenge to the deeply rooted practices of segregation, forcing many to confront racism. He displayed a courageous agitated demeanor. His memoirs reveal that his ultimate challenge was "to destroy wrongs, and at the same time write beautiful music."[44]

Appendix I

WILL MARION COOK COMPOSITIONS

Any Old Place in Yankee-land Is Good Enough for Me
Lyrics, Alex Rogers; Music, Cook and Chris Smith
New York: Gotham-Attucks, 1908; 1935

As the Sunflower Turns to the Sun
Lyrics, Richard Grant; Music, Cook
New York: Gotham-Attucks, 1904

Bon Bon Buddy
Lyrics, Alex Rogers; Music, Cook
New York: Gotham-Attucks, 1907; 1934

Brown-Skin Baby Mine
Lyrics, Cook and Cecil Mack; Music, Cook
New York: G. Schirmer, 1902

By-Gone Days Are Best
Lyrics, L. Lamprey; Music, Cook
New York: Jos. W. Stern, 1900

Clorindy March and Two-Step (piano)
Music, Cook
New York: M. Witmark, 1898

Clorindy, Origin of the Cake Walk (piano arr. by F. W. Meacham)
Music, Cook
New York: M. Witmark, 1899

Clorindy, Origin of the Cake Walk (piano arr. by T. P. Trinkaus for mandolins and
guitar)
Music, Cook
New York: M. Witmark, 1900

Creole Dance (piano)
Music, Marion
New York: M. Witmark, 1898

Cruel Daddy
    Lyrics, Anon.; Music, Cook
    New York: Jos. W. Stern, 1915; 1942

Cruel Papa; Fox Trot (piano)
    Music, Cook
    New York: Jos. W. Stern, 1914; 1941

Cruel Papa; Fox Trot (orch. arr. by Stephen Jones)
    Music, Cook
    New York: Jos. W. Stern, 1915; 1942

Czar of Dixie Land
    Lyrics, Paul Laurence Dunbar; Music, Cook
    New York: Jos. W. Stern, 1901

Dainty
    Lyrics, Paul Laurence Dunbar; Music, Cook
    New York: A. Payne, 1909; 1937

Daisy Deane
    Lyrics, Richard Wilkins and Cook; Music, Cook
    New York: John H. Cook, 1904

Darktown Barbecue
    Lyrics, Cook; Music, Cook
    New York: John H. Cook, 1904

Darktown Is Out Tonight
    Lyrics, Cook; Music, Marion
    New York: M. Witmark, 1899

Darktown Is Out Tonight, Two-Step (orch. arr. by Robert Recker)
    Music, Marion
    New York: M. Witmark, 1899

Darktown Is Out Tonight (arr. by George Lechler for zither)
    Music, Marion
    New York: M. Witmark, 1899

Darktown Is Out Tonight, March and Two-Step (arr. by G. L. Lansing for 2 banjos)
    Music, Marion
    New York: M. Witmark, 1900

Darktown Is Out Tonight, Two-Step for Piano (arr. by F. W. Meacham)
    Music, Marion
    New York: M. Witmark, 1899

Dar's Mah Mandy
    Lyrics, William Moore; Music, Cook
    Chicago: Will M. Cook, 1907

Dinah
    Lyrics, Alex Rogers; Music, Cook
    New York: Gotham-Attucks, 1907

Down de Lover's Lane
    Lyrics, Paul Laurence Dunbar; Music, Cook
    New York: Jos. W. Stern, 1900

Dreamin' Town (Mandy Lou)
   Lyrics, Paul Laurence Dunbar; Music, Cook
   New York: John H. Cook, 1904

Ev'rybody Loves
   Lyrics, Cook; Music, Cook
   New York: Will M. Cook, 1930

Exhortation: A Negro Sermon
   Lyrics, Alex Rogers; Music, Cook
   New York: G. Schirmer, 1912; 1940

An Explanation
   Lyrics, James W. Johnson; Music, Cook
   New York: G. Schirmer, 1914; 1941

Gal O'Mine
   Lyrics, Cecil Mack; Music, Cook
   New York: Artmusic, 1918; 1944

Ghost Ship; the Slave Ship
   Lyrics, Cook; Music, Cook
   New York: Will M. Cook, 1929

Girl from Vassar
   Lyrics, Cook; Music, Cook
   New York: Jos. W. Stern, 1901

Good Evenin'
   Lyrics, Paul Laurence Dunbar; Music, Cook
   New York: Harry Von Tilzer, 1902

Harlem Band
   Lyrics, Mercer Cook; Music, Lenoir Cook and Will M. Cook
   New York: Will M. Cook, 1929

Harlem Is Hell
   Lyrics, Mercer Cook; Music, Will M. Cook
   Washington, D.C.: Will Marion Cook, 1932

Hot Foot
   Lyrics, Paul Laurence Dunbar; Music, Cook
   Washington, D.C.: Will Marion Cook, 1901

Hottest Coon in Dixie
   Lyrics, Paul Laurence Dunbar; Music, Marion
   New York: M. Witmark, 1898

Hurrah for Captain Kidd
   Lyrics, Paul Laurence Dunbar; Music, Cook
   New York: Harry Von Tilzer, 1902

If the Sands of All the Seas Were Peerless Pearls
   Lyrics, James W. Johnson; Music, Cook
   New York: Jerome Remick, 1914; 1941

I'm Comin' Virginia
   Lyrics, Cook; Music, D. Heywood
   New York: Robbins Music, 1927

In Bandanna Lan'
  Lyrics, Mord Allen; Music, Cook
  New York: Gotham-Attucks, 1907

In De Evenin
  Lyrics, Richard Grant; Music, Cook
  New York: Harry Von Tilzer, 1910; 1937

It's Allus de Same in Dixie
  Lyrics, Richard Grant; Music, Cook
  New York: John H. Cook, 1904

I Want to Live and Die in Dixie Land
  Lyrics, Cecil Mack; Music, Cook
  New York: Empire Music, 1915; 1943

Jewel of the Big Blue Nile
  Lyrics, J. Mord Allen; Music, Cook
  New York: John H. Cook, 1908

Julep Song
  Lyrics, Richard Grant; Music, Cook
  New York: York Music Co., 1904

Jump Back (Negro Love Song)
  Lyrics, Paul Laurence Dunbar; Music, Marion
  New York: M. Witmark, 1898

Just a Little Bit of Heaven Called Home
  Lyrics, Mercer Cook; Music, Will M. Cook
  New York: Metro-Goldwyn-Mayer, 1934

Just the Same
  Lyrics, Alex Rogers; Music, Cook
  New York: Gotham-Attucks, 1907

Kinky
  Lyrics, Mord Allen and Ed Green; Music, Cook
  New York: Gotham-Attucks, 1908

Leader of the Colored Aristocracy
  Lyrics, James W. Johnson; Music, Cook ·
  New York: Harry Von Tilzer, 1902

Let's Save the U.S.A., to Hell with Over There (Over Here)
  Lyrics, Mercer Cook I and Mercer Cook II; Music, Cook
  New York: Will M. Cook, 1941

A Little Bit of Heaven Called Home
  Lyrics, Mercer Cook; Music, Will M. Cook
  New York: G. Schirmer, 1933; 1939

The Little Gypsy Maid
  Lyrics, Harry B. Smith and Cecil Mack; Music, Cook
  New York: Harry Von Tilzer, 1902

Lotus Blossoms (for piano)
  Music, Cook and B. Nierman
  New York: John H. Cook, 1904

Love in a Cottage Is Best
Lyrics, Cook; Music, Cook
New York: M. Witmark, 1898; 1925

Love Is the Tend'rest of Themes
Lyrics, Cook; Music, Cook
New York: Howley, Haviland, 1896

Love Looks Not at Estate
Lyrics, Cook; Music, Cook
Brooklyn: Will M. Cook, 1904

Love Me with a Tiger Love
Lyrics, Addison Burkhardt; Music, Cook
New York: Harry Von Tilzer, 1910; 1938

Lovie Joe
Lyrics, Cook; Music, Joe Jordan
New York: Harry Von Tilzer, 1910; 1937

Lulu
Lyrics, R. C. McPherson; Music, Cook
New York: Gotham Music, 1905

Maggie Magee
Lyrics, Al Smith; Music, Cook
New York: John H. Cook, 1905

Mammy
Lyrics, Lester A. Walton; Music, Cook,
New York: Artmusic, 1916; 1943

Mammy's 'Lasses Candy Chile
Lyrics, Cecil Mack; Music, Cook
New York: Maurice Shapiro, 1909; 1937

Mandy Lou
Lyrics, R. C. McPherson; Music, Cook
New York: Gotham Music, 1905

Molly Green
Lyrics, Cecil Mack; Music, Cook
New York: Harry Von Tilzer, 1902

Molly Green; Waltz on Melodies from *In Dahomey,* M. Retford arr. Boosey and
Co.'s Journal for Military Bands no. 32
Lyrics, Cecil Mack; Music, Cook
London: Will M. Cook, 1906

My Alabama Dan
Lyrics, Cook; Music, Cook
Washington, D.C.: Will Marion Cook, 1912; 1940

My Lady
Lyrics, Paul Laurence Dunbar and Cook; Music, Cook
New York: G. Schirmer, 1912; 1940

My Lady Frog
Lyrics, Will Accooe and Cook; Music, Cook
New York: Harry Von Tilzer, 1902

My Lady Nicotine
Lyrics, F. Clifford Harris; Music, Cook
New York: Harry Von Tilzer, 1910; 1937

My Lady Nicotine; Waltzes (piano) Eugene Platzmann, arr.
Music, Cook
New York: Will Marion Cook, 1910

My Lady's Lips Am Like de Honey
Lyrics, James W. Johnson; Music, Cook
New York: G. Schirmer, 1915; 1942

My Lady's Lips Am Like de Honey, Fox Trot (orch. arr. S. Jones)
Lyrics, Andrew B. Sterling; Music, Cook
New York: Howley, Dresser, 1904

My Little Irish Canary
Lyrics, Andrew B. Sterling; Music, Cook
New York: Howley, Dresser, 1904

On Emancipation Day
Lyrics, Paul Laurence Dunbar; Music, Cook
New York: Harry Von Tilzer, 1902

On Emancipation Day, March and Two-Step (for piano)
Music, Cook
New York: Harry Von Tilzer, 1902

Oo! Oo!! Oo!!! It's Very Strange
Lyrics, Mord Allen; Music, Cook
New York: John H. Cook, 1908

Parthenia Johnson
Lyrics, James W. Johnson; Music, Cook
New York: John H. Cook, 1908

Pensacola (The) Mooch
Lyrics, Ford T. Dabney; Music, Ford T. Dabney and Cook
New York: Harry Von Tilzer, 1910; 1937

Possum Am de Best Meat After All
Lyrics, Paul Laurence Dunbar; Music, Cook
New York: Jos. W. Stern, 1901

Rain-Song (men's chorus)
Lyrics, Alex Rogers; Music, Cook
New York: G. Schirmer, 1912; 1940

Rain-Song (high voice)
Lyrics, Alex Rogers; Music, Cook
New York: G. Schirmer, 1912

Rain-Song (mixed voices) (arr. by W. Riegger)
Lyrics, Alex Rogers; Music, Cook
New York: G. Schirmer, 1912

Red, Red Rose
Lyrics, Alex Rogers; Music, Cook
New York: Gotham-Attucks, 1908; 1935

Returned
  Lyrics, Paul Laurence Dunbar; Music, Cook
  New York: Harry Von Tilzer, 1902

Romance
  Lyrics, Harry B. Smith; Music, Cook
  New York: Jos. W. Stern, 1900

She's Dancing Sue
  Lyrics, Charles S. Sager; Music, Cook and Will Accooe
  New York: Harry Von Tilzer, 1902

Slumber Song
  Lyrics, R. C. McPherson; Music, Cook
  New York: John H. Cook, 1904

Spread de News
  Lyrics, Cook; Music, Cook
  Brooklyn: Will M. Cook, 1904

Springtime
  Lyrics, Phil. H. Armstrong; Music, Cook
  New York: G. Schirmer, 1914; 1941

Squirrel Song
  Lyrics, Richard Grant; Music, Cook
  New York: John H. Cook, 1904

A Summah Night
  Lyrics, Paul Laurence Dunbar; Music, Cook
  New York: Harry Von Tilzer, 1906

Sweet Dreams, You Can't Come Back
  Lyrics, Alex Rogers; Music, Cook and William McCoy
  New York: Cook and Rogers, 1911; 1938

Sweetie Dear
  Lyrics, Will Marion Cook; Music, Joe Jordan
  New York: Barron and Thompson, 1906; 1934

Swing Along
  Lyrics, Cook; Music, Cook
  New York: G. Schirmer, 1912

Swing Along (2-part boys' chorus) Jeffrey Marlowe, arr.
  Lyrics, Cook; Music, Cook
  New York: G. Schirmer, 1943

Swing Along (men's chorus)
  Lyrics, Cook; Music, Cook
  New York: G. Schirmer, 1912

Swing Along (high voice)
  Lyrics, Cook; Music, Cook
  New York: G. Schirmer, 1912; 1940

Swing Along (4-part chorus) Frank R. Rix, arr.
  Lyrics, Cook; Music, Cook
  New York: G. Schirmer, 1914; 1942

Swing Along, March, Charles Brunover, arr.
  Music, Cook
  Milwaukee: Wm. C. Stahl, 1924

Swing Along (orch. arr. by Maurice Baron)
  Music, Cook
  New York: G. Schirmer, 1924

Swing Along (3-part women's chorus, Carl Deis, arr.)
  Lyrics, Cook; Music, Cook
  New York: G. Schirmer, 1951; 1979

Swing Along (school mixed chorus adapted by Ralph Baldwin)
  Lyrics, Cook; Music, Cook
  New York: G. Schirmer, 1928

That'll Be All Right Baby
  Lyrics, Cook; Music, Cook
  New York: Spaulding & Gray, 1896

There's a Place in the Old Vacant Chair
  Lyrics, Cook; Music, Cook
  New York: Gotham Music, 1905

Troubled in Mind—Negro Spiritual
  Lyrics, Mercer Cook; Music, arr. by Will M. Cook
  New York: G. Schirmer, 1929

Until Then
  Lyrics, Alex Rogers; Music, Cook
  New York: Gotham-Attucks, 1907

Ups and Downs
  Lyrics, Mercer Cook; Music, Will M. Cook
  New York: Will M. Cook, 1927

Vassar (The) Girl
  Lyrics, Cook; Music, Cook
  New York: Will M. Cook, 1927

We're Marching On
  Lyrics, Cook; Music, Cook
  W. Bedford, Mass.: George Broome, 1896

We's A Comin'
  Lyrics, Cook; Music, Cook
  New York: Will Marion Cook, 1904

Whatever the Hue of Your Eyes
  Lyrics, Harry B. Smith; Music, Cook
  New York: Jos. W. Stern, 1900

What Makes Me Love You the Way I Do
  Lyrics, R. C. McPherson; Music, Cook
  New York: Cook and McPherson, 1911

What Would You Be A' Doing
  Lyrics, W. S. Estren; Music, E. Parke and Cook
  New York: Harry Von Tilzer, 1902

Where the Lotus Blossoms Grow
  Lyrics, Joseph C. Farrell; Music, Cook
  New York: John H. Cook, 1904

Who Dat Say Chicken in Dis Crowd?
  Lyrics, Paul Laurence Dunbar; Music, Marion
  New York: M. Witmark, 1898

Who Dat Say Chicken in Dis Crowd? Polka Two-Step (orch. arr. by W. H. Mackie)
  Music, Marion
  New York: M. Witmark, 1898

Whoop 'er Up
  Lyrics, Andrew Sterling; Music, Cook
  New York: Harry Von Tilzer, 1910; 1937

Wid de Moon, Moon, Moon
  Lyrics, William Moore; Music, Cook
  New York: G. Schirmer, 1907; 1935

Wid de Moon, Moon, Moon (men's voices, Ralph L. Baldwin, arr.)
  Lyrics, William Moore; Music, Cook

Appendix 2

SONGS BY COOK PERFORMED IN MUSICAL SHOWS

Africana

I'm Coming Virginia

Bandanna Land

Any Old Place in Yankee Land
   Is Good Enough for Me
Bon Bon Buddy
Just the Same
Kinky
Red, Red Rose
Until Then

The Boys and Betty

Whoop 'er Up

The Casino Girl

By-Gone Days Are Best
Down de Lover's Lane
Romance
Whatever the Hue of Your Eyes

Clorindy

Darktown Is Out Tonight
Hottest Coon in Dixie
Jump Back
Love in a Cottage Is Best
Who Dat Say Chicken in Dis Crowd?

Cohan and Harris' Minstrels

Mammy's 'Lasses Candy Chile

Darkydom

Dreaming Town
The Ghost Ship
I Want to Live and Die in Dixie Land
The Jewel of the Big Blue Nile
Mammy
My Lady Nicotine
My Lady's Lips

The Girl from Dixie

As the Sunflower Turns to the Sun

In Dahomey

Brown-Skin Baby Mine
Caboceers' Entrance
Czar of Dixie Land
Girl from Vassar
Good Evenin'
Hurrah for Captain Kidd
Leader of the Colored
   Aristocracy
Molly Green
My Lady Frog
On Emancipation Day
Returned
She's Dancing Sue

In Dahomey (continued)

Society
Swing Along

The Deacon and the Lady

Love Me with a Tiger Love

In the Jungles

The Jewel of the Big Blue
   Nile

In Zululand

Wid de Moon, Moon, Moon

Jes Lak White Fo'ks

Down De Lover's Lane
Girl from Vassar
Love Looks Not at Estate
Spread de News
We's A Comin'

The Man from Bamm

Red, Red Rose
Sweetie, Dear

Miss Calico

I'm Coming Virginia

Mrs. Black Is Back

By-Gone Days Are Best

My Friend from Georgia

The Ghost Ship

The New Yorkers

Dat's All, Ragtime Girl

The Sons of Ham

Down de Lovers' Lane

The Southerners

As the Sunflower Turns to the Sun
Daisy Deane
Dandy Dan
Darktown Barbecue
Good Evenin'
It's Allus de Same in Dixie
Julep Song
Mandy Lou; Dreamin' Town
Parthenia Johnson
Slumber Song
Squirrel Song
Swing Along
Where the Lotus Blossoms Grow

The Traitor

Down de Lovers' Lane

The Wild Rose

The Little Gypsy Maid
What Would You Be A-Doing

Ziegfeld Follies of 1910

Lovie Joe

Appendix 3

SOUTHERN SYNCOPATED
ORCHESTRA'S PERSONNEL

Will Marion Cook	violin/composer-arranger/conductor
James Arthur Briggs, Robert Jones	trumpet
John Forrester	trombone
Anthony Rivera, Sidney Bechet	clarinet
Ferdinand Coxito	saxophone
Milford Warren	French horn
Ambrose Smith	piano
Joseph Caulk, Henry Saparo, Carroll Morgan, Lawrence Morris	bandoline
Paul Wyer, Angelina Rivera	violin
Joseph Porter	cello
Santos Rivera	double bass
Robert Young	drums
Benton E. Peyton	tympani

The players who were also featured as vocalists or members of vocal groups were Joseph Caulk, Henry Saparo, Carroll Morgan, Joseph Porter, Benton E. Peyton, Lawrence Morris, Robert Young, and Angelina Rivera. Additional vocalists with the group were: Earl McKinney, E. C. Rosemond, John Payne, Robert Williams, and Hattie King Reavis. George Lattimore served as the business manager for the orchestra.

Other performers, who do not appear on this list but have been included in other listings of the orchestral personnel performing in Europe are:[1]

Mattie Gilmore, Pierre de Caillaux	piano
Lawrence Morris	banjo
Pedro Vargas	double bass
Bert Marshall	drums
Frank Withers, Jacob Patrick, Ellis Jackson	trombone
Bertin Depestre Salnave	flute
Mazie Mullins	saxophone
George Smith, Ralph Jones	violin

According to the earliest extant program of the orchestra from Philharmonic Hall, September 26, 1919, the following musicians had been added:

Edward Patrick ....trumpet
Jacob Patrick, George Rogers ....trombone
John George Russell ....clarinet
Frank A. Dennie ....saxophone
Mattie Gilmore, Pierre De Caillaux ....piano
Pedro Vargas ....double bass

Frank Dennie also sang, and William D. Burns, George Baker, Joseph Hall, William T. Tatten, and Lottie Gee were added vocalists. On October 14, 1919, the violinists Frank Tate and George Smith arrived in Britain and joined the orchestra.

Appendix 4

ITINERARY FOR THE SOUTHERN SYNCOPATED ORCHESTRAL TOURS

First SSO American Tour—1919

January 30 . . . . Lancaster, Penn.
February 4 . . . . Johnstown, Penn.
February 5 . . . . Alatoona, Penn.
February 6 . . . . Pittsburgh, Penn.
February 7 . . . . Pittsburgh, Penn.
February 24 . . . . Harrisburg, Penn.
February 25 . . . . Philadelphia, Penn.
February 26 . . . . Williamsport, Penn.

Second SSO American Tour—1919

April 4 . . . . Titusville, PA
April 5 . . . . Oil City, PA
April 6 . . . . Akron, OH
April 7 . . . . Canton, OH
April 8 . . . . Canton, OH
April 9 . . . . Alliance, OH
April 10 . . . . Youngstown, OH
April 11 . . . . Sandusky, OH
April 12 . . . . Elyria, OH
April 13 . . . . Columbus, OH
April 15 . . . . Lima, OH
April 16 . . . . Toledo, OH
April 17 . . . . Toledo, OH
April 20 . . . . Chicago, IL

Appendix 5

SOUND RECORDINGS OF
WILL MARION COOK COMPOSITIONS

Title	Performer(s)	Label	Issue No.	Matrix No.	Year And Place
Any Old Place in Yankee Land	Edward Meeker	Edison		mx10189	
Bon Bon Buddy	Billy Murray	Victor	5433		
Bon Bon Buddy (refrain)	Zonophone Band	Zon-O-Phone	5166-A		
Cannibal King	Dan Quinn	Edison		mx1008	
Darktown Is Out Tonight	Edgar A. Cantrell	Edison Bell		mx6124	4/1906 London
	Danny Barker	New World	254		
	Missouri Minstrels	Victor	35321		5/1914
	Dan Quinn				
	Met Orch. and Gram	Edison	6905		
	Minstrel Chorus	Ber Gram Victor	027		
	Met. Orch.		A253		
Darktown (orch.& chorus)	Ethiop. Minstrels	Monarch	M1834		
Down De Lover's Lane	Peerless Quartet	Victor	17097-B		
	w/o Paul Robeson	Victor	7430-A	mxOEA7694	5/9/39 London
	w/L. Brown				
	Paul Robeson w/o				6/15/28 London
	Carroll Gibbons				
Exhortation	C. Thompson/Europe's Singing	Pathe	022084B	N.F.	
	Serenaders Orch.				
	Reed Miller w/o	Columbia	A1158	mx39325	
		Victor	17695A		
	Ivan Browning w/E. Blake	EBM	3		1972
	Paul Robeson w/L. Brown	Victor	3409		2/27/30 London

Title	Perform-Er(S)	Label	Issue No.	Matrix No.	Year And Place
I'm Comin' Virginia	Jo Stafford/Her Man of Jazz	V Disc	895A	mx02327	
	"Wild Bill" Davison/His Commodores	Commodore	628A		
	Fletcher Henderson/His Commodores	Columbia	1059-D	mx144133	
	Harold Lambert	Romeo	444	mx2562A2	
	Woody Herman/His Orch. Steady Nelson	Decca	2817a	mx66673A	
	Bunny Berigan/& His Blue Boys	Decca	18116B	mx60231A	
	Ethel Waters/Her Singing Orch. with Cook	Columbia	14170DM	mx142643	
	Charlie Barnet/His Orch/F. Leary & Quartet	Bluebird	B-11417-b	mx-11417B	
I'm Comin' Virginia	Paul Whiteman/His Orch. with vocal refrain	Victor	20751-B		
	Paul Whiteman/Swing Wing/Jack Teagarden The Modernaires	Decca	2145B	mx64616A	
	Al Friedman and His Orch. The Rollickers	Edison	52102	mx11901	11/1927
Lovie Joe	Arthur Collins w/o Elizabeth Brice w/o Charles A. Prince	Columbia	A953	mx4997	4/20/17
		Victor	5838		New York
Mandy Lou	Hayden Quartet	Victor	4544		
My Little Gypsy Maid	Marie George	FAV	1-66028		c.1909

(continued)

Title	Perform-Er(S)	Label	Issue No.	Matrix No.	Year And Place
My Little Irish Canary	Edward H. Favor w/o	Columbia	1712	mx1712-6	
On Emancipation Day	Anon. Baritone	Columbia	1028		
	Arthur Collins	Edison	8097		
	Spencer & Ossman/banjo	Victor			1/1918
Rain Song	Eubie Blake, piano	Rythmodik	J19124		
	Afro-American Folk-Song Singers	Columbia	A1538		
Red, Red Rose	John Barnes Wells	Edison	1435		
	Clough with Hayden Quartet	Victor	35085		
Swing Along	Orpheus Quartet	Victor	17899		5/1918
	Afro-American Folk-Song Singers	Columbia	A1538	mx39274	
	Orpheus Quartet w/o	Edison	80313-R	mx39274	
	Binghamton Kiwanis Quartet	Columbia	229-D	-1-9	
Swing Along	Paul Robeson w/o Ray Noble	OB	6523-1		5/2/33
		HMV	B-8018		London
Who Dat Say Chicken In Dis Crowd?	Sousa Band w/ Arthur Pryor	Berliner	01208		4/1900
					Phil.
	Met. Orch./Kendle &Kelley	Berliner	0911		
	Met. Orch.	Victor	A289		
	Arthur Collins	Edison	5475		
Whoop 'Er Up	Ada Jones w/o	Columbia	A954	mx49462-2	
Wid de Moon, Moon, Moon	Abbie Mitchell	Station			
	Radio Broadcast tape	WABC			7/13/37

According to the Illinois Writers Project, the Umbrian Glee Club recorded "The Rain Song," "Exhortation," and "Swing Along" for the Brunswick Recording Company.

NOTES

Chapter 1

1. Constance McLaughlin Green, *The Secret City: A History of Race Relations in the Nation's Capital* (Princeton, N.J.: Princeton University Press, 1967), 78.

2. Unless otherwise indicated, this and other biographical information was gleaned from Will Marion Cook's unfinished "Autobiographical Notes," given to the author by the late Mercer Cook. See also Marva Griffin Carter, "The Life and Music of Will Marion Cook" (Ph. D. diss., University of Illinois at Urbana-Champaign, 1988), 386–421.

3. "The Cook Family in History," *The Negro History Bulletin* 11 (June 1946): 214; Gerri Major and Doris E. Saunders, *Black Society* (Chicago: Johnson Publishing, 1976), 168.

4. Rayford W. Logan, *Howard University—The First Hundred Years 1867–1967* (New York: New York University Press, 1969), 49.

5. *National Republican* (Washington, D.C.), n.d., "John Hartwell Cook," Oberlin College Archives.

6. "John Hartwell Cook," Oberlin College Archives.

7. Cook's autobiographical notes do not reveal why his mother chose to venture to these two locales.

8. Documentation on William and Jane Lewis acquired from Patrice Glass, Local History and Genealogy Department, Chattanooga-Hamilton County Bicentennial Library. Biography File with correspondence from William J. Lewis of Philadelphia, December 3, 1975; *The Chattanooga Times*, September 3, 1896; January 26, 1947, 20; February 13, 1947, 10; W. R. Pittenger, *The Great Locomotive Chase*, [n.p., n.d.], 245. Discrepancies occur in the number and relation of family members freed by Bill Lewis. In another account he is credited with purchasing his freedom and that of his spouse at $1,000 each. He bought his six-year-old son for $400; his mother and aunt for $150 each because of their advanced ages; and two brothers for $1,000 each. A slave trader purchased his sister for him for only $400. Because of the laws of the day, he was obliged to pay a white man to legalize his transactions. Jane Lewis is believed to have been of Cherokee descent and to have had long straight black hair.

9. Mercer Cook, interview by author, Washington, D.C., June 12, 1983.

Chapter 2

1. Virginius Dabney, *Virginia—The New Dominion* (Garden City, N.Y.: Doubleday, 1971), 252; "The Cook Family in History," *The Negro History Bulletin* 11 (June 1946): 214; Gerri Major and Doris E. Saunders, *Black Society* (Chicago: Johnson Publishing, 1976), 196.

2. John Barnard, *From Evangelicalism to Progressivism at Oberlin College 1866–1917* (Columbus: The Ohio State University Press, 1969), 3.

3. Ibid., 41.

4. Ibid., 28.

5. The town of Oberlin had a longstanding reputation of liberalism toward blacks, to the point that it was dubbed "Nigger" town. See Nat Brandt, *The Town That Started the Civil War* (Syracuse, N.Y.: Syracuse University Press, 1990). Despite this reputation, the idea that the college had a large black enrollment was more myth than reality. "They made up four or five percent of the student body between 1840 and 1860, rose to seven percent or eight percent during the decade after the Civil War, and then declined to five or six percent." See W. E. Bigglestone, "Oberlin College and the Negro Student, 1865–1940," *The Journal of Negro History* 56 (July 1971): 198.

6. Josie W. Roberts, "Oberlin—The Pioneer Liberal College of America," *Abbott's Monthly* (Feb. 1931): 59–60; see also W. E. Bigglestone, "Oberlin College and the Negro Student," 198; S. Frederick Starr, "Oberlin's Ragtimer: Will Marion Cook," *Oberlin Alumni Magazine* (Fall 1989), 13.

7. George Frederic Thompson Cook (1835–1912) was born in Washington, D.C., on June He enrolled as a preparatory student in Oberlin in 1853, entering as a freshman in 1855. He left college in his junior year at the outbreak of the war but nevertheless was granted the honorary degree of Master of Arts in 1877. One of the most distinguished black graduates of the college, for more than thirty years, beginning in 1868, he was Superintendent of Colored Schools in Washington, D.C. He never married and died of bronchitis in his Washington home on August 14, 1912. "Annual Report 1914–1915," George Cook File, Box 152, Former/Grads, Oberlin College Archives.

8. Mr. Doolittle studied for a short time in Cincinnati and later spent a year in private study abroad before instructing violin at Oberlin. *The Oberlin Alumni Magazine* 10, no. 1 (Oct. 1913), 7; The Oberlin College Archives do contain records verifying the years in which William Cook was a student at the conservatory; however, they do not have transcripts revealing courses actually taken and grades received. Oberlin Conservatory's founder, J. P. Morgan, translated Richter's book in 1867 and titled it *The Manual of Harmony*.

9. Ibid., 15. The details of Oberlin Conservatory's curriculum have been acquired from this source, 14–27.

10. "Frederick Giraud Doolittle," Folder in the Oberlin College Archives, Oberlin, Ohio.

11. Barnard, *From Evangelicalism to Progressivism*, 51, 54–55, 65, 67;. King tried to bridge the gap between the traditional conception of a personal God and the new idea of a God at work with humankind to better the world (76).

12. Bigglestone, "Oberlin College and the Negro Student," 200.

13. Barnard, *From Evangelicalism to Progressivism*, 6.

14. Mary Church Terrell, *A Colored Woman in a White World* (1940; reprint, New York: G. K. Hall, 1996), 26.

15. *Oberlin Review* 12, no. 8 (January 5, 1884), 94.

16. *Oberlin Review* 12, no. 17 (May 10, 1884), 201.

17. Ibid 12, no. 11 (February 16, 1884), 130.

18. Ibid. 11, no. 16 (April 26, 1884), 191.

19. *The Cleveland Gazette*, October 2 and 16, 1886.

20. Ibid., December 18, 1886, 4.

21. Ibid., January 22, 1887.

22. Ibid., February 12, 1887.

23. Ibid., January 22, 1887.

24. Ibid., March 26, 1887.

25. Ibid., January 1, March 23, and April 16, 1887.

26. Arna Bontemps and Jack Conroy, *Anyplace But Here* (New York: Hill and Wang, 1969), 93. Unfortunately, Bontemps does not give the source of his information.

27. Terrell, *Colored Woman in a White World*, 44; Barnard, *From Evangelicalism to Progressivism*, 20.

28. Correspondence from W. E. Bigglestone, Archivist, Oberlin College Archives, October 3, 1979, Box 2 File 28/2.

29. Unfortunately, there are no extant church records.

30. In Cook's autobiographical notes, he describes this critic as "a Bostonian who had written a book on Negro singers, composers and instrumentalists." Presumably, this was James Trotter, the author of *Music and Some Highly Musical People*, published in 1881.

31. Ronald Taylor, *Berlin and Its Culture* (New Haven, Conn.: Yale University Press, 1997), 90. Unless otherwise noted, this source provided me with the historical context for understanding William Cook's experiences in Berlin.

32. Quoted in Taylor, *Berlin and Its Culture*, 150–151.

33. Ibid., 206.

34. Berlin was later than other European cities to establish such a school of music. Paris's Conservatoire de Musique had been in existence since 1795, Vienna's Konservatorium der Gesellschaft der Musikfreunde had existed since 1817, and London's Royal Academy of Music since 1822.

35. Andreas Moser, *Joachim Biography*, 1904, 203. It was the most important artistic academy of the Prussian state and remained such until the end of the monarchy in 1918. It benefited considerably from financial state support.

36. Imogen Fellinger to Thomas L. Riis, Ann Arbor, Mich., December 22, 1980. Personal Files of Thomas L. Riis, Boulder, Col. Further confirmed at the Berlin Hochschule library.

37. Margaret Campbell, *The Great Violinists* (New York: Doubleday, 1981), 79.

38. Franz Farga, *Violins and Violinists* (New York: Frederick A. Praeger, 1950), 219.

39. Terrell, *Colored Woman in a White World*, 44.

40. Will Marion Cook Obituary, *Time Magazine*, July 31, 1944, 90.

41. Marva Griffin Carter, "The Life and Music of Will Marion Cook" (Ph.D. diss., University of Illinois at Urbana-Champaign, 1988), 420.

42. The exact duration of Cook's stay in Germany has yet to be verified. His autobiographical notes specify three years. Some erroneous accounts indicate that he remained there as long as nine years. It is also possible that he studied there intermittently. (See "The Cook Family," *Negro History Bulletin*, 214). His passport application of May 17, 1919, indicates that he resided in Berlin from 1889 to 1902. (Passport Office, U. S. Department of State, Washington, D.C.)

43. "Persons and Achievements to Be Remembered in February," *The Negro History Bulletin* (Feb. 1939): 35. This undocumented source indicates that Cook returned to the United States because of ill health. It was Mercer Cook's belief that his father's funds were depleted. (Interview with the author, July 10, 1983.)

44. *The Freeman,* September 13, 1890, 2; for a complete slate of officers see *The New York Age,* September 27, 1890, 1.

45. *The New York Age,* September 27, 1890, 1.

46. *The New York Age,* October 25, 1890, 1.

47. According to information provided by his widow. W. E. Bigglestone, Oberlin College Archivist, personal letter.

Chapter 3

1. Elliott M. Rudwick and August Meier, "Black Man in the 'White City': Negroes and the Columbian Exposition, 1893," *Phylon* 26, no. 4 (Winter 1965), 354.

2. Ida B. Wells. *The Reason Why the Colored American Is Not in the World's Columbian Exposition,* Chicago, 1893. (Pamphlet located at the Chicago Historical Society)

3. Rayford W. Logan and Michael R. Winston, eds., *Dictionary of American Negro Biography* (New York: W. W. Norton, 1982), 186.

4. *The Freeman,* February 11, 1893, 5.

5. *The Freeman,* August 12, 1893, 2.

6. Rudwick and Meier, "Black Man in the 'White City,' 359–360; *Cleveland Gazette,* July 15 and 22, 1893; *Topeka Call,* July 15, 1893.

7. *Daily Inter Ocean* (Chicago), August 26, 1893, 2.

8. *Daily Inter Ocean* (Chicago), August 26, 1893, 1 and 2.

9. *Daily Inter Ocean* (Chicago), August 26, 1893, 2.

10. *The Chicago Tribune,* August 26, 1893, 3.

11. *Daily Columbian* (Chicago), August 24 and 26, 1893.

12. William McFeely, *Frederick Douglass* (New York: W. W. Norton, 1991), 370–372; Douglass quoted in "The World in Miniature," *Indianapolis Freeman,* September 1, 1892; and "Appeal of Douglass," *Chicago Tribune,* August 26, 1893. It is interesting to note that Douglass refers to *your* country, rather than to *our* country.

13. *Daily Columbian* (Chicago), August 26, 1893.

14. *The Freeman,* August 12, 1893, 2.

15. *Daily Inter Ocean* (Chicago), August 26, 1893, 2.

16. *The Conservator* (Chicago), September 9, 1893. "Sissieretta Jones Folder," Library Division, Moorland-Spingarn Research Center, Howard University. I am indebted to Thomas Riis for sending me this clipping in correspondence on May 31, 1981.

17. Eugene Levy, *James Weldon Johnson—Black Leader Black Voice* (Chicago: University of Chicago Press, 1973), 37.

18. Arna Bontemps and Jack Conroy, *They Seek a City* (Garden City, N.Y.: Doubleday, 1945), 92.

19. Dreck Spurlock Wilson, "Black Involvement in Chicago's Previous World's Fairs," Ms., World Columbian Exposition of 1893, (Chicago, 1984), 6.

20. Ibid.

21. Maurice Peress, *Dvořák to Duke Ellington: A Conductor Explores America's Music and Its African American Roots* (New York: Oxford University Press, 2004), 37–39. Cook interviews found in *Chicago Defender,* May 1, 1915, and *Illinois*

Record, May 14, 1898. See Lawrence Gushee, "The Nineteenth-Century Origins of Jazz," *Black Music Research Journal* 14, no. 1 (Spring 1994):1–24.

22. James Weldon Johnson, *Black Manhattan* (1930; reprint, New York: Atheneum, 1972), 95, 98; Lynne Emery, "Black Dance and the American Musical Theatre to 1930," in *Musical Theatre in America*, ed. Glenn Loney (Westport, Conn.: Greenwood Press, 1984), 303.

23. Levy, *James Weldon Johnson*, 39.

24. Henry Edward Krehbiel, *Afro-American Folksongs* (1913; reprint, New York: Frederick Ungar, 1967), 60 64–65.

25. Wilson, "Chicago's Previous World's Fairs," 19.

26. Michael Beckerman, ed., "Letters from Dvořák's American Period: A Selection of Unpublished Correspondence Received by Dvořák in the United States," in *Dvořák and His World* (Princeton, N.J.: Princeton University Press, 1993) 198–199. More recently, Maurice Peress gives a vivid description of this handwritten letter which he viewed on three sheets of Hotel Lakota stationary at the Dvořák Archives in Prague. (See Peress, *Dvořák to Duke Ellington*, 31–32.)

Chapter 4

1. N. Robert Aborn, "The Influence on American Musical Culture of Dvořák's Sojourn in America" (Ph.D. diss., Indiana University, 1965), 150, 187.

2. Maurice Peress, *Dvořák to Duke Ellington: A Conductor Explores America's Music and Its African American Roots* (New York: Oxford University Press, 2004), 44–51.

3. Jan van Straaten, *Slavonic Rhapsody: The Life of Antonín Dvořák* (New York: Allen, Towne and Heath, 1948), 179–80.

4. See *Chicago* Tribune, August 13, 1893; reprinted in John Clapham, *Dvořák* (New York: W. W. Norton, 1979), 201; Thomas L. Riis, "Dvořák and His Black Students," in David R. Beveridge, ed., *Rethinking Dvořák: Views from Five Countries* (Oxford: Clarendon Press, 1996), 265–273.

5. Aborn, "Dvořák's Sojourn in America," 174; Harry Rowe Shelley, "Dvořák As I Knew Him," *The Etude* 31 (Aug. 1913): 541–542.

6. "The National Conservatory of Music of America," *Harper's Weekly* 34, no. 1773 (December 13, 1890): 970.

7. See *Chicago Tribune*, August 13, 1893; reprinted in John Clapham, *Dvořák* (New York: W. W. Norton, 1979), 201; Riis, "Dvořák and his Black Students," 265–273.

8. John C. Tibbetts, ed., *Dvořák in America: 1892–1895* (Portland, Ore.: Amadeus Press, 1993), 18.

9. Peress, *Dvořák to Duke Ellington*, 44–51.

10. Will Marion Cook, "Clorindy, the Origin of the Cakewalk," *Theatre Arts Magazine* (September 1947): 61 (published posthumously, Cook died in 1944); reprinted in Eileen Southern, ed., *Readings in Black American Music*, 2nd ed. (New York: W. W. Norton, 1983), 228.

11. "Writings by Will Marion Cook," MCP Box 157-9 Folder 15.

12. Quoted in Maud Cuney-Hare, *Negro Musicians and Their Music* (1936; reprint, New York: Da Capo Press, 1974), 59.

13. Michael Beckerman, "Dvořák's 'New World' Largo and 'The Song of Hiawatha,'" in *Nineteenth Century* Music 16, no. 1 (Summer 1992): 36.

14. Sam Dennison, *Scandalize My Name: Black Imagery in American Popular Music* (New York: Garland, 1981), 281.

15. A letter from Cook to Claude Barnett, September 20, 1921, referred to George W. Broome as his "old pal." (See the Claude Barnett Papers of the Associated Negro Press, Chicago Historical Society.) "We're Marching On" may well have been Broome's only publication. He is not on file at the Copyright Office in Washington, D.C., nor is he listed in the Medford City Directory for 1895–1896, which includes West Medford. Thanks to Wayne D. Shirley, Music Specialist at the Library of Congress for providing this information.

Chapter 5

1. Quoted by Mercer Cook, "From *Clorindy* to *The Red Moon* and Beyond." Paper presented at "Black America On Stage" Symposium, The Graduate Center of the City University of New York, October 26, 1978.

2. Ann Charters, *Nobody—The Story of Bert Williams* (New York: Macmillan, 1970), 51.

3. Cook, "From *Clorindy* to *The Red Moon*."

4. James Weldon Johnson, *Along This Way—The Autobiography of James Weldon Johnson* (1933; reprint, New York: Viking, 1968), 172–173.

5. Ibid., 177.

6. Cook and Dunbar agreed with M. Witmark and Sons to divide royalties from *Clorindy* for the first four weeks of any production Dunbar would receive $15 and Cook $25. For further consecutive weeks in America and Canada Dunbar would receive $20 and Cook $30 on a basis of 40 and 60 percent. For England and foreign countries Dunbar would receive 27 percent and Cook 73 percent. (Contract signed by Cook and Dunbar July 15, 1895, located in the Paul Laurence Dunbar Collection, Box 6, 181 and on Microfilm 25 Roll Number 2, The Ohio Historical Society, Columbus Ohio).

7. "Writings by Will Marion Cook," MCP Box 157-9 Folder 15.

8. Addison Gayle, Jr., *Oak and Ivy—A Biography of Paul Laurence Dunbar* (Garden City, N.Y.: Doubleday, 1971), 167.

9. Dunbar's account suggested that the piano was used in the compositional process; however, Cook notes that the writing was not aided by an instrument. The piano seems to have been in the parlor and their writing took place in the kitchen, where they also drank and ate. See Will Marion Cook, "Clorindy, the Origin of the Cakewalk," in *Readings in Black American Music*, ed. Eileen Southern, (2nd ed., New York: W. W. Norton, 1983), 227–233.

10. Cook, "Clorindy, the Origin of the Cakewalk," 229.

11. Ibid., 230.

12. Ibid., 231.

13. Various descriptions of this work were given in the press. *The Colored American* (Washington, D.C., July 9, 1898, p. 6) called this work "a Negro musical farce in one act," and *The New York Dramatic Mirror* (July 23, 1898, p. 17) referred to it as "a negro operetta." *The Freeman* (February 15, 1902, p. 5) described it as a "first-class, ragtime, musical cakewalk."

14. *The New York Dramatic Mirror,* August 27, 1898, p.16.

15. Cook, "Clorindy, the Origin of the Cakewalk," 232.

16. "Clorindy Notes," MCP Box 157-9 Folder 9.

17. James Weldon Johnson, *Black Manhattan,* 3rd ed. (New York: Atheneum, 1972), 103.

18. *The New York Dramatic Mirror,* July 6, 1898, p. 16.

19. Will Marion Cook, "Autobiographical Notes," MCP Box 157-9 Folder 6.

20. Will Marion Cook, "Notes on Belle Davis," MCP Box 157-9 Folder 11.

21. *The New York Dramatic Mirror*, July 16, 1898, p. 16.

22. Ironically, Isidore Witmark was the first to hear the *Clorindy* audition, with Cook's unpolished piano playing and singing. He turned it down. By the time E. E. Rice agreed to produce it, however, Cook had been able to draft singers and dancers to give a more impressive audition. Isidore Witmark and Isaac Goldberg, *From Ragtime to Swingtime* (1939; reprint, New York: Da Capo Press, 1976), 448–449.

23. Cook, "Clorindy, The Origin of the Cakewalk," 233.

24. Words and Music by Will Marion, "Darktown Is Out To-Night" (New York: M. Witmark & Sons, 1898).

25. Edward A. Berlin, *King of Ragtime: Scott Joplin and His Era* (New York: Oxford University Press, 1994), 79.

26. Sam Dennison, *Scandalize My Name—Black Imagery in American Popular Music* (New York: Garland , 1982), 364.

27. Ibid.

28. *The Colored American*, Washington, D.C., September 3, 1898, p. 8. My thanks to Dr. Doris McGinty for this citation.

29. *The New York Dramatic Mirror*, September 3, 1898, p. 18; September 10, 1898, p. 17; October 1, 1898, p. 20.

30. Cook, "Clorindy, the Origin of the Cakewalk," 227.

31. *The New York Dramatic Mirror*, October 29, 1898, p. 20.

32. *The New York Dramatic Mirror*, November 19, 1898, p. 18.

33. *The New York Dramatic Mirror*, December 3, 1898, p. 18.

34. *The New York Dramatic Mirror*, December 10, 1898, p. 18; December 17, 1898, p. 18.

35. *The New York Dramatic Mirror*, November 19, 1898, p. 18.

36. *The New York Dramatic Mirror*, January 21, 1899, p. 19. As late as April 1900, the title *Clorindy or The Origin of the Cake Walk* reappears, under the management of Sam Corker, playing at Swanson's Ripple Villa in Atlantic City. It apparently was well received. (*The Freeman*, April 21, 1900).

37. Abbie Mitchell, "Autobiographical Notes of 40 Years on Stage," MCP Box 157-7 Folder 24.

38. Cook, "From *Clorindy* to *The Red Moon*."

39. "Clorindy Notes," MCP Box 157-9 Folder 9.

40. Ibid.

41. Ibid.

42. There are unsubstantiated claims that the Cooks also married in Washington, D.C. The marital records of all New York City boroughs and the District of Columbia have been investigated, to no avail.

43. Isidore Witmark and Isaac Goldberg. The Story of the House of Witmark: From Ragtime to Swingtime (New York: Lee Furman, 1939), 195–196.

44. Mabel Rowland, ed., *Bert Williams—Son of Laughter* (New York: English Crafters, 1923), 37.

45. Tom Fletcher, *100 Years of the Negro in Show Business* (1954; reprint, New York: Da Capo Press, 1984), 230.

46. Henry G. Sampson, *Blacks in Blackface* (Metuchen, N.J.: Scarecrow Press, 1980), 278.

47. *The New York Times*, April 3, 1900, p. 9.

48. Unidentified clipping, D. F. P., December 19, 1899, *Policy Players* folder, Harvard Theater Collection; ad for Williams and Walker's first big show, *The Policy Players*, circa 1900 in Sampson, *Blacks in Blackface*, 80.

49. *The Colored American*, November 18, 1899, p. 5.

50. Abbie Mitchell, "Autobiographical Notes of 40 Years on Stage,"MCP Box 157-7 Folder 24.

51. Ibid., unless otherwise indicated.

52. The birth and marriage sequence of events was further confirmed with Mercer Cook in an interview with the author.

53. Abbie Mitchell, "Autobiographical Notes of 40 Years on Stage," MCP Box 157-7 Folder 24.

54. Johnson, *Along This Way*, 175.

55. *The New York Times*, June 26, 1900, p. 7.

56. For more discussion with musical examples, see Thomas L. Riis, *More Than Just Minstrel Shows: The Rise of Black Musical Theatre at the Turn of the Century*, Institute for Studies in American Music Monographs: No. 33 (New York: City University of New York, 1992), 38–39.

57. *The New York Dramatic Mirror*, August 25, 1900, p. 19.

58. The act of ridiculing individuals, groups, ideas, or institutions results in feelings of superiority on the part of the joke tellers. See Lawrence W. Levine, *Black Culture and Black Consciousness* (New York: Oxford University Press, 1979), 308.

Chapter 6

1. Abbie Mitchell, "The Negro in the Theatre," MCP Box 157-7 Folder 25.

2. Synopsis of *In Dahomey* found on a program of the New York Theatre for the week of March 9, 1903, Museum of the City of New York, Theatre Archive.

3. Abbie Mitchell, "The Negro in the Theatre," MCP Box 157-7 Folder 25.

4. James Weldon Johnson, *Along This Way* (1933; reprint, New York: Viking Press, 1968), 175. *The Cannibal King* libretto is housed at The Library of Congress. It indicates that the composer is unknown and that its authors are Bob Cole and J. W. Johnson, 1901. There are four Cook songs referenced in the *Dahomey* libretto, however: "The Leader of the Colored Aristocracy," "Vassar Girl," "For Florida," and "Spread de News" (a.k.a. "Captain Kidd").

5. Before Broadway, *In Dahomey* was scheduled to appear in Cincinatti, November 30–December 6, 1902; Louisville, Kentucky, November 24–29; Pittsburg, November 3–9; Cleveland, November 10–17; Columbus, Ohio, December 8–10; Muncie, Indiana, December 11; Chicago, December 15–21; Bloomington, December 22; Peoria, Illinois, December 23; Alton, Illinois, December 24; Springfield, Illinois, December 25; Decatur, Illinois, December 26; Jacksonville, Illinois, December 27, St. Louis, December 28–January 3, 1903; and Kansas City, Missouri, January 4–11, 1903. See *The Freeman*, November 22, 1902.

6. Unidentified clipping, Bert Williams Vertical File, Schomburg Center, New York Public Library.

7. *The New York Times*, February 19, 1903, *In Dahomey* Folder, Harvard Theater Collection (HTC); *The Freeman*, April 4, 1903, p. 9.

8. *Boston Transcript*, March 21, 1905, *In Dahomey* Folder, HTC.

9. Sylvester Russell, quoted in Henry T. Sampson, *The Ghost Walks: A Chronological History of Black Show Business 1865–1910* (Metuchen, N.J.: Scarecrow Press, 1988), 268–269.

10. See an exhaustive treatment of the history and many variants of *In Dahomey* in Thomas L. Riis, ed., "The Genesis of *In Dahomey*," in *The Music and Scripts of* In Dahomey, Vol. 5, Music of the United States of America (Madison: A-R Editions, 1996).

11. Joseph Holloway defines Africanisms as "those elements of culture found in the New World that are traceable to an African origin." Joseph Holloway, ed., *Africanisms in American Culture* (Bloomington: Indiana University Press, 1991), ix.

12. See Riis, ed., "The Genesis of *In Dahomey*," xviii–xxi.

13. "The business of the day was to begin with the procession of Caboceers," an old traditional ceremony. Sir Richard Burton, *A Mission to Gelele King of Dahome*, ed. C. W. Newbury (New York: Frederick A. Praeger, 1966), 129.

14. *The New York Herald*, October 21, 1902, *In Dahomey* Folder, HTC.

15. Nathan Irvin Huggins, *Harlem Renaissance* (New York: Oxford University Press, 1971), 281.

16. Eric J. Sundquist, *To Wake the Nation: Race in the Making of American Literature* (Cambridge, Mass.: Belknap Press, 1993), 291–294.

17. George W. Walker, "The Real 'Coon' on the American Stage," *Theatre Magazine* supplement (August 1906), 225.

18. Ibid., i–ii.

19. *The New York Herald*, March 6, 1922.

20. *The New York Times*, February 19, 1903, *In Dahomey* Folder, HTC.; Vincent Smith, "Bert Williams: Why Nobody?" (M.A. thesis, University of Maryland, 1979), 15.; Unidentified clipping, February 19, 1903, *In Dahomey* Folder, HTC.

21. Alex Rogers, "I'm a Jonah Man" (New York: M. Witmark & Sons, 1903); reprinted in Ann Charters, *Nobody—The Story of Bert Williams* (New York: Macmillan, 1970), 71.

22. Charters, *Nobody*, 105.

23. William McFerrin Stowe, Jr., "Damned Funny: The Tragedy of Bert Williams," *Journal of Popular Culture* 10 (Summer 1976): 5.

24. *Boston Herald*, March 21, 1905, *In Dahomey* Folder, HTC.

25. *Williams and Walker Scrapbook*, April 29, 1903, p. 11. The New York Public Library, Lincoln Center for the Performing Arts, Billy Rose Theater Collection.

26. *The Tattler*, May 20, 1903, p. 99.

27. *The Sketch* [London], October 2, 1903, p. 412.

28. Jeffrey P. Green, "*In Dahomey* in London in 1903," in *The Black Perspective in Music* 11, no. 1 (Spring 1983): 32.

29. Ibid.

30. Mabel Rowland, ed., *Bert Williams—Son of Laughter* (New York: English Crafters, 1923), 50.

31. Unidentified clipping, May 18, 1903, *In Dahomey* Folder, HTC.

32. *The Sketch*, [London], May 27, 1903, p. 198.

33. *The Tattler*, "Written, Composed, and Played by Coloured Coons: A Chat with the Composer of *In Dahomey*," no. 99, May 20, 1903, p. 300. Located in the *In Dahomey* File, Theatre Museum, London.

34. "Correspondence," MCP Box 157-2 Folder 10.

35. *The Tattler*, May 20, 1903, p. 99.

36. Words and Music by Will Marion Cook, "Swing Along," reprinted in Riis, ed., *The Music and Scripts of* In Dahomey, 155–162.

37. "Correspondence," MCP Box 157-2 Folder 10.

38. Mercer Cook, "From *Clorindy* to *The Red Moon* and Beyond." Paper presented on a "Black American On Stage" panel, C.U.N.Y., October 26, 1978.

39. Unidentified clipping, May 21, 1903, *In Dahomey* Folder, HTC.

40. Quoted in Green, "*In Dahomey* in London," 29, 31–32.

41. *Washington Bee*, October 10, 1903, and April 20, 1907.

42. Riis, ed. *The Music and Scripts of* In Dahomey, lxix.

43. In the same year, Harry von Tilzer was responsible for writing the music for such songs as "In the Sweet Bye and Bye," "The Mansion of Aching Hearts" (a sequel to "A Bird in a Gilded Cage"), "Jennie Lee," "I Just Can't Help Loving That Man," and "When Kate and I Were Coming through the Rye," among others. See Maxwell F. Marcuse, *Tin Pan Alley in Gaslight* (Watkins Glen, N.Y.: Century House, 1959), 282–283.

44. Quoted in Green, "*In Dahomey* in London," 26.

45. *Daily News* [London], May 16, 1903.

46. No newspaper clipping title, n.d. [1903], HTC.

47. *The Tattler*, May 20, 1903, p. 99.

48. *Daily News*, May 16, 1903, p. 6.

49. *The Tattler*, May 20, 1903, p. 99.

50. Ibid.

51. Riis, ed. *The Music and Scripts of* In Dahomey, lx.

52. Ibid.; for an analysis of who composed which segments of "The Czar," xxxiii.

53. *New York* Telegraph, June 24, 1903.

54. Abbie Mitchell, "A Negro Invasion of Buckingham Palace in 1903," MCP Box 157-7 Folder 29.

55. *The Era*, June 20, 1903, p. 12.

56. Gates, Jr., and West, *The African American Century*, 40.

57. Mitchell, "Negro Invasion," April 20, 1904, MCP Box 157-7 Folder 29.

Chapter 7

1. Letter from Will Marion Cook to Booker T. Washington, New York City, March 29, 1901, reprinted in Louis R. Harlan and Raymond W. Smock, eds., *The Booker T. Washington Papers*, Vol. 6 (Chicago: University of Illinois Press, 1981), 67–68.

2. "Writings by Mercer Cook," MCP Box 157-4 Folder 6. When Will Marion lived in Chattanooga with his maternal grandparents, he indicated, he heard *real* Negro melodies for the first time. The Fisk Jubilee experience seems to contradict the Chattanooga one.

3. Letter from Cook to Washington. Harlan and Smock, *Booker T. Washington Papers*, 67.

4. James Weldon Johnson, *Black Manhattan* (3rd ed., New York: Atheneum, 1972), 120–121.

5. Ibid., 122; Alain Leroy Locke, *The Negro and His Music* (New York: Arno Press, 1969), 65; Edgar A. Toppin, *A Biographical History of Blacks in America Since 1528* (New York: David McKay, 1969), 272.

6. Gunther Schuller, *Early Jazz* (New York: Oxford University Press, 1968), 183.

7. *The Freeman*, July 8, 1905.

8. Eileen Southern, *Biographical Dictionary of Afro-American and African Musicians*, (Westport, Conn.: Greenwood Press, 1982), 270.

9. *The Freeman*, November 4, 1905.

10. *The Freeman*, January 20, 1906.

11. Tom Fletcher, *100 Years of the Negro in Show Business* (1954; reprint, New York: Da Capo Press, 1984), 129.

12. Mabel Rowland, *Bert Williams* (1923; reprint, New York: Negro Universities Press, 1969), 71–72.

13. Gerald Bordman, *American Musical Theatre: A Chronicle* (New York: Oxford University Press, 1978), 219.

14. Ann Charters, *Nobody—The Story of Bert Williams* (New York: Macmillan, 1970), 83. According to *The Freeman* (September 9, 1905), several donkeys and a few lions were also added to provide a realistic effect.

15. Mabel Rowland, ed., *Bert Williams—Son of Laughter* (New York: English Crafters, 1923), 66–67.

16. *The New York Times*, February 21, 1906, p. 9.

17. "*Abyssinia,*" *The Theatre Magazine*, April 1906, xiv.

18. *The Freeman*, February 29, 1908.

19. Unidentified clipping, February 1906, *Abyssinia* Folder, HTC.

20. Unidentified clipping, August 18, 1906, *Abyssinia* Folder, HTC.

21. Henry T. Sampson, *Blacks in Blackface: Source Book on Early Black Musical Shows* (Metuchen, N.J.: Scarecrow Press, 1980), 115.

22. Undated excerpt included among the critical reviews in a souvenir program from the Pekin Theatre, November 22, 1907. Personal collection.

23. L. Lucas, "The Negro in Illinois Theater," from the *Illinois Writers Project—Theatre*, Vivian G. Harsh Collection, Mss./IWP/42,13, Carter G. Woodson Branch, Chicago Public Library.

24. Lucas, "The Negro in Illinois Theatre," 15–16.

25. "J. Ed Green—Director of Amusements, New Pekin Theatre, Chicago," *Alexander's Magazine* 3, no. 4, (Feb. 15, 1907): 190 (reprint, New York: Negro Universities Press, 1969).

26. Reprinted article from *The Inter Ocean* (1907) published as an advertisement in a Pekin Theatre Program, November 22, 1907.

27. Lucie F. Pierce, "The Only Colored Stock Theatre in America," *The Theatre Magazine* 8 (Jan. 1908): 28.

28. Mercer Cook, personal letter, August 17, 1983. He summarizes Will Marion Cook's notes on his Pekin Theatre experience. Abbie Mitchell's move is further documented in *The Freeman*, November 24, 1906.

29. "Robert (Bob) Motts," Eileen Southern, ed., *Biographical Dictionary of Afro-American and African Musicians* (Westport, Conn.: Greenwood Press, 1982), 283.

30. Mercer Cook, personal letter, August 17, 1983.

31. *New York Age*, February 20, 1908, p. 6.

32. Ibid., p. 10.

33. Unidentified clipping, 1908, *Bandanna* Land Folder, HTC.

34. *Boston Globe*, September 6, 1908, *Bandanna Land* Folder, HTC.

35. Ibid.

36. *Song Libretto of Williams and Walker's "Bandanna Land."* Book and lyrics by J. A. Shipp and Alex Rogers. Music by Will Marion Cook and Bertha Williams. (New York: Gotham-Attucks Music Co., 1907), 7. Located in the Music Library of the University of Illinois at Urbana. The two songs appear to be virtually the same except that the G. Schirmer 1912 edition of "Rain-Song" is in c minor and the Gotham-Attucks 1907 edition is in d minor. There are also a few text differences.

37. Words by Alex Rogers, music by Will Marion Cook, "Rain-Song" (New York: G. Schirmer, 1912).

38. Williams starred in a series of moderately successful one-reel comedies for Biograph in 1914, and the poker routine was also part of the film "Late Hours." It has been preserved in the film short "Natural Born Gambler," made in 1916.

39. Tom Fletcher, *100 Years of the Negro in Show Business* (New York: Burdge, 1954), 239–240.

40. *The Freeman,* August 22, 1908. More recently, a jazzed version of "Bon Bon Buddy" was included in the touring *Williams and Walker,* with the Broadway stars Ben Harney and Vondie Curtis-Hall. (See review in *The Atlanta Constitution,* June 17, 1987, p. C2.)

41. *New York Age,* August 27, 1908, p. 6.

42. In fact a crusade was inaugurated against the dance by the print media, churches, and authorities of several cities. *New York Age,* September 24, 1908, p. 6.

Chapter 8

1. Paul Laurence Dunbar, "We Wear the Mask," in *The Norton Anthology: African American Literature,* ed., Henry Louis Gates, Jr., and Nellie Y. McKay (New York: W. W. Norton, 1997), 896.

2. Eileen Southern, *Biographical Dictionary of Afro-American and African Musicians* (Westport, Conn.: Greenwood Press, 1982), 3–4, 212, 337.

3. James Weldon Johnson, *Along This Way: The Autobiography of James Weldon Johnson* (1933; reprint, New York: Viking Press, 1968), 172–173.

4. Will Marion Cook, "*Clorindy*: The Origin of the Cakewalk," *Theatre Arts* (Sept. 1947): 61–65. Reprinted in *Readings in Black American Music,* ed. Eileen Southern (2nd ed., New York: W. W. Norton, 1983), 233.

5. Cook, "*Clorindy*: The Origin of the Cakewalk," 232.

6. Addison Gayle, Jr., *Oak and Ivy: A Biography of Paul Laurence Dunbar* (Garden City, N.Y.: Doubleday, 1971), 87–88.

7. Gayle, *Oak and Ivy,* 17–18.

8. George Rawick, *The American Slave: A Composite Autobiography,* vol. 1, Alabama Narratives (Westport, Conn.: Greenwood Press, 1972), 51, 96, 100, 206, 279, quoted in Joseph Boskin, *Sambo—The Rise and Demise of an American Jester* (New York: Oxford University Press, 1986), 49.

9. W. E. B. Du Bois, *The Souls of Black Folk* (1903; reprint, New York: New American Library, 1969), 45.

10. Words and music by Will Marion Cook, "Swing Along" (New York: G. Schirmer, 1912).

11. Eric Lott, *Love and Theft: Blackface Minstrelsy and the American Working Class* (New York: Oxford University Press, 1995), 25, 243. Lott further credits Michael Rogin for a similar point. In *Black Skin, White Masks,* Frantz Fanon remarks that in the white imagination, "the Negro . . . *is* a penis," 170.

12. Du Bois, *The Souls of Black Folk,* 45.

13. Mel Watkins, *On the Real Side: Laughing Lying, and Signifying, the Underground Tradition of African-American Humor That Transformed American Culture, from Slavery to Richard Pryor* (New York: Simon & Schuster, 1994), 126.

14. Interview with Mercer Cook, July 24, 1983, Silver Spring, Md.

15. Words by Harry B. Smith and Cecil Mack, music by Will Marion Cook, "The Little Gypsy Maid" (New York: Harry Von Tilzer, 1902).

16. Words by Will Marion Cook and Cecil Mack, music by Will Marion Cook, "Brown-Skin Baby Mine" (New York: G. Schirmer, 1902).

17. Gerald Bordman, *American Musical Theatre: A Chronicle* (New York: Oxford University Press, 1978), 181.

18. See *New York Age*, October 28 ,1915, p. 6; and *Freeman*, October 23, 1915, p. 4.

19. Words by Lester A. Walton, music by Will Marion Cook, "Mammy" (New York: Artmusic, 1916).

20. For more discussion of songs used as "alerting" mechanisms for Underground Railroad escapes, see Eileen Southern, *The Music of Black Americans: A History* (3rd ed.; New York: W. W. Norton, 1997), 142–145.

21. Watkins, *On the Real Side,* 76.

22. *The New York Age,* December 9, 1915.

23. *The New York Age, January 24, 1916.*

24. Gayle, *Oak and Ivy,* 35.

25. Barry N. Schwartz and Robert Disch, *White Racism: Its History, Pathology, and Practice* (New York: Dell, 1970), 165.

26. A recording of Abbie Mitchell singing "Red Red Rose" is among the restricted Cook Papers at the Moorland-Spingarn Research Center of Howard University, "Abbey [sic] Mitchell, Hammerstein, WABC, 12/10/37," Box 157-19, Item 2.

27. See Paul Charosh and Robert A. Fremont, eds., *Song Hits from the Turn of the Century* (New York: Dover, 1975), 101–110.

28. Interview with Mercer Cook.

29. This folk saying appears in many variations, including slave songs and blues lyrics. See Julius Lester, *To Be a Slave* (New York: Scholastic, 1968), 101.

Chapter 9

1. *New York Telegraph,* n.d., Abbie Mitchell Scrapbook, Locke Collection, Billy Rose Theatre Collection, New York Public Library at Lincoln Center.

2. Unnamed news clipping, August 5, 1905, Abbie Mitchell Scrapbook, Box 157-8 Folder 22.

3. *New York Age,* August 6, 1908, p. 6.

4. *New York Telegraph,* May 20, 1909, Abbie Mitchell Scrapbook, Envelope No. 1484. The quotation from Abbie Mitchell is from Abbie Mitchell Scrapbook, Box 157-8 Folder 22.

5. Isadore Witmark and Isaac Goldberg, *The Story of the House of Witmark— From Ragtime to Swingtime* (New York: Lee Furman, 1939), 195–196.

6. Rudi Blesh, *Combo: USA (Eight Lives in Jazz)* (New York: Chilton Book Co., 1971), 194–195.

7. Correspondence from James Weldon Johnson to William C. Graves indicating whether or not Cook would be a viable candidate to head a proposed music school in New York City. James Weldon Johnson Collection, William C. Graves, Series No. I, Folder No. 172, Beinecke Library, Yale University.

8. James Weldon Johnson, *Along This Way: The Autobiography of James Weldon Johnson* (1933; reprint, New York: Viking Press, 1961), 173.

9. See Reid Badger, *A Life in Ragtime: A Biography of James Reese Europe* (New York: Oxford University Press, 1995); James Weldon Johnson, *Black Manhattan* (3rd ed., New York: Atheneum, 1972); 122; Maud Cuney-Hare, *Negro Musicians and Their Music,* 1936 (reprint, New York: Da Capo Press, 1974, 140; and Alain LeRoy Locke, *The Negro and His Music* (New York: Arno Press, 1969), 65.

10. *The Chicago Defender,* July 19, 1944.

11. *The New York Age,* April 28, 1910.

12. Tom Fletcher, *100 Years of the Negro in Show Business* (New York: Burdge, 1954), 264.

13. *The New York Age,* September 24, 1948.

14. Natalie Curtis, "The Negro's Contribution to the Music of America," in *The Craftsman,* February 1913; reprinted in Allen Schoener, ed., *Harlem on My Mind* (New York: Random House, 1968), 26–27.

15. Olly Wilson, "The Black-American Composer and the Orchestra in the Twentieth Century," *The Black Perspective in Music,* 14, no. 1, Special Issue (Winter 1986): 26–34.

16. Fletcher, *100 Years,* 261.

17. Maurice Peress, *Dvořák to Duke Ellington* (New York: Oxford University Press, 2004), 13.

18. *The New York Age,* May 9, 1912. See reprint of this and other pertinent articles in "In Retrospect: Black Music Concerts in Carnegie Hall, 1912–1915," *The Black Perspective in Music* 6 no. 1 (Spring 1978): 71–88; *The New York Times,* March 20, 1912.

19. *The Evening Post* (New York), March 13, 1914; reprinted in Robert Kimball and William Bolcom, *Reminiscing with Sissle and Blake* (New York: Viking Press, 1973), 61.

20. James Weldon Johnson, *Along This Way* (1933; reprint, New York: Viking Press, 1968), 173.

21. *The New York Age,* May 9, 1912. The first Carnegie Hall "Concert of Negro Music" held on May 2, 1912, was: [Badger, *A Life in Ragtime,* 264–265]

Part One

1. "The Clef Club March" .... Europe
   The Clef Club Orchestra
2. "Lit'l Gal" ... J. Rosamond Johnson, words by Paul Laurence Dunbar
   Sung and played by the composer
3. a. "Dance of the Marionettes"......................... Woolford
   b. "You're Sweet to Your Mammy Just the Same" .... Johnson
   The Versatile Entertainers Quintette
4. a. "Tout a Vous"... Tyers
   b. "Panama—characteristic dance"....................... Tyers
   Orchestra conducted by the composer
5. a. "Jean" .... Burleigh
   b. "Mon Coeur s'Ouvre ta Voix" from Samson
   and Delilah .... Saint-Saens
   (A last-minute substitution for Stephen Foster's "Old Folks at Home")
   Miss Elizabeth Payne, Contralto
6. "Benedictus" .... Bohlen
   Choir of St. Phillips's Church
   Paul C. Bohlen, Organist

Part Two

7. "Swing Along"... Cook
   Clef Club Chorus
8. "Danse Heroique" .... Johnson
   Piano Solo by the composer

9. a. "Hula—Hawaiian Dance" .... Europe
   b. "On Bended Knee"................................ Burleigh
      Clef Club Orchestra
10. "By the Waters of Babylon"...................... Coleridge-Taylor
    Choir of St. Phillip's Church
11. a. "Dearest Memories"
    b. "The Belle of the Lighthouse"
    c. "Take Me Back to Dear Old Dixie"
    d. "Old Black Joe"
       The Royal Poinciana Quartette
12. "The Rain Song" .... Cook, words by Alex Rogers
    Clef Club Chorus and Deacon Johnson's Martinique Quartette
13. a. "Lorraine Waltzes"................................. Europe
    b. "Strength of the Nation," dedicated to the proposed
       Colored Regiment................................. Europe
       Clef Club Orchestra

22. Ibid.

23. Fletcher, *100 Years*, 260.

24. Noble Sissle, "Memoirs of Lieutenant 'Jim' Europe," October 1942, 22–23, NAACP Records 1940–1955, Group II, J Box 56, General Miscellany, Library of Congress, 33. This was not an eye-witness account, but one Europe conveyed to Sissle some years later.

25. *The New York Age*, January 1, 1914.

26. Badger, *A Life in Ragtime*, 74–75. See reprinted program schedule of Exposition events in Joshua Berrett, "The Golden Anniversary of the Emancipation Proclamation," *The Black Perspective in Music* 16 (Spring 1988): 76–77.

27. Will Marion Cook and Alex Rogers, *Songs of Sunny Lands and Black Bohemia* or *Darkydom* (a forty-minute sketch of Negro songs and dances), August 15, 1911. Typewritten libretto located at the Library of Congress, Music Division.

28. *The Freeman*, October 23, 1915, p. 4.

29. One *Variety* reviewer described them as "a funnier team than Williams and Walker" (November 5, 1915, p. 18).

30. *The Freeman*, October 23, 1915, p. 4.

31. Ibid.

32. *Variety*, November 5, 1915, p. 18.

33. *New York Age*, October 28, 1915, p. 6, and *The Freeman*, October 23, 1915, p. 4.

34. Words by James W. Johnson, music by Will Marion Cook, "My Lady's Lips Am Lik de Honey" (New York: G. Schirmer, 1915).

35. *New York Age*, January 6, 1934, p. 6.

36. Ibid.

37. *The Freeman*, October 23, 1915, p. 4.

38. *New York Age*, October 28, 1915, p. 6.

39. *The Freeman*, October 23, 1915, p. 4.

40. *The New York Tribune,* November 22, 1914; *The Evening Post* (New York), March 13, 1914.

41. Irene Castle, *Castles In the Air* (1958; reprint, New York: Da Capo, 1980), 115.

42. Irene Castle McLaughlin, "Jim Europe—A Reminiscence," *Opportunity* (March 1930): 90–91.

43. James Reese Europe, "A Negro Explains 'Jazz,'" *Literary Digest* 61, no. 4 (April 26, 1919): 28; reprinted Eileen Southern, ed., *Readings in Black American Music,* 2nd ed. (New York: W. W. Norton, 1983), 239.

44. "The Great Marion Incident," an undated, unidentified clipping, MCP Box 157-9 Folder 42.

45. Europe, "A Negro Explains 'Jazz,'" 29.

46. Kimball and Bolcom, *Reminiscing with Sissle and Blake,* 65.

47. *St. Louis Post-Dispatch,* June 10, 1918, reprinted in Kimball and Bolcom, *Reminiscing with Sissle and Blake,* 67–68. Noble Sissle describes a specific concert program given by the army band on Lincoln's birthday in France and the audience's favorable response, particularly to ragtime.

48. Leroy Ostransky, *Jazz City—The Impact of Our Cities on the Development of Jazz* (Englewood Cliffs, N.J.: Prentice-Hall, 1978), 211.

49. For details of the murder, see Badger, *A Life in Ragtime,* 214–216.

50. Kimball and Bolcom, *Reminiscing with Sissle and Blake,* 72.

51. *The New York Times,* May 12, 1919.

Chapter 10

1. Eric Foner, ed., *America's Black Past: A Reader in Afro-American History* (New York: Harper & Row, 1970), 380.

2. Tom Fletcher, *100 Years of the Negro in Show Business* (New York: Burdge, 1954), 187.

3. Olly Wilson, "The Black-American Composer and the Orchestra in the Twentieth Century," *The Black Perspective in Music* 14, no. 1, Special Issue (Winter 1986): 26–34.

4. Fletcher, *100 Years in Show Business,* 187.

5. Youngstown *Daily Vindicator,* February 21, 1919, p. 11; April 11, 1919, p. 31; *Canton Daily News,* April 8, 1919, p. 8.

6. Quoted in Chris Goddard, *Jazz Away from Home* (New York: Paddington Press, 1979), 52.

7. Natalie Spencer, "Tales of the Syncopated Orchestra, *Dancing Times* (Feb. 1921): 411.

8. *The New York Age,* March 22, 1919, p. 6.

9. *Chicago Daily Tribune,* April 21, 1919, p. 21; April 29, 1919, p. 21.

10. Goddard, "Arthur Briggs," *Jazz Away from Home,* 282.

11. Howard Rye, "The Southern Syncopated Orchestra," in *Under the Imperial Carpet: Essays in Black History 1780–1950* (Crawley, England: Rabbit Press, 1986), 218.

12. The orchestra recruited additional players while abroad, causing their number to increase from 25 to 35. *Variety* 55, no. 9 (July 25, 1919): 4.

13. Fletcher, *100 Years,* 268; Program of SSO's European Season.

14. Interview of Arthur Briggs by James Lincoln Collier, February 25–26, 1982, The Institute of Jazz Studies, Jazz Oral History Project, Rutgers University, New Brunswick, N.J., 95, MCP Box 157-9 Folder 25. See appendix C for a complete listing of the orchestral personnel.

15. Ernest Ansermet, "Sur un Orchestre Negre," reprinted in *Escrits Sur La Musique* (Neuchatels Suisse: A la Baconniere, 1971), 172–173;,178; Ernest Ansermet, "Prologue: Sidney Bechet in Europe, 1919," ed. Martin Williams, trans. Walter E. Schapp, reprinted in *The Art of Jazz* (New York: Oxford University Press, 1959), 3–4, 6; Ernest Ansermet, "Bechet and Jazz Visit Europe, 1919," ed. Ralph de Toledano, trans. Walter E. Schapp, reprinted in *Frontiers of Jazz* (1947; 2nd ed. New York: Frederick Ungar, 1962), 112, 116–117.

16. Sidney Bechet, *Treat It Gentle* (New York: Hill and Wang, 1960), 127; Albert McCarthy, *Big Band Jazz* (New York: G. P. Putnam's Sons, 1974), 309.

17. Bechet, *Treat It Gentle*, 128; *Chicago Defender*, January 3, 1920, p. 7.

18. Jean-Christophe Averty, "Sidney Bechet 1919–1922," *Jazz Hot*, no. 250 (May 1969): 23.

19. Bertrand Demeusy, "The Bertin Depestre Salnave Musical Story," *Storyville 78*, (August–September, 1978): 209; *Variety* 59, no. 1 (May 28, 1920): 2. Letter from Arthur Briggs to Marva Carter, November 20, 1980, Paris, France.

20. Jean-Christophe Averty, "Sidney Bechet 1919–1922," *Jazz Hot*, no. 250 (May 1960): 23; Rye, "SSO," 228–229; *Variety* (August 20, 1920): 2; Lattimore disclosed the details of the battle with Cook over the SSO in *The New York Age*, April 24, 1920, p. 6.

21. *Variety* 61, no. 5 (December 24, 1920): 2.

22. *The New York Age*, October 15, 1921, p. 1; *Variety* 64, no. 8 (October 14, 1921): 2; *Glasgow Herald*, October 10, 1921, p. 9, quoted in Edward S. Walker, "A New Look at the S. S. O.," *Storyville* 51 (February–March 1974): 96; *The Times* (London), October 10, 1921, p. 10, lists 35 to 37 SSO members; whereas the *Glasgow Herald*, October 10, 1921, p. 9, mentions 32.

23. Edward S. Walker, "The Southern Syncopated Orchestra," *Storyville* 42 (August–September 1972): 207–208; McCarthy, *Big Band Jazz*, 309.

24. Ted Heath, *Listen to My Music* (London: Frederick Muller, 1957), 31.

25. This message appeared on a poster of the New York Syncopated Orchestra reproduced in Samuel B. Charters and Leonard Kunstadt, *Jazz—A History of the New York Scene* (Garden City, N.Y.: Doubleday, 1962), 75–76.

Chapter 11

1. *Chicago Defender*, March 23, 1923; Walter C. Allen, *Hendersonia: The Music of Fletcher Henderson and His Musicians: A Bio-Discography*, (Highland Park, N.J., Walter C. Allen, 1973), 44–45.

2. Oberlin Archive File 28/2/Box 2.

3. Walter C. Allen, *Hendersonia*, 45.

4. *The New York Age*, May 29, 1923.

5. *The New York Age*, July 21, 1923.

6. *The New York Age*, July 28, 1923.

7. *The New York Age*, January 19, 1924; January 26, 1924.

8. Eileen Southern, *Biographical Dictionary of Afro-American and African Musicians* (Westport, Conn.: Greenwood Press, 1982), 82.

9. *The New York Age*, January 9, 1926.

10. *The New York Age*, November 5, 1927.

11. *The New York Age*, December 10, 1927.

12. *The New York Age*, February 23, 1929.

13. *The New York Age*, April 6, 1929; Gerald Bordman, *American Musical Theatre: A Chronicle*, (New York: Oxford University Press, 1978), 455; Letter from Mercer Cook to Daniel I. McNamara of ASCAP, August 31, 1950, ASCAP Correspondence File.

14. *The New York Age*, January 4, 1930; January 18, 1930.

15. *The Freeman*, May 8, 1915; *Crisis* 10 June 10, 1915; *The New York Age*, February 7, 1931; March 21, 1931; June 4, 1932.

16. March 10, 1932, handwritten date indicated on manuscript. Personal collection.

17. *The New York Age*, June 4, 1932.

18. Tom Whaley—Reel III, Smithsonian Institution Jazz Oral History Project, Rutgers University Archive, The Institute of Jazz Studies, March 1980.

19. *The New York Age*, January 6, 1934.

20. *Journal and Guide (Norfolk)*, August 11, 1934; *Chicago Defender*, August 11, 1934.

21. *Washington Bee*, September 14, 1935, clipping from (Music) Vertical File. The Library Division, Moorland-Spingarn Research Center, Howard University.

22. Letter to Alain Locke from Cook, July 28, 1936, Alain Locke Papers, Manuscript Division, Moorland-Spingarn Research Center, Howard University.

23. *Black Dispatch*, August 6, 1938, clipping from Will Marion Cook Vertical File, The Library Division, Moorland-Spingarn Research Center, Howard University.

24. Claude Barnett Papers, Chicago Historical Society.

25. "Writings by Abbie Mitchell," MCP Box 157-7 Folder 24.

26. Ibid.

27. Edward Kennedy Ellington, *Music Is My Mistress*, (Garden City, N.Y.: Doubleday, 1973), 96–97.

28. There is an extant program in The Schomburg Collection of a Carnegie Hall performance on Sunday, November 18, featuring Sissieretta Jones. Although the year is not mentioned, on the basis of the repertory used and the assisting performers for the program, the most likely year is 1893. Will Marion Cook's name, however, does not appear on this program. See Willia Estelle Daughtry's "Sissieretta Jones: A Study of the Negro's Contribution to Nineteenth Century American Concert and Theatrical Life" (Ph.D. dissertation, Syracuse University, 1968) 56, 202.

John Graziano has confirmed that Will Marion Cook was a participant in a Carnegie Hall Concert with Sissieretta Jones on February 13, 1893, as a fundraiser for the World's Fair in Chicago. See *New York Review*, February 13, 1893.

29. "Arthur Briggs" in Chris Goddard's *Jazz Away from Home* (New York: Paddington Press, 1979), 281. Tom Whaley's version places Cook in Chicago playing with the symphony band [?]. He was not made first violinist, so he broke his violin and refused to play again. See Smithsonian Institution Jazz Oral History Project, Tom Whaley—Reel III, March 1980, 56 and 58. Located in the Rutgers Institute of Jazz Studies Archive.

There is no known record of verification that Cook ever played with the Boston Symphony Orchestra or the Chicago Symphony Orchestra. There is the possibility, however, that he might have played in "a Boston or Chicago orchestra" rather than *the* Boston or Chicago Symphony Orchestra.

30. Bechet, *Treat It Gentle*, (New York: Hill and Wang, 1960), 125.

31. Tom Fletcher, *100 Years of the Negro in Show Business* (1954; reprint, New York: Da Capo Press, 1984), 259.

32. Lester A. Walton, "Will Marion Cook," *New York Age*, May 7, 1908, p. 6.

33. Will Marion Cook autobiographical notes, personal collection.

34. *The Afro-American*, October 22, 1938. Cook Vertical File, The Library Division, Moorland-Spingarn Research Center, Howard University. This poem was excerpted from Cook's unfinished autobiography, which he aptly titled "A Hell of a Life."

35. This letter appeared in the black press under the caption, "Noted Musician Assails White Author's Works," *New York News*, October 29, 1927. Cook Vertical File, Schomburg Collection, and James Weldon Johnson Collection, Beinecke Library, Yale University.

36. Correspondence to Claude C. Barnett of the Negro Associated Press, June 14, 1941, Claude C. Barnett Papers, Chicago Historical Society.

Will Marion Cook may have suffered from a manic-depressive disorder during most of his life and career. This would account for his sporadic creative output, his breakdown, and prolonged ill health.

37. *Pittsburg Courier*, November 4, 1944, p. 7. Will Marion Cook Vertical File, The Library Division, Moorland-Spingarn Research Center, Howard University.

38. Will Marion Cook Vertical File, The Library Division, Moorland-Spingarn Research Center, Howard University.

Chapter 12

1. James Weldon Johnson, *Along This Way* (1933; New York: Viking Press, 1968), 173.

2. *The Freeman*, May 2, 1903, p. 5.

3. Ibid., March 3, 1906, p. 5.

4. *The New York Age*, June 11, 1914, p. 6.

5. John Graziano, "Sentimental Songs, Rags and Transformations: The Emergence of the Black Musical, 1895–1910," in *Musical Theatre in America: Papers and Proceedings of the Conference on the Musical Theatre in America*, ed. Glenn Loney (Westport, Conn.: Greenwood Press, 1984), 221.

6. From an article by Kurt Schindler on "Will Marion Cook" which appeared in *Schirmer's Bulletin of New Music*, October 15, 1912. "Writings about Will Marion Cook," MCP Box 157-9 Folder 34.

7. Apparently Jordan wept as he listened from outside the theater to the thunderous applause for the song's first performance—as a Negro he had not been permitted to enter the theater. {Terry Waldo, *This Is Ragtime* [New York: Hawthorn Books, 1976], 127.}

8. *Lost Sounds: Blacks and the Birth of the Recording Industry 1891–1922*, Archeophone 1005 (St. Joseph, Ill.: Archeophone Records, 2005). This group appeared in concert on November 21, 1913, at Washington's Metropolitan A.M.E. Church; on February 28, 1914, at the Howard Theater in Washington, D.C.; and at the Carnegie Hall Concert for New York's Music School Settlement for Colored People on March ll, 1914. (See Tim Brooks, *Lost Sounds: Blacks and the Birth of The Recording Industry, 1890–1919* [Urbana: University of Illinois Press, 2005], 294–295.)

9. Ibid.

1. Even though he was legally married to Abbie Mitchell for only a short time, the two maintained a close professional and personal relationship until his death. Soon after Abbie Mitchell's marriage to William Charles Phillips during the summer of 1910, she announced her retirement from the stage to become a housewife. Her new husband objected to her remaining on the stage, and she initially complied with his wishes. (*New York Age*, August 18, 1910, p. 6.) However, by the next year Abbie Mitchell was performing in a theatrical production by Will Marion Cook. (*New York Age*, August 18, 1910, p. 6.)

2. *New York Age*, July 29, 1944; *Chicago Defender*, July 29, 1944.

3. Located at 4611 Benning Road, SE, in the District of Columbia, this is the last remaining large black cemetery in the city. Since it was founded in 1895, many persons of local and national acclaim have been interred there, including the Reverend Sterling Brown, John Wesley Cromwell, Daniel Payne Murray, and John Mercer Langston (Will Marion's namesake). Today the cemetery stands locked and abandoned as a result of negligence, political disputes, and lack of funds. I was unable to locate a marker for Will Marion Cook. (Sandra Fitzpatrick and Maria R. Goodwin, *The Guide to Black Washington* [3rd printing; New York: Hippocrene Books, 1993], 58).

4. Darlene Clark Hine, ed., *Black Women in America: An Historical Encyclopedia* (New York: Carlson, 1993), 802–803. See the Mercer Cook Papers.

5. "Biographical Sketch of Clarence Cameron White," n.d., 1–2 Washington Conservatory of Music Records Box 122-44 Folder 679; Manuscript Division, Moorland-Spingarn Research Center, Howard University.

6. Clarence Cameron White, handwritten note of sympathy to the Cook family, July 22, 1944. "Abbie Mitchell," Box 157-7 Folder 14.

7. Edward Kennedy Ellington, *Music Is My Mistress* (New York: Doubleday, 1973), 97.

8. James Lincoln Collier, *The Making of Jazz* (New York: Dell, 1978), 244–245.

9. Mark Tucker, "The Genesis of *Black, Brown and Beige*," and Scott De-Veaux, "*Black, Brown and Beige* and the Critics," in *Black Music Research Journal* 13, no. 2 (Fall 1993): 72–73; 128.

10. Meyer Weinberg, ed., *W. E. B. DuBois: A Reader* (New York: Harper & Row, 1970), xv.

11. Mercer Cook, interview by author, Washington, D.C., June 14, 1983.

12. Al Rose, *Eubie Blake* (New York: Schirmer, 1979), 42.

13. Lawrence T. Carter, *Eubie Blake—Keys of Memory* (Detroit: Balamp Publishing, 1979), 80.

14. Mercer Cook, "Will Marion Cook: He Helped Them All," *Crisis* (October 1944): 322.

15. Ibid., 432–433.

16. Eileen Southern, The Music of Black Americans: A History (3rd ed., New York: W. W. Norton, 1983), 422–423; Eileen Southern, Biographical Dictionary of Afro-American and African Musicians (Westport, Conn.: Greenwood Press, 1982), 203.

17. W. C. Handy, "Cook Was My Ideal," *New York Daily News*, July 1944, MCP Box 157-9 Folder 27.

18. *Chicago Defender*, July 29, 1944.

19. Correspondence from Hall Johnson to Will Marion Cook, August 14, 1941. Mercer Cook Papers, Series H, Box 157-8.

20. Correspondence from Arthur Briggs to Mercer Cook, February 4, 1979, MCP Box 157-1 Folder 28.

21. Natalie Spencer, "Tales of the Syncopated Orchestra," *Dancing Times* (February 1921): 409.

22. Taylor Gordon, *Born to Be* (New York: Covici-Friede Publishers, 1929), 141.

23. Perry Bradford, *Born with the Blues* (New York: Oak Publications, 1965), 98.

24. Ibid., 16.

25. Cook, "He Helped Them All," 322, 328.

26. Ibid, 322.

27. David Ewen, *All the Years of American Popular Music* (Englewood Cliffs, N.J.: Prentice-Hall, 1977), 398.

28. *The Afro-American,* November 18, 1950. Clipping obtained from the Claude Barnett Papers, Chicago Historical Society.

29. See chapter on Broadway Years in Robert Oberfirst's *Al Jolson—You Ain't Heard Nothin' Yet* (New York: A. S. Barnes, 1982), 97–188.

30. Writings by Will Marion Cook, MCP Box 157-9 Folder 15.

31. *Chicago Defender,* July 23, 1944.

32. William M. Banks, *Black Intellectuals: Race and Responsibility in American Life* (New York: W. W. Norton, 1996), 47. See also Alfred A. Moss, Jr., *The American Negro Academy—Voice of the Talented Tenth* (Baton Rouge: Louisiana State University Press, 1981).

33. Du Bois quotes taken from W. E. B. Du Bois, "The Conservation of Races," *W. E. B. Du Bois Speaks: Speeches and Addresses, 1890–1919,* ed. Philip S. Foner (1897; New York, 1970), 77, 84. Anthony Appiah, "The Uncompleted Argument: Du Bois and the Illusion of Race, in *The Idea of Race* (Indianapolis: Hackett Publishing Co., 2000), 120. I am grateful to Dwight Andrews for bringing this article to my attention.

34. Quoted in James G. Spady's, "Indigene = Folksi Equations in the Black Arts," *The Black Scholar* (November/December 1978): 29.

35. Sterling Brown, interview by author, Washington, D.C., August 3, 1983.

36. Négritude is a word coined by the West Indian poet Aime Cesaire which means self-confirmation. It has been called the African personality. It represents "a certain way of speaking, singing, and dancing; of painting and sculpturing, and even of laughing and crying." It points to a humanistic value. See Leopold Sedar Senghor, "Négritude: A Humanism of the Twentieth Century," Fred Lee Hord, et al., *I Am Because We Are: Readings in Black Philosophy* (Amherst: University of Massachusetts Press, 1995), 45–46.

37. Mercer Cook and Stephen E. Henderson, *The Militant Black Writer in Africa and the United States* (Madison: University of Wisconsin Press, 1969), 3.

38. An open letter printed in *The New York News,* October 29, 1927.

39. *Pittsburg Courier,* July [?], 1944, clipping from MCP Box 157-9 Folder 42.

40. *The New York Times,* December 26, 1926, VII, 8:2.

41. See Marshall and Jean Stearn, *Jazz Dance: The Story of American Vernacular Dance* (1968; reprint, New York: Schirmer, 1979), 12–13, 83–84, 110–112, for documentation of the African origin and early appearance of the Charleston in the South as well as the southern roots of the Black Bottom dance among Negroes.

42. *The New York Age,* February 9, 1911, p. 6.

43. W. E. B. Du Bois, "Agitation," in *The Crisis* 1, no. 1 (November 1910): 21; reprinted in Julius Lester, ed., *The Seventh Son: The Thought and Writings of W. E. B. Du Bois* (New York: Random House, 1971), 3–4.

44. Will Marion Cook to Claude Barnett of the Associated Negro Press, August 1, 1941, Chicago Historical Society.

Appendix 3

1. Edward S. Walker, "The Southern Syncopated Orchestra," *Storyville* 42 (August–September 1972): 204. This roster was determined through gathering information from Robert Goffin's *Jazz from the Congo to the Metropolitan* (Garden City, N.Y.: Doubleday, 1944), 70; Howard Rye, "The Southern Syncopated Orchestra," *Under the Imperial Carpet—Essays in Black History 1780–1950,* ed. Rainer Lotz and Ian Pegg (Crawley, England: Rabbit Press, 1986), 218.

SELECT BIBLIOGRAPHY

Books and Articles

Aborn, M. Robert. "The Influence on American Musical Culture of Dvořák's Sojourn in America." Ph.D. diss., Indiana University, 1965.

Allen, Walter C. *The Music of Fletcher Henderson and His Musicians: A Bio-Discography.* Jazz Monographs No. 4, Highland Park, N.J.: Walter C. Allen, 1973.

Anderson, Jervis. *This Was Harlem—A Cultural Portrait, 1900–1950.* New York: Farrar Straus Giroux, 1982.

Ansermet, Ernest. "Bechet and Jazz Visit Europe, 1919." ed. Ralph de Toledano, Trans. Walter E. Schapp. Reprinted in *Frontiers of Jazz.* 2nd ed. New York: Frederick Ungar, 1962, 115–122.

———. "Prologue: Sidney Bechet in Europe, 1919." Reprinted in *The Art of Jazz,* ed. Martin Williams. Trans. Walter E. Schapp. New York: Oxford University Press, 1959, 3–6.

———. "Sur un Orchestra Négre." *Ecrits sur La Musique.* Neuchâtel, Suisse: A la Bacconié, 1971, 171–178.

Averty, Jean-Christophe. "Sidney Bechet 1919–1922." *Jazz Hot,* no. 250 (May 1969): 22–23.

Badger, Reid. *The Great American Fair: The World's Columbian Exposition and American Culture.* Chicago: Nelson Hall, 1979.

———. *A Life in Ragtime: A Biography of James Reese Europe.* New York: Oxford University Press, 1995.

Bardolph, Richard. *The Negro Vanguard.* Westport, Conn: Negro Universities Press, 1959.

Bechet, Sidney. *Treat It Gentle.* New York: Hill and Wang, 1960.

Beckerman, Michael, ed. *Dvořák and His World.* Princeton, N.J.: Princeton University Press, 1993.

———. "Dvořák's 'New World' Largo and *The Song of Hiawatha,"* in *Nineteenth Century Music* 16, no. 1 (Summer 1992): 35–48.

———. *New Worlds of Dvořák: Searching in America for the Composer's Inner Life.* New York: W. W. Norton, 2003.

———. "The Real Value of Yellow Journalism: James Creelman and Antonìn Dvořák." *The Musical Quarterly* 77, no. 4 (Winter 1993): 749–768.

Berger, Morroe, Edward Berger, and James Patrick. *Benny Carter: A Life in American Music,* Vol. I. Metuchen, N.J.: Scarecrow Press, 1982.

Berlin, Edward A. *King of Ragtime: Scott Joplin and His Era.* New York: Oxford University Press, 1994.

———. *Ragtime: A Musical and Cultural History.* Berkeley: University of California Press, 1980.

Beveridge, David R., ed. *Rethinking Dvořák: Views from Five Countries.* New York: Oxford University Press, 1996.

Bigglestone, W. E. "Oberlin College and the Negro Student, 1865–1940." *The Journal of Negro History* 56, no. 3 (July 1971): 198–219.

Blesh, Rudi, and Harriet Janis. *They All Played Ragtime.* 4th ed. New York: Oak Pub., 1971.

Bloom, Ken. *American Song—The Complete Musical Theatre Companion,* Vols. 1 and 2. New York: Facts on File Publications, 1985.

Bond, Frederick W. *The Negro and the Drama.* Washington, D.C.: The Associated Publishers, 1940.

Bontemps, Arna, and Jack Conroy. Anyplace But Here. Reprint. New York: Hill and Wang, 1966.

———. *They Seek a City.* Garden City, N.Y.: Doubleday, 1945.

Bordman, Gerald. *American Musical Theatre: A Chronicle.* New York: Oxford University Press, 1978.

Bradford, Perry. *Born with the Blues.* New York: Oak Pub., 1965.

Brawley, Benjamin. *The Negro Genius: A New Appraisal of the Achievement of the American Negro in Literature and the Fine Arts.* New York: Dodd, Mead & Co., 1937.

———. *Paul Laurence Dunbar: Poet of His People.* Port Washington, N.Y.: Kennikat Press, 1936.

Brunn, H. O. *The Story of the Original Dixieland Jazz Band.* Baton Rouge: Louisiana State University Press, 1960.

Burg, David F. *Chicago's White City of 1893.* Lexington: The University Press of Kentucky, 1976.

Burton, Sir Richard. *A Mission to Gelele King of Dahome.* New York: Frederick A. Praeger, 1966.

Butcher, Margaret Just. *The Negro in American Culture.* New York: Alfred A. Knopf, 1957.

Caemmerer, H. P. *Washington—The National Capital.* Washington, D.C.: U. S. Government Printing Office, 1932.

Campbell, Margaret. *The Great Violinists.* Garden City, N.Y.: Doubleday, 1981.

Carter, Lawrence T. *Eubie Blake: Keys of Memory.* Detroit: Balamp, 1979.

Carter, Marva Griffin. "The Life and Music of Will Marion Cook." Ph.D. diss., University of Illinois at Urbana, 1988.

———. "Removing the 'Minstrel Mask' in the Musicals of Will Marion Cook." *Musical Quarterly* 84, no. 2 (Summer 2000): 206–220.

Charters, Ann. *Nobody: The Story of Bert Williams.* New York: Macmillan, 1970.

Charters, Samuel B., and Leonard Kunstadt. *Jazz: A History of the New York Scene.* New York: Doubleday, 1962.

Chase, Gilbert. *America's Music.* Revised 3rd ed. Urbana: University of Illinois Press, 1987.

Chilton, John. *Jazz.* New York: David McKay, 1979.

————. *Sidney Bechet: The Wizard of Jazz.* New York: Oxford University Press, 1987.

Claghorn, Charles Eugene. *Biographical Dictionary of American Music.* New York: Parker Publishing, 1973.

Clapham, John. *Antonín Dvořák: Musician and Craftsman.* New York: St. Martin's Press, 1966.

————. *Dvořák.* New York: W. W. Norton, 1979.

Cockrell, Dale. *Demons of Disorder: Early Blackface Minstrels and Their World.* Cambridge, UK: Cambridge University Press, 1997.

Collier, James Lincoln. *The Making of Jazz.* New York: Dell, 1978. "The Cook Family in History." *The Negro History Bulletin* 9 (June 1946): 195–196 213–215.

Cook, Will Marion. "Clorindy, the Origin of the Cakewalk." *Theatre Arts* (September 1947): 61–65.

Crawford, Richard. *America's Musical Life: A History.* New York: W. W. Norton, 2001.

Cripps, Thomas. *Slow Fade to Black: The Negro in American Film, 1900–1942.* New York: Oxford University Press, 1977.

Cron, Theodore O., and Burt Goldblatt. *Portrait of Carnegie Hall.* New York: Macmillan, 1966.

Cuney-Hare, Maud. *Negro Musicians and Their Music.* 1936. Reprint, New York: Da Capo Press, 1974.

Cunningham, Virginia. *Paul Laurence Dunbar and His Song.* New York: Biblo and Tannen, 1969.

Dabney, Virginius. *Virginia—The New Dominion.* Garden City, N.Y.: Doubleday, 1971.

Demeusy, Bertrand. "The Bertin Depestre Salnave Musical Story." *Storyville* 78. Trans. Howard Rye. (August–September 1978): 207–219.

Dennison, Sam. *Scandalize My Name: Black Imagery in American Popular Music.* New York: Garland, 1982.

Douglass, Frederick. *Life and Times of Frederick Douglass.* 1892. Reprint, Toronto: Crowell-Collier, 1969.

DuBois W. E. Burghardt. "The Freedmen's Bureau." *Reconstruction in Retrospect: Views from the Turn of the Century, ed.* Richard N. Current. Baton Rouge: Louisiana State University Press, 1969: 52–72.

————. *The Souls of Black Folk.* 1903. Reprint, New York: The American Library, 1969.

Ellington, Edward Kennedy. *Music Is My Mistress.* New York: Doubleday, 1973.

Emery, Lynne Fauley. *Black Dance in the United States from 1619 to 1970.* New York: National Press, 1972.

Engel, Lehman. *The American Musical Theater.* New York: Macmillan, 1967.

Ewen, David. *All the Years of American Popular Music.* Englewood Cliffs, N.J.: Prentice-Hall, 1977.

Farga, Franz. *Violins & Violinists.* New York: Frederick A. Praeger, 1950.

Fletcher, Tom. *100 Years of the Negro in Show Business.* New York: Burdge, 1954.

Floyd, Samuel A., Jr. and Marsha J. Reisser. *Black Music Biography.* White Plains, N.Y.: Kraus International, 1987.

Fox, Charles. "Now You Has Jazz." *Rïalitïs,* no. 282 (May 1974): 64–71.

Franklin, John Hope. *From Slavery to Freedom.* 2nd rev. ed. New York: Alfred A. Knopf, 1965.

Fredrickson, George M. *The Black Image in the White Mind.* New York: Harper & Row, 1971.

Gaines, Kevin. "Duke Ellington, *Black, Brown and Beige, and the Cultural Politics of Race*," in *Music and the Racial Imagination.ed.* Ronald Radano and Philip V. Bohlman. Chicago: University of Chicago Press, 2000, 585–604.

Gates, Henry Louis, Jr., and Nellie Y. McKay, eds. *The Norton Anthology of African American Literature.* New York: W. W. Norton, 1997.

Gayle, Addison, Jr. *Oak and Ivy: A Biography of Paul Laurence Dunbar.* Garden City, N.Y.: Doubleday, 1971.

Gilbert, Douglas. *American Vaudeville: Its Life and Times.* New York: Whittlesey House, 1940.

Goddard, Chris. *Jazz Away from Home.* New York: Paddington Press, 1979.

Goldberg, Isaac. *Tin Pan Alley: A Chronicle of American Popular Music.* 1930. Reprint, New York: Frederick Ungar, 1961.

Gordon, Taylor. *Born to Be.* New York: Covici-Friede, 1929.

Gossett, Thomas F. *Uncle Tom's Cabin and American Culture.* Dallas: Southern Methodist University Press, 1985.

Green, Jeffrey P. *Edmund Thornton Jenkins: The Life and Times of an American Black Composer.* Westport, Conn.: Greenwood Press, 1982.

Gregory, James M. *Frederick Douglass: The Orator.* Springfield, Mass.: Wiley, 1893.

Hallett, Robin. *Africa Since 1875: A Modern History.* Ann Arbor: University of Michigan Press, 1974.

Hamm, Charles. *Music in the New World.* New York: W. W. Norton, 1983.

———. *Yesterdays: Popular Song in America.* New York: W. W. Norton, 1979.

Handy, D. Antoinette. *Black Women in American Bands and Orchestras.* Metuchen, N.J.: Scarecrow Press, 1981.

Harlan, Louis R., and Raymond W. Smock, eds. *The Booker T. Washington Papers,* Vol. 10. Urbana: University of Illinois Press, 1981.

Haskins, James. *Black Theater in America.* New York: Thomas Y. Crowell, 1982.

Heath, Ted. *Listen to My Music.* London: Frederick Muller, 1957.

Hill, Errol, ed. *The Theater of Black Americans,* Vol. I. Englewood Cliffs, N.J.: Prentice Hall, 1980.

Howe, Mark Anthony De Wolfe. *The Boston Symphony Orchestra 1881–1931.* New York: Da Capo Press, 1978.

Hughes, Langston, and Milton Meltzer. *Black Magic: A Pictorial History of the Negro in American Entertainment.* Englewood Cliffs, N.J.: Prentice-Hall, 1967.

———. *A Pictorial History of the Negro in America.* 3rd rev. by C. Eric Lincoln and Milton Meltzer. New York: Crown Publishers, 1968.

Huggins, Nathan Irvin. *Harlem Renaissance.* New York: Oxford University Press, 1971.

Hummel, David. *The Collector's Guide to the American Musical Theatre.* Metuchen, N.J.: Scarecrow Press, 1984.

Isaac, Edith J. R. *The Negro in the American Theatre.* New York: Theatre Arts, 1947.

Jablonski, Edward. *The Encyclopedia of American Music.* Garden City, N.Y.: Doubleday, 1981.

Jasen, David A., and Gene Jones. S*preadin' Rhythm Around: Black Popular Songwriters, 1880–1930.* New York: Schirmer, 1998.

Johnson, James Weldon. *Along This Way: The Autobiography of James Weldon Johnson.* 1933. Reprint, New York: The Viking Press, 1968.

———. *Black Manhattan.* 3rd ed. New York: Atheneum, 1972.

Katkov, Norman. *The Fabulous Fanny: The Story of Fanny Brice.* New York: Alfred A. Knopf, 1953.

Kenney, William Howland III. "The Influence of Black Vaudeville on Early Jazz." *The Black Perspective in Music* 14, no. 3 (Fall 1986): 233–248.

Kimball, Robert, and William Bolcom. *Reminiscing with Sissle and Blake.* New York: The Viking Press, 1973.

Kislan, Richard. *The Musical: A Look at the American Musical Theater.* Englewood Cliffs, N.J.: Prentice-Hall, 1980.

Knight, Arthur. *Disintegrating the Musical: Black Performance and American Musical Film.* Durham, N.C.: Duke University Press, 2002.

Krehbiel, Henry Edward. *Afro-American Folksongs.* 2nd ed. New York: Frederick Ungar, 1967.

Langston, John Mercer. *From the Virginia Plantation to the National Capital.* New York: Arno Press and *The New York Times,* 1969.

Levine, Lawrence W. *Black Culture and Black Consciousness.* New York: Oxford University Press, 1979.

———. *Highbrow/Lowbrow: The Emergence of Cultural Hierarchy in America.* Cambridge, Mass.: Harvard University Press, 1988.

Levy, Eugene. *James Weldon Johnson: Black Leader, Black Voice.* Chicago: University of Chicago Press, 1973.

———. "Ragtime and Race Pride: The Career of James Weldon Johnson." *Journal of Popular Culture* I (1968): 357–370.

Lewis, David Levering. *W. E. B. DuBois: Biography of a Race: 1868–1919.* New York: Henry Holt., 1993.

———. *When Harlem Was in Vogue.* New York: Alfred A. Knopf, 1981.

Lewis, Lloyd. *Chicago: The History of Its Reputation, Part I.* New York: Harcourt, Brace, 1929.

Locke, Alain, ed. *The New Negro.* 6th ed. New York: Atheneum, 1974.

Logan, Rayford W. *Howard University: The First Hundred Years, 1867–1967.* New York: New York University Press, 1969.

Loney, Glenn, ed. *Musical Theatre in America.* Westport, Conn.: Greenwood Press, 1984.

Long, Richard. "Black Music Biography." *Black Music Research Journal* (1986): 49–56.

Lott, Eric. *Love and Theft: Blackface Minstrelsy and the American Working Class.* New York: Oxford University Press, 1993.

Lueders, Edward. *Carl Van Vechten.* New York: Twayne Pub., 1965.

Mahar, William J. *Behind the Burnt Cork Mask: Early Blackface Minstrelsy and Antebellum American Popular Culture.* Urbana: University of Illinois Press, 1999.

Major, Gerri (with Doris E. Saunders). *Black Society.* Chicago: Johnson Publishing, 1976.

Marcuse, Maxwell F. *Tin Pan Alley in Gaslight.* Watkins Glen, N.Y.: Century House, 1959.

Mates, Julian. *America's Musical Stage: Two Hundred Years of Musical Theatre.* Westport, Conn.: Greenwood Press, 1985.

Mattfeld, Julius. *Variety Music Cavalcade: Musical Historical Review, 1620–1969.* 3rd ed. Englewood Cliffs, N.J.: Prentice-Hall, 1971.

McCarthy, Albert. *Big Band Jazz.* New York: G. P. Putnam's Sons, 1974.

McFeely, William S. *Frederick Douglass.* New York: W. W. Norton, 1991.

McLaughlin, Irene Castle. "Jim Europe: A Reminiscence." *Opportunity* (March 1930): 90–91.

McLean, Albert F. Jr. *American Vaudeville as Ritual.* Lexington: University of Kentucky Press, 1965.

Meier, August. *Negro Thought in America 1880–1915: Racial Ideologies in the Age of Booker T. Washington.* 4th ed. Ann Arbor: University of Michigan Press, 1969. *The New York Times Theatre Reviews 1870–1919.* 6 vols. New York: Arno Press and *The New York Times,* 1976.

Oberfirst, Robert. *Al Jolson: You Ain't Heard Nothin' Yet!* New York: A. S. Barnes, 1982.

Osgood, Henry O. *So This Is Jazz.* New York: Da Capo, 1978.

Ostransky, Leroy. *Jazz City: The Impact of Our Cities on the Development of Jazz.* Englewood Cliffs, N.J.: Prentice-Hall, 1978.

Ottley, Roi, and William Weatherby. *The Negro in New York.* New York: New York Public Library, 1967.

Paige, Diane and Michael Beckerman. "Does It Still Pay to Study Music?" *The Musical Quarterly* 81, no. 1 (Spring 1997): 64–80.

Papich, Stephen. *Remembering Josephine.* New York: Bobbs-Merrill, 1976.

Pettigrew, Thomas F., ed. *Racial Discrimination in the United States.* New York: Harper & Row, 1975.

Phillips, Waldo. "Paul Laurence Dunbar: A New Perspective." *Negro History Bulletin* 29, no. 1 (October 1965): 7–8.

Riis, Thomas Laurence. "Bob Cole: His Life and Legacy to Black Musical Theatre," *The Black Perspective in Music* 13, no. 2 (Fall 1985): 135–150.

———. *Just Before Jazz: Black Musical Theater in New York, 1890 to 1915.* Washington, D.C.: Smithsonian Institution Press, 1989.

Robb, Frederic H. H. *The Negro in Chicago 1779–1929,* Vols. 1–2. Chicago: Washington Intercollegiate Club of Chicago, 1929.

Roberts, Josie W. "Oberlin—The Pioneer Liberal College of America." *Abbott's Monthly* (February 1931): 59–60, 93.

Root, Deane Leslie. "American Popular Stage Music, 1860–80." Ph.D. diss., University of Illinois, 1977.

Rose, Al. *Eubie Blake.* New York: Schirmer Books, 1979.

Rossiter, Johnson, ed. *A History of the World's Columbian Exposition, Vol. 1.* New York: D. Appleton, 1897.

Rowland, Mabel. *Bert Williams: Son of Laughter.* 1923. Reprint, New York: Negro Universities Press, 1969.

Rubin, Emanuel. "Jeannette Meyers Thurber and the National Conservatory of Music." *American Music* 8, no. 3 (Fall 1990): 295–325.

Rudwick, Elliott M., and August Meier. "Black Man in the 'White City': Negroes and the Columbian Exposition, 1893." *Phylon,* 26, 4 (Winter 1965): 354–361.

Rye, Howard. "The Southern Syncopated Orchestra," in *Under the Imperial Carpet: Essays in Black History 1780–1950.* Crawley, England: Rabbit Press, 1986.

Sampson, Henry T. *Blacks in Blackface: A Source Book on Early Black Musical Shows.* Metuchen, N.J.: The Scarecrow Press, 1980.

Schafer, William J., and Johannes Riedel. *The Art of Ragtime.* Baton Rouge: Louisiana State University Press, 1973.

Schechter, William. *The History of Negro Humor in America.* New York: Fleet Press, 1970.

Schuller, Gunther. *Early Jazz: Its Roots and Musical Development.* New York: Oxford University Press, 1968.

Shelly, H. R. "Dvořák As I Knew Him." *The Etude* 31 (August 1913): 541–542.

Shirley, Wayne D. "The House of Melody: A List of Publications of the Gotham-Attucks Music Company at the Library of Congress." *The Black Perspective in Music* 15, no. 1 (Spring 1987): 79–112.

Simond, Ike. *Old Slack's Reminiscence and Pocket History of the Colored Profession from 1865 to 1891.* 1891. Reprint, Bowling Green, Ohio: Popular Press, 1974.

Skvorecky, Josef. *Dvořák in Love: A Light-hearted Dream.* Trans. Paul Wilson. Toronto:Lester & Orpen Dennys, 1983.

Smith, Cecil. *Musical Comedy in America.* New York: Theatre Arts Books, 1950.

Smith, Vincent Douglas. "Bert Williams: Why Nobody?" M.A. thesis, University of Maryland, 1979.

Southern, Eileen. *Biographical Dictionary of Afro-American and African Musicians.* Westport, Conn.: Greenwood Press, 1982.

———. "In Retrospect: Black-Music Concerts in Carnegie Hall, 1912–1915." *The Black Perspective in Music* 6, no. 1 (Spring 1978); 71–88.

———. *The Music of Black Americans: A History,* 3rd ed. New York: W. W. Norton, 1983.

———. ed. *Readings in Black American Music.* 2nd ed., New York: W. W. Norton, 1983.

Stearns, Marshall W. *The Story of Jazz.* New York: Oxford University Press, 1956.

——— and Jean Stearns. *Jazz Dance.* New York: Macmillan, 1968.

Stowe, Harriet Beecher. *Uncle Tom's Cabin or Life Among the Lowly.* 1852. Reprint, Garden City, N.Y.: Doubleday, 1960.

Stowe, William M., Jr. "Damned Funny: The Tragedy of Bert Williams." *Journal of Popular Culture* 10, no. 1 (Summer 1976): 5–13.

Swain, Joseph P. *The Broadway Musical: A Critical and Musical Survey.* New York: Oxford University Press, 1990.

Taylor, Ronald. *Berlin and Its Culture.* New Haven, Conn.: Yale University Press, 1997.

Tibbetts, John C., ed. *Dvořák in America, 1892–1895.* Portland, Ore.: Amadeus Press, 1993.

Toll, Robert C. *Blacking Up: The Minstrel Show in Nineteenth-Century America.* New York: Oxford University Press, 1974.

Toppin, Edgar A. *Biographical History of Blacks in America Since 1528.* New York: David McKay, 1969.

Tucker, Mark. *Ellington: The Early Years.* Urbana: University of Illinois Press, 1991.

Wade, Harold, Jr. *Black Men of Amherst.* Amherst, Mass.: Amherst College Press, 1976.

Walker, Edward Samuel. "A New Look at the SSO." *Storyville,* no. 51 (February/March 1974): 95–97.

———. "The Southern Syncopated Orchestra." *Storyville* 42 (August/September 1972): 204–208.

Watkins, Mel, ed. *Inside the Minstrel Mask: Readings in Nineteenth-Century Blackface Minstrelsy.* Hanover, N.H.: University Press of New England, 1996.

———. *On the Real Side: Laughing, Lying, and Signifying—The Underground Tradition of African-American Humor that Transformed American Culture, from Slavery to Richard Pryor.* New York: Simon & Schuster, 1994.

Whyte, James H. *The Uncivil War: Washington During the Reconstruction 1865–1878.* New York: Twayne Pub., 1958.

Wiggins, Lida Keck. *The Life and Works of Paul Laurence Dunbar.* 1896. Reprint, Millwood, N.Y.: Kraus, 1975.

Wilder, Alec. *American Popular Song.* New York: Oxford University Press, 1972.

Wilson, Olly. "The Black-American Composer and the Orchestra in the Twentieth Century." *The Black Perspective in Music* 14, no. 1, Special Issue (Winter 1986): 26–34.

Witmark, Isidore, and Isaac Goldberg. *The Story of the House of Witmark: From Ragtime to Swingtime.* New York: Lee Furman, 1939.

Wittke, Carl. *Tambo and Bones: A History of the American Minstrel Stage.* Durham, N.C.: Duke University Press, 1930.

Woll, Allen. *Dictionary of the Black Theatre: Broadway, Off-Broadway, and Selected Harlem Theatre.* Westport, Conn.: Greenwood Press, 1983.

Zanger, Jules. "The Minstrel Show as Theater of Misrule." *Quarterly Journal of Speech* 60, no. 1 (1974): 33–8.

Music Collections

Appelbaum, Stanley, ed. *Show Songs from "The Black Crook" to "The Red Mill"— Original Sheet Music for 60 Songs from 50 Shows, 1866–1906.* New York: Dover, 1974.

Charosh, Paul, and Robert A. Fremont, eds. *Song Hits from the Turn of the Century: Complete Original Sheet Music for 25 Songs.* New York: Dover, 1983.

Charters, Ann, ed. *The Ragtime Songbook: Songs of the Ragtime Era by Scott Joplin, Hughie Cannon, Ben Harney, Will Marion Cook, Alex Rogers and Others.* New York: Oak, 1965.

Fremont, Robert A., ed. *Favorite Songs of the Nineties: Complete Original Sheet Music for 89 Songs.* New York: Dover, 1973.

Jackson, Richard, compiler. *Popular Songs of Nineteenth-Century America: Complete Original Sheet Music for 64 Songs.* New York: Dover, 1976.

Jasen, David A. *"Alexander's Ragtime Band" and Other Favorite Song Hits, 1901–1911.* New York: Dover, 1987.

Riis, Thomas L., ed. *Songs and Scripts from "In Dahomey."* Madison,Wis.: A-R Editions, 1997.

INDEX

Johnson, James Weldon, 26, 28, 33, 37, 42, 54, 56, 57, 65, 92, 116, 123, 127
Johnson, Jimmie, 108
Johnson, J. Rosamond, 27, 33, 37, 57, 95, 96, 123
Jolson, Al, 86, 125
Jones, George, 102
Jones, Sissieretta Jones, 24, 26, 37, 48, 112, 164n28. *See also* Black Patti Troubadours
Joplin, Scott, 26–27
   Treemonisha, 65
Jordan, Joe, 70, 73–74, 75, 118, 119
   "Sweetie Dear" ("Pekin Rag,"), 74

Kahn, Otto, 125
Kalkbrenner, Friedrich, 17
Keith, Prowse of London, 67
Kemp, Bobby, 70
King, Albert L., 15
King, Henry Churchill, 13
Kneisel (string) Quartet Club, 15
Krehbiel, Henry E., 27
KKK (Ku Klux Klan), 7

Lafayette Theatre, 107, 108, 109, 122
Langston, John Mercer, 20, 62, 166n3
Lattimore, George, 104
Lederer, George W., 44, 86
Leipzig Conservatory, 13
Lenwood Quartet, 102
Lewis, William (maternal grandfather), 7, 147n8
Lewis, Jane (maternal grandmother), 147n8
Lincoln, Abraham, 62
Liszt, Franz, 17, 18
Little Foxes, The, 122
Locke, Alain, 109, 127
Longfellow, Henry Wadsworth, 32
   "The Song of Hiawatha," 32
Loomis, Harvey Worthington, 30
Lyles, Aubrey, 74

McAdoo, Orpheus, 22
McConnell, Will, 38
McGinty, Doris, 153n28
McIntosh, Hattie, 57
McKay, Claude, 127

McLean, Evelyn, 93
Madeline, Marie, 77
Mallory, Frank, 46
Mannes, David, 94
Mannes School of Music, 94
Marshall, Leona, 74
Marshall's, Jimmie hotel, 37, 69
Mason, Billy, 106
Memphis Students (a.k.a. Nashville Students and Tennessee Students), 69, 93, 122
Mendelssohn, Felix
   Elijah, 15
   "Wedding March," 119
Metropolitan Orchestra (New York), 15
Meyerbeer, Giacomo, 18
Miller, Flournoy E., 74
Miller, Irvin C., 74
Miller and Lyles, 96
   The Mayor of Dixie, 74
   Runnin' Wild, 108
Miller, Quintard, 74
Mills, Florence, 108
minstrelsy, 44, 67, 71, 76, 80, 94, 102
Mitchell, Abbie, 56, 62, 70, 86, 88,
   breadwinner's role, 111
   early years, 47
   Clorindy audition, 47
   divorced Cook, 92
   dramatic roles, 122
   father figure in Cook, 49
   firstborn arrival, 52
   joins *Clorindy*, 48, 49
   makes final rites for Cook, 121
   marital difficulties, 91
   memoirs on Cook eccentricities, 111
   other marriages, 121, 166n1
   second pregnancy, 56
   The Southerners, 91
   stage clothes ruined by Cook, 91
   Tuskegee Institute position, 122
Monroe, James, 13
Monroe, Willard, 121
Morehouse, Henry L., 125
Morgan, John Mrs., 17
Moscheles, Ignaz, 17
Motts, Robert 73
Mozart, Wolfgang Amadeus, 18
Mulatto, 122